Two week
loan

Please return on or before the last
date stamped below.
Charges are made for late return.

JAPAN, NAFTA AND EUROPE

Also by T. David Mason and Abdul M. Turay

* US–JAPAN TRADE FRICTION: Its Impact on Security
  Cooperation in the Pacific Basin (*co-editors*)

 *Also from the same publishers

Japan, NAFTA and Europe

Trilateral Cooperation or Confrontation?

Edited by

T. David Mason
Professor of Political Science
University of Memphis

and

Abdul M. Turay
Professor of Economics
Radford University

382·0952(07)

382·0952(07)

382·0952(07)

382·0952(07)

382·0952(07)

382·0952(07)
J

Selection and editorial matter © T. David Mason and Abdul M. Turay 1994
Chapters 1–8 and 10 © Macmillan Press Ltd 1994
Chapter 9 © Nobuo Matsunaga 1994
Chapter 11 © Kenneth B. Pyle 1994

All rights reserved. No reproduction, copy or transmission of
this publication may be made without written permission.

No paragraph of this publication may be reproduced, copied or
transmitted save with written permission or in accordance with
the provisions of the Copyright, Designs and Patents Act 1988,
or under the terms of any licence permitting limited copying
issued by the Copyright Licensing Agency, 90 Tottenham Court
Road, London W1P 9HE.

Any person who does any unauthorised act in relation to this
publication may be liable to criminal prosecution and civil
claims for damages.

First published in Great Britain 1994 by
MACMILLAN PRESS LTD
Houndmills, Basingstoke, Hampshire RG21 2XS
and London
Companies and representatives
throughout the world

A catalogue record for this book is available
from the British Library.

ISBN 0–333–62485–8

10 9 8 7 6 5 4 3 2
03 02 01 00 99 98 97 96 95

Printed and bound in Great Britain by
Antony Rowe Ltd, Chippenham, Wiltshire

First published in the United States of America 1994 by
Scholarly and Reference Division,
ST. MARTIN'S PRESS, INC.,
175 Fifth Avenue,
New York, N.Y. 10010

ISBN 0–312–12393–0

Library of Congress Cataloging-in-Publication Data
Japan, NAFTA, and Europe : trilateral cooperation or confrontation? /
edited by T. David Mason and Abdul M. Turay.
p. cm.
Includes bibliographical references (p.   ) and index.
ISBN 0–312–12393–0
1. Japan—Foreign economic relations—North America. 2. North
America—Foreign economic relations—Japan. 3. Japan—Foreign
economic relations—European Union countries. 4. European Union
countries—Foreign economic relations—Japan. 5. Trade blocs—North
America. 6. Trade blocs—European Union countries. 7. Trade blocs-
-Asia. I. Mason, T. David (Thomas David), 1950– . II. Turay,
Abdul M.
HF1602. 15.N7J354 1994
337.5207—dc20   94–27908
                                                       CIP

1 5 JAN 1996

Contents

List of Tables   vii
Preface   viii
Acknowledgements   xii
Notes on the Contributors   xiii
List of Abbreviations   xvi

1   NAFTA and the Single European Act
    Kenneth M. Holland   1

2   The Canada–US Free Trade Agreement:
    Implications for the Global Trading Regime
    William Dymond   38

3   'Europe 1992' and Japan's Relations with Western Europe
    John R. McIntyre   58

4   The Impact of 'Europe 1992' on Japan's Relations with
    Europe: A German View
    Klaus W. Grewlich   93

5   'Europe 1992' and Japan: A British Perspective
    Frank Cassell   108

6   Trade Blocs and the Prospects for Japan's Relations with
    Eastern Europe
    Abdul M. Turay   114

7   Trade Blocs and the Prospects for Japan's Relations with
    Russia
    Gordon B. Smith   141

8   Prospects for an Asian Trade Bloc: Japan, the Association
    of South-east Asian Nations and the Asian Newly
    Industrializing Economies
    Shigeko Fukai   164

9   A Japanese Perspective on the Pacific Rim in the 1990s
    Nobuo Matsunaga   189

10   The Impact of Trade Blocs on the Future of Japan's
      Relations with China
      T. David Mason   195

11   Can Japan Lead in the International System?
      Kenneth B. Pyle   219

Index   243

List of Tables

1.1	Penetration of US and Canadian markets, 1981–83 and 1989–91	14
3.1	Japan's trade with the USA and the EC	73
3.2	Japan's trade balance with major trading partners, 1984–88	74
3.3	Japan's FDI by country, fiscal years 1984–88	76
6.1	The status of economic reform in the CSFR, Hungary and Poland	118
6.2	Export trade between Canada, Mexico and the USA, 1990	121
6.3	Bulgarian imports and exports, 1984–90	124
6.4	CSFR's imports and exports, 1984–90	126
6.5	Hungary's imports and exports, 1984–90	128
6.6	Romania's imports and exports, 1984–90	130
7.1	Soviet exports to Japan and imports from Japan, 1965–87	148
7.2	Soviet exports to Japan, 1975–87	151
10.1	Japanese trade with China, 1972–90	200

Preface

This volume is the product of a research symposium entitled 'Japan–North America–Western Europe: Trilateral Cooperation or Confrontation?' The symposium was held in Jackson, Mississippi, in the autumn of 1989 under the sponsorship of the Center for International Security and Strategic Studies (CISS) at Mississippi State University.

The original idea for the symposium was to bring together a group of scholars from Europe, Japan and North America to explore the impact that the emergence of trade blocs in North America and Europe might have on Japan's position as an economic power in the global economy. The competition from the Canada–US Free Trade Agreement, from NAFTA (the North America Free Trade Agreement) and from the Single European Act ('Europe 1992') would fundamentally alter trade relations among member nations of each regional bloc and between them and their major trading partners, including Japan.

The critical question was whether these two trade blocs would divert or create trade for Japan. Certainly the elimination of trade barriers in North America would make each nation's goods more competitive in the other's market and thereby give them a competitive boost relative to Japanese goods. Likewise the integration of the European Community (EC) into a single market devoid of barriers to the movement of goods and services, labour and capital among the member nations would enhance the competitiveness of European products relative to Japanese goods in the single European market. However, eliminating trade barriers within each of these blocs should also stimulate economic growth in the member nations and thereby create new opportunities for Japanese exports.

The conventional wisdom seemed to be that the trade-creating effects of economic growth would more than offset any Japanese losses resulting from the competitive edge gained by producers within the blocs. Moreover, Japanese firms adopted a strategy of expanded investment in North America and the EC as a hedge against the potential decline in the competitiveness of their products. The remaining questions were, first, whether the two trade blocs would erect barriers to goods produced outside their boundaries at the same time as they were eliminating barriers to trade within those boundaries. Despite assurances to the contrary from the EC, the possibility of 'Europe 1992' (EC 92) becoming 'Fortress Europe' was a source of concern in national capitals and corporate boardrooms outside Europe and the subject of extensive debate in the press, in international organizations and in the academic community. Second was the question of whether, in response to the emergence of these two trade blocs, Japan would press for an Asia–Pacific trade bloc that would include some combination of the Asian NICs (Newly Industrializing Countries), ASEAN (the Association of South-east Asian Nations), and perhaps Australia and New Zealand.

These were the issues that provided the focus for the CISS. However, since that time, the international system has undergone dramatic transformations which have altered the context of many of the original analyses presented at the symposium. During the autumn of 1989, democratic movements in Eastern Europe succeeded in overthrowing Communist Party domination and introducing market reforms and democratic institutions throughout most of the nations of that region. Following a failed coup attempt in August of 1991, the Soviet Union disintegrated as a sovereign political entity as its constituent republics declared their independence. Thus, at the same time as Western Europe and North America were taking steps to integrate their economies more thoroughly, the Soviet bloc disintegrated and the former member nations rushed to liberalize their economies and integrate themselves into a global economy that was itself undergoing rapid and profound structural transformations.

These events altered the parameters of the analyses in this volume and necessitated the revision of several chapters, the updating of all chapters (several times), and the addition of two new chapters. Of particular significance is the fact that in December 1992 the Canada–US Free Trade Agreement was augmented with the addition of Mexico to the free trade area under what has now come to be known as NAFTA. Events continue to unfold rapidly as the international system is still in a transition phase. However, we think that, at the time of writing, the chapters in this volume have been refined to the point that they at least provide an analytical framework within which one can analyse the further evolution of events in Japan's relations with the emerging trade blocs in North America and Europe, and the implications for these relations of the further transformation of the international system brought about by the changes taking place in the nations of Eastern Europe and the former Soviet Union.

Kenneth Holland begins the book with a description of the terms of both NAFTA and the Single European Act (SEA). He then presents a far-reaching analysis of the likely impact of these agreements on trade and investment flows within each of the blocs and between them and Japan. His general conclusion is that the benefits of reducing internal trade barriers will more than offset any potential trade-diverting effects for Japan. These optimistic conclusions are echoed in William Dymond's legal and institutional analysis of the Canada–US Free Trade Agreement and its implications for the multilateral trade regime. John McIntyre follows this with a thorough and compelling analysis of the politics within the EC over the reforms required to effect the goal of EC economic integration. While his general outlook is optimistic, his chapter highlights the complex political tensions both among the EC members and within several of the member nations over just how far and how rapidly the integration of national economies should be allowed to proceed. Klaus Grewlich and Frank Cassell add to this picture the German and British perspectives, respectively, on the obstacles to and benefits of European integration.

With Abdul Turay's chapter, we shift our focus to the impact of trade blocs on the other regions of the world. His chapter explores the risks and opportunities of EC integration for the nations of Eastern Europe as they undertake the liberalization of their own domestic economies and the integration of their economies with the global economic system. He foresees considerable potential, especially in certain sectors, for the rapid development of trade ties between Japan and Eastern Europe. Of special significance is the prospect of the capital- and technology-starved Eastern European economies becoming a target for Japanese manufacturing investments, both to penetrate the newly opened markets of Eastern Europe and to produce goods there for export to the EC. Gordon Smith follows this with an analysis of the prospects for trade between Japan and Russia in the aftermath of the collapse of the Soviet Union and the emergence of trade blocs in Europe and North America. His analysis shows that the apparent affinity for trade between Japan and Russia based on natural resources for technology has been overstated in the past, and the collapse of the Soviet Union has done little or nothing to enhance these prospects.

Shigeko Fukai presents an analysis of the prospects for the emergence of an Asian trade bloc in response to NAFTA and EC 92. Since Japan and the Asian NICs have achieved their economic success on the basis of trade, the formation of trade blocs in the two most lucrative markets of the world are of special concern to these nations, especially to the extent that NAFTA and EC 92 have trade-diverting effects on the Asian nations. Fukai argues that there has already been considerable progress towards integration of the Asia–Pacific economies, and further integration is being pursued both through intergovernmental efforts and through rapid growth in trade and investment flows within the region. At the same time, most of the Asian nations still fear the prospects of Japanese regional hegemony. Nobuo Matsunaga reinforces many of Fukai's conclusions in his analysis of the prospects for Asia–Pacific economic cooperation and integration. David Mason follows this with an analysis of the special case of Japan's relations with China.

While China continues to experience high rates of economic growth and continues to attract large volumes of foreign investment, Mason argues that the emergence of trade blocs and the collapse of the Soviet Union will create new opportunities for Japan that may have the effect of diverting some of Japan's interest in expanded economic ties with China. The Tiananmen Square incident of 1989 and the uncertainty surrounding the impending leadership transition in China should add to this caution. Finally Kenneth Pyle focuses on Japan itself by asking whether, given the transformation of the global economic system witnessed in the last decade, Japan is prepared to assume a leadership role in the post-Cold War international system. His analysis is prospective and provides a fitting conclusion to this volume.

We, the editors of this volume, are indebted first and foremost to Janos Radvanyi, Director of CISS, for his tireless work on the conception of the project and the direction of the symposium. Without his initiative and persistence, this project and the book that follows would not have materialized.

We are also indebted to the Japan–US Friendship Commission and its Executive Director, Lindsey Sloan, for their generous grant which made it possible to bring this collection of scholars together for the symposium. The Chamber of Commerce of Jackson, Mississippi, through its Executive Director Paul Latture, was instrumental in securing local support for the symposium. Nana Goto Bellerud assisted in editing early drafts of most of the chapters and was especially valuable in translation and transliteration of Japanese words, terms and phrases. Charles Bond, Tan Tsai and Catherine Vellake of CISS also played invaluable roles in arranging the conference and in arranging for the transcription of several of the manuscripts presented at the symposium. Lisa Aplin and Cindy Henson of the Department of Political Science at Mississippi State University also assisted the editors in the preparation of drafts of several of the chapters. Tom Mason assisted in printing and copying the final drafts of all the chapters. Finally, we are indebted to Belinda Holdsworth, our publishing editor at Macmillan, for her extraordinary patience with us as we went through several revisions of several of the chapters to account for rapidly evolving changes in the international system generally and in the relations among the nations that are the subject matter of this volume. Of course, we and the individual chapter authors remain responsible for any errors in fact or interpretation contained in the chapters that follow.

T. DAVID MASON
ABDUL M. TURAY

Acknowledgements

The editors and publishers wish to acknowledge with thanks:

Chapter 9, 'A Japanese Perspective on the Pacific Rim in the 1990s', by Nobuo Matsunaga, previously appeared under the same title in the *Japan Review of International Affairs*, Volume 6 (1992), in a special issue on 'Asia-Pacific Partnerships'. It is reprinted here with the permission of the author.

Chapter 11, 'Can Japan Lead in the International System?', by Kenneth B. Pyle, is reprinted with the permission of Kenneth B. Pyle from *The Japanese Question: Power and Purpose in a New Era* (Washington, DC: American Enterprise Institute, 1992).

Notes on the Contributors

Frank Cassell received a BSc in economics at the London School of Economics in 1953. From 1953 until 1965 he worked as a financial journalist on the *News Chronicle* and then *The Banker*. He began his government service career in 1965, in Her Majesty's Treasury, and served as Economic Adviser to Home Finance Divisions, Chief Balance of Payments Forecaster, Head of Monetary Policy Division, Head of Finance Economic Unit, Head of Medium-Term and Policy Analysis Group, and Deputy Secretary in charge of Public Finances. Since 1988 he has been Economic Minister in the British Embassy in Washington, DC, and Executive Director for the UK at the International Monetary Fund and the World Bank. Mr Cassell is the author of numerous articles on banking and international finance as well as the book *Gold or Credit?*

William A. Dymond received BA and MA degrees from the University of Toronto. In 1967 he joined the Department of External Affairs, serving as First Secretary of the Canadian Mission to the United Nations in Geneva and as Minister-Counsellor in the Canadian Mission to the European Commission in Brussels. In 1983 Mr Dymond became the Director of European Community Division of the Department of External Affairs and in 1984 the Senior Advisor and Coordinator, Canada/US Trade Task Force. He assumed his present position as Minister-Counsellor in the Canadian Embassy in Washington in 1987.

Shigeko N. Fukai received degrees in law from Chuo University and the University of Tokyo. In 1967 she received her MA in International Relations from the University of Denver and in 1977 a PhD in Political Science from the University of Tennessee. After serving as a member of the faculty at Arizona State University and Auburn University, Dr Fukai assumed her present position as Director of the Japan Program, Center for International Commerce at Auburn University in 1987. Dr Fukai is the author of numerous journal articles and book chapters.

Klaus Grewlich holds a Juris Doctor degree from the University of Freiberg, Docteur en Sciences Economique from the University of Lausanne, Switzerland, and an LLM degree from the University of California, Berkeley. He has held positions in the European Space Agency, the OECD Secretariat in Paris, and in the Cabinet of the EC Commission in Brussels. He is currently Director-General of the International Affairs Department of Telekom.

Kenneth Holland is Professor of Political Science, University of Memphis. He holds a PhD from the University of Chicago, an MA from the University of Virginia and a BA from Furman University. He has held visiting positions at the University of Wisconsin–Madison, the University of Calgary and Skidmore College. He is the recipient of numerous awards, including a Fulbright Fellowship to research and lecture in Japan, Faculty Research Grants from the governments of Canada and Quebec, a Study Visit Grant from the German Academic Exchange Service and a Woodrow Wilson Fellowship. He is the author or editor of four books, including two published by Macmillan, *Judicial Activism in Comparative Perspective* and *The Political Role of Law Courts in Modern Democracies*. His many articles have appeared in such journals as *Quarterly Journal of Ideology, Canadian Journal of Law and Society, Constitution, American Bar Foundation Research Journal, Policy Studies Journal, Justice System Journal* and *Law and Policy Quarterly*.

T. David Mason received his PhD in Political Science from the University of Georgia in 1982. From 1981 to 1992 he served as a faculty member in the Department of Political Science at Mississippi State University, with additional duties as Co-Director of the Japan Program of the CISS and as Research Associate with the Social Science Research Center at that university. In 1992 he joined the faculty at the University of Memphis. He has published a number of articles in journals such as *American Political Science Review, Political Behavior, Asian Affairs, International Studies Quarterly* and *Comparative Political Studies*. He is co-editor of the book *US–Japan Trade Friction: Its Impact on Security Cooperation in the Pacific Basin*.

Nobuo Matsunaga is President and Director of the Japan Institute for International Affairs, Adviser to the Minister of Foreign Affairs, and Envoy of the Government of Japan. He is a graduate of Tokyo University and began serving in Japan's Foreign Ministry in 1945. While in that Ministry he served as Director-General of the Treaties Bureau, Director of the Personnel Division and from 1976 to 1978 as Deputy Vice-Minister and Vice-Minister of Foreign Affairs. He has also served as Japan's Ambassador to Mexico and to the USA. His writings on Japan's foreign relations are widely published.

John R. McIntyre earned degrees from Jacksonville University, McGill University, Northeastern University and Strasbourg University, and received his PhD from the University of Georgia. He is on the faculty of the Georgia Institute of Technology and is the author of numerous journal articles and books, including *Technology Transfer and the Strategic Dimensions of East-West Trade*; *International Space Policy: Legal, Economic, and Strategic Options for the Twentieth Century and Beyond*; and *Managing U.S. Export Control Policy: Trading in Advanced Technology*.

Kenneth B. Pyle is a graduate of Harvard College and received his PhD in Japanese history from Johns Hopkins University in 1965. Dr Pyle served as Director of the Henry M. Jackson School of International Studies at the University of Washington from 1978 to 1988. He was the founding editor of the *Journal of Japanese Studies* and has been President of the Society for Japanese Studies since 1978. He is the author of numerous articles, reports, reviews and books, including *The New Generation in Meiji Japan: Problems of Cultural Identity, 1885–1895* and *The Making of Modern Japan*.

Gordon B. Smith earned a BS degree from Iowa State University and MS and PhD degrees in political science from Indiana University. In 1975–76 he was a Fulbright Exchange Professor at Leningrad State University Law School. Dr Smith has also served as a Fellow of the Harvard University Russian Research Institution, the Kennan Institute for Advanced Russian Studies, and as a Visiting Scholar at the Centre for Russian and East European Studies at the University of Birmingham in England and the Slavic Research Centre of Hokkaido University in Sapporo, Japan. He is currently on the faculty of the University of South Carolina. He has published numerous books and articles on the Soviet Union.

Abdul M. Turay is the Head of the Department of Economics at Radford University. He received degrees from Morehouse College and Atlanta University and earned his PhD in economics from the University of Oklahoma. In 1978 he joined the faculty of Mississippi State University and also served as a Senior Fellow with the university's CISS. He is Editor of *Mid-South Journal of Economics and Finance* and the author of numerous articles, reviews, and book chapters on international economics. He is co-editor of the book *US–Japan Trade Friction: Its Impact on Security Cooperation in the Pacific Basin*.

List of Abbreviations

APEC	Asia-Pacific Economic Cooperation
ASEAN	the Association of South-East Asian Nations
CAP	Common Agricultural Policy
CIS	Commonwealth of Independent States
CISS	Center for International Security and Strategic Studies
CMEA	Council of Mutual Economic Assistance
COCOM	Coordinating Committee on Multilateral Export Controls
CSFR	Czech and Slovak Federated Republic
EAI	Enterprise for the Americas Initiative
EC	European Community
EC 92	Europe 1992 (the Single European Act)
EEA	European Economic Area
EFTA	European Free Trade Association
EPA	Economic Planning Agency
FAIR	Foundation for Advanced Information and Research
FDI	Foreign Direct Investment
FTA	Canada–US Free Trade Agreement
GATT	General Agreement on Tariffs and Trade
GDP	Gross Domestic Product
GNP	Gross National Product
GSP	Generalized System of Preferences
GST	Goods and Services Tax
IMF	International Monetary Fund
INF	Intermediate Nuclear Forces
JERC	Japan Economic Research Centre
JETRO	Japan External Trade Relations Organization
LDP	Liberal Democratic Party
MFN	Most Favoured Nation
MITI	Ministry for International Trade and Industry
MTN	Multinational Trade Negotiations
NAFTA	North American Free Trade Agreement
NDP	New Democratic Party
NICs	Newly Industrializing Countries
NIEs	Newly Industrializing Economies
NTB	Non-tariff Barriers
ODA	Official Development Assistance

OECD	Organization for Economic Cooperation and Development
OPEC	Organization of Petroleum Exporting Countries
OPTAD	Organization of Pacific Trade and Development
PAFTA	Pacific Free Trade Area
PAFTAD	Pacific Trade and Development
PBCC	Pacific Basin Cooperation Concept
PBEC	Pacific Basin Economic Council
PCC	Pacific Cooperation Committee
PECC	Pacific Economic Cooperation Conference
PMC	Post-Ministerial Conference
PTA	Preferential Trade Area
R&D	Research and Development
SEA	Single European Act
VER	Voluntary Export Restraint

1 NAFTA and the Single European Act
Kenneth M. Holland

On 1 January 1993, Europe achieved an unprecedented level of economic integration as the last tariff barriers fell among the twelve members of the EC. On 17 December 1992, an agreement creating an even larger free trade area called the North America Free Trade Area, embracing Canada, the USA and Mexico, was signed by the three nations. As beneficiaries of the multilateral trading system operating under the General Agreement on Tariffs and Trade (GATT), the nations of East Asia and the Pacific naturally view these developments with alarm. They fear that regional trading blocs are motivated by protectionist sentiment, that they may become an alternative to global free trade, and that their effects are essentially trade-diverting instead of trade-creating. Although countries outside the two blocs have some reason to be concerned, their anxieties are disproportionate to the real danger. This chapter presents an overview and assessment of the SEA and NAFTA in order to lay the foundations for subsequent chapters which explore the impact of these agreements on specific nations and regions of the global community. This overview should provide the analytical context within which to analyse crucial issues created by the emergence of trade blocs. In particular, this volume is concerned with the question of whether the efforts to integrate the economies of Western Europe and North America in fact enhance the openness of the international trade regime, increase the total volume of world trade and complement the Uruguay Round of the GATT negotiations completed in 1993. Later chapters will focus especially on whether the emergence of trade blocs works to the benefit of Japan, Australia and the NICs of the Republic of Korea, Taiwan, Hong Kong and ASEAN which are, as a group, the most important and most rapidly growing trading states that are not members of these two trade blocs.

THE ORIGIN OF THE SINGLE EUROPEAN ACT

Determined to prevent future wars among the nations of Western Europe, France, West Germany, Italy and the Benelux countries (Belgium, the Netherlands and Luxembourg) signed the Treaty of Rome in 1957, estab-

lishing the EC. The agreement envisaged full realization of a common
market by 1 January 1970 (a goal not achieved until 1993). Economic
integration was seen as an instrument to achieve the founding states'
overarching political objective of ending armed conflict. A series of acces-
sions began in 1973 when the EC embraced Great Britain, Ireland and
Denmark as new members. In order to stabilize their currencies, in 1979 EC
members established the European Monetary System, in which they agreed
to maintain their exchange rates within narrow bands, and instituted direct
popular election of members of the European Parliament. With the admission of Greece in 1981 and Spain and Portugal in 1986, the EC achieved its
present membership of twelve states.

In the 1970s, however, the effort to achieve the economic and political
integration of Europe stalled, and commentators began talking of
'Eurosclerosis', a condition of social and political rigidity which was causing Western Europe to fall behind the USA and Japan. The centre of the
world's gravity seemed inexorably to be shifting from the Atlantic to the
Pacific, leaving Europe in a backwater. Signs of the EC's competitive
disadvantage were a widening technology gap, weak economic growth and
endemic unemployment.[1] Europeans realized that a third industrial revolution had occurred and that their survival depended upon their ability to
compete with Japan and the USA, the world's two commercial, industrial
and technological superpowers.

In 1985 Jacques Delors, a former French finance minister, assumed the
presidency of the European Commission, a body which proposes policies to
the Council of Ministers. He provided the effective leadership needed to
move the Commission and the governments of the twelve member states
towards the goal of European unity.[2] Agreeing with Delors that Europe
needed a bold and innovative response to the Pacific challenge, the EC
leaders promised a concerted effort to free the flow of goods, services,
people and capital throughout the Community by the end of 1992. Thus was
born the project known as EC 92. Delors outlined the programme in an EC
Commission White Paper entitled *Completing the Internal Market*.[3] The
White Paper stated that approximately 300 directives would be passed to
abolish all physical, technical and fiscal barriers to trade among the twelve.
Significantly, the Single Act allows certain decisions relating to the internal
market to be made by less than unanimous vote. The act was adopted by the
EC Council of Ministers and went into effect on 1 July 1987.[4]

Meeting in Edinburgh, Scotland, in December 1992, EC leaders trium-
phantly proclaimed the completion on schedule of the single market. While
not all member countries had adopted all of the directives passed by the
European Council, by 1 January 1993 much had been achieved. Most

highway border controls had been eliminated. Governments were accepting each other's technical standards. However, there were some failures, such as a delay in the liberalization of the transport industry and trade in automobiles. Manufacturers continue to enjoy monopolies in their home countries, and sales of Japanese cars remain severely restricted by import quotas. The EC says it will open the market in the year 2000, but imposing obstacles exist to the goal's achievement.[5] The EC 92 programme does not actually achieve a single market analogous to that existing within France, the USA or Japan yet, on the whole, services, capital, persons and goods are all moving more freely.

The Maastricht Treaty

In Delors' opinion, the single market was not sufficient to achieve European economic and political integration. Therefore, in 1988 he called for the creation of a single central bank and a single currency. Meeting in 1990, the European Council issued a remarkable statement proclaiming that peace and security in Europe might require the transformation of the EC into a monetary and political union. In December 1991 the EC's prime ministers and presidents met in Maastricht, the Netherlands, and voted to give the Community broader powers, a central bank and a common currency. As an amendment to the Treaty of Rome, this Treaty of Political Union had to be ratified by each of the twelve EC members, a process which was completed in October 1993. With ratification, the EC became the European Union (EU). The treaty regards monetary union as the crucial second phase in European integration but also contains a framework for coordinating defence and foreign policies. The European central bank and currency are to be established by 1999. In order to qualify for monetary union, all countries must meet strict goals for reducing government spending, budget deficits and inflation. Italy, Portugal, Spain and Greece will have great difficulty achieving these goals. If they are not met, Germany, France and the Benelux countries are likely to agree on a single currency by the turn of the century.[6]

The Role of the Cold War's End

Competition in the global market is not the only force catalysing European integration. The collapse of Communism in Eastern Europe and the end of the Cold War between the West and the Soviet Union have set in motion a series of largely unanticipated developments within the EU, the first of which was the decision of formerly neutral countries – Austria, Switzer-

land, Finland and Sweden – to seek membership of the EU. In response to
the signing of the Treaty of Rome, several European states had formed the
European Free Trade Association (EFTA) in 1960. In 1972 and 1973 the
EC and EFTA successfully negotiated a trade pact. In 1991, when neutrality
no longer made sense, the two trade associations agreed to form a European
Economic Area (EEA) by 1993. The EEA came into being on January 1,
1994. The EEA is a seventeen-country trade bloc, consisting of the twelve
EC countries and five wealthy EFTA members. Four EFTA members,
Austria, Finland, Norway and Sweden, have already applied for EU mem-
bership and the two others – Switzerland and Iceland – as well as Liechten-
stein have indicated an intention to apply in the future. Malta, Cyprus and
Turkey have also applied for full membership.

Second is the turning of the Warsaw Pact countries towards the West.
The EU has associated members not only in the EEA but also in Eastern
Europe, where it has partnership agreements as well. In December 1991,
Hungary, Poland and Czechoslovakia signed association contracts with the
EC, governing political and economic cooperation, trade relations and
freedom of movement. The separation of Czechoslovakia into the Czech
and Slovak Republics on 1 January 1993 is affecting their relationship to the
EU, with early associational and eventual full membership more likely for
the more market-oriented Czech Republic. The prospect of ties to the EU,
of course, lowered the cost of partition for both partners and may have
contributed to the break-up, as Canadian membership in NAFTA may be
fueling Quebec separatism.

The third factor is the Maastricht treaty itself, which was a product of the
'Europhoria' which swept the continent after the unification of Germany,
the collapse of Communism in Eastern Europe and the Soviet Union, and
the end of the Cold War. This outburst of pride ended the *malaise* that had
lingered since the early 1980s and helped give the European masses a stake
in the Delors Plan, a privilege which they had not previously enjoyed in
Commission policies. Some observers believe that the addition of Central
and Eastern European countries to the EU is likely to result in greater
European political integration and a centralization of power in Brussels,
since the poorer members of the EU rely on the centre to redistribute wealth
within the Community and are the greatest champions of economic union
and delegation of greater powers to the centre.[7]

The final element is the unification of Germany. Although unification has
demanded higher levels of spending and taxation by the former West
Germany and has led to high interest rates there, it is expected that within
a few years unification will have produced an even stronger and more
influential Germany within the EU.

Difficulties in Implementing the Single Market

Despite the Europhoria of the early 1990s, a number of impediments to European unity remain, including the problem of enforcement of EU directives. Although governments which refuse to comply with EU single-market rules can be taken before the European Court of Justice, they cannot be compelled to obey the Court's decision. This tribunal interprets the constituent treaties of the EU as well as the regulations and directives of the European Commission. In theory, its decisions have the force of law, override conflicting national laws and judicial decisions, and are binding on the courts of member states. More than 100 Court rulings against EU governments, however, remain unenforced.[8] Moreover, many US and Japanese firms fear that they will be the principal victims of non-compliance. Pressure on EU governments to pass stricter environmental protection and consumer safety legislation also threatens to fragment the single market. The 'greens' in Germany, for instance, have blocked construction of an oil pipeline to the Czech Republic, leaving that nation totally dependent upon uncertain oil supplies from the former Soviet Union.

The second source of problems is, ironically, the end of the Cold War. The opening of the borders of the Warsaw Pact countries, for instance, has allowed a flood of refugees to enter the EU countries, and some members with exclusionary policies are reluctant to yield further control over immigration to the Commission.[9] As witnessed by the Yugoslav civil war, the partition of Czechoslovakia and the outbreak of separatist movements in the former Soviet Union, the collapse of the Communist rule has made Europeans more aware of their diversity. Despite the progress made in integrating Western Europe, there is not yet a common sense of European identity.

Another consequence of the collapse of Communism is the unification of Germany. This has generated fears of German domination of the political and monetary union. Germany's economic power is revealed in the fact that in the past decade Germany had a trade surplus with its eleven EU partners of $200 billion, while Great Britain ran a $100 billion trade deficit.[10] The nation perhaps most fearful of the Germans is Denmark, which turned down the Maastricht Treaty on 2 June 1992 by a margin of 51 per cent to 49 per cent. Because unanimity of the member states is required for this treaty to go into effect, the Danish Government was forced to find some way of reversing this vote in order to prevent the collapse of the movement towards political and monetary union. In a second vote on 18 May 1993, the treaty was ratified by Danish voters by a margin of 57 per cent to 43 per cent. Two days later, the British House of Commons passed it, thus averting a looming crisis for the movement towards European unity.

The other side of German domination of Europe is the reluctance of Germans to give up their strong and stable mark. The German mark has now replaced the US dollar as the standard currency of Europe. Germans are reluctant to relinquish the resulting benefits and advantages in exchange for a weaker European currency, and neither are they enthusiastic about subjecting themselves to a central bank governed by representatives of weaker economies that are plagued by slow growth and inflation.[11]

A third obstacle to European integration is the British reluctance to yield any further portion of its sovereignty to the EU. The tactic which British Prime Minister, John Major, has chosen is to support the 'widening' of the Community by adding new members, such as Poland, as soon as possible. He believes 'widening' will come at the expense of its 'deepening', delaying adoption of a common currency and empowerment of Brussels to issue standardizing regulations for the member states.[12] Delors' response is that the preservation of the free market, from which Britain expects to benefit, requires augmentation of the powers of the EU administration and a compromise of the principle of national sovereignty.

A fourth impediment is public opinion. In a Community poll taken before the Maastricht Treaty, 80 per cent of the respondents supported the efforts being made to unify Western Europe.[13] However, a poll conducted in June 1992 showed that most citizens of Britain, France and Germany, the EC's largest economies, think Maastricht will make them worse off.[14] Most political leaders, however, remained strongly in favour of the pact.

LIKELY EFFECTS OF THE SINGLE EUROPEAN ACT AND MAASTRICHT

Early in the process of achieving a single market, the EC commissioned a major study entitled 'The Costs of Non-Europe', published in 1988 as the Cecchini Report. According to this report, economic integration of Europe should result in an impressive 4.5 per cent annual economic growth rate for the Community, a rate which substantially exceeds the anticipated performance of the US and Japanese economies.[15] One of the most substantial potential benefits to European firms of the single market will be their ability to leverage funds to support research and development to a far greater extent than before.[16] By removing internal barriers to trade, the SEA increases the chance of successful European response to US and Japanese competition in cars, trucks, consumer electronics, electronic components, chemicals, aerospace and computers, and developing country competition in textiles and clothing. The principal benefit to European industry of the

EC 92 programme, however, is the stimulation to investment and the introduction of competition to new areas, such as services and telecommunications.[17] Nevertheless, the extent of the single market will still remain far short of that which exists in the USA or Japan.

A potential drag on economic growth is the controversial labour policy which is attached to the SEA. In 1989, the governments controlled by leftist parties proposed a social plan in response to what they perceived as Delors' pro-business initiative. Included are proposals on worker consultation, working time, subcontracting and benefits (that is, giving part-time workers the same benefits as full-time employees). So far Britain has blocked the adoption of these labour directives, which prior to 1994 required unanimous approval. However, under the Maastricht Treaty, they can be approved by majority vote of the member states.[18]

The opening of markets within the EU member states as a result of the SEA presents valuable opportunities for US and Japanese exporters. Exports are becoming more and more important to the US economy. In fact, the USA is the largest exporter in the world. In 1992 US exports totalled $439.3 billion, 30 per cent more than total Japanese exports.[19] Exports account for 8 million US jobs. The EU's domestic market is as large as that of the USA and Japan combined. In 1990 the USA exported $109 billion worth of merchandise to Western Europe, twice its exports to Japan. US exports to the EC between 1986 and 1992 nearly doubled, in part due to the announcement of the EC 92 project and the run up to its completion. The USA moved from a $22.5 billion trade deficit with the EC in 1986 to a $16.7 billion surplus in 1991, partially offsetting its huge trade deficit with Japan, China and Organization of Petroleum Exporting Countries (OPEC). The total US trade deficit in 1992 was $96.3 billion, more than half of it with Japan. The trade surplus with Europe is particularly important to the USA, as the heavy indebtedness of the Third World inhibits export potential there.

The USA sees a number of advantages flowing from EC 92, including a unified market, a single set of standards, a reduction in product testing and certification rules, the opening of public procurement opportunities, liberalization of services (especially in banking, investment and insurance), the end of quantitative restrictions on US imports (such as quotas on automobile imports), improvements in competition policy, freer circulation of capital, and generally a more 'level playing field' for US firms.[20] The unified market will lead many medium-sized US companies to do business in Europe for the first time, and it will induce US firms already there to expand operations to all twelve countries. Opening EU government procurement to bids by US firms alone promises substantial increases in sales for them; EU government purchases total more than $600 billion a year but, prior to the SEA, 85 per cent of this business was closed to US and Japanese firms.

US industry is benefiting from several of the EU single market directives, including those involving computer software, banking, automobiles and telecommunications services, especially cellular communications. Since the establishment of the single market, the European Commission has worked to reduce government subsidies to national industries, or 'champions', in order to establish a level playing field in Europe. Some of the EU directives implementing the SEA, however, pose problems for US businesses. The data privacy directive, for instance, could impede banking, insurance, credit and direct marketing industries. Another directive allows public utilities to discriminate against US and Japanese products. In addition, there are directive quotas on non-European broadcast programming and an import regime which gives preference to African agricultural produce.[21] Nevertheless, in general, US business leaders believe that EC 92 is good for US exporters and investors and that Community directives are, as a rule, well-designed to increase foreign direct investment (FDI) and trade flows with the rest of the world.[22] Europe has become a magnet for US direct investment. The importance of investment is highlighted by the fact that about 34 per cent of all US exports to the EU go directly to the subsidiaries of US companies.

Europe is also a formidable trading rival. The EU accounts for more than 15 per cent of the world's exports, compared to 12 per cent for the USA and 9 per cent for Japan.[23] The SEA means that by having a home market of continental proportions, Europe will be able to take advantage of its economies of scale for the first time and thus increase its worldwide competitiveness. As the countries of Eastern Europe are brought into the EU, cheaper, labour-intensive goods will compete with comparable goods manufactured in Asia and Mexico. For example, Volkswagen, Europe's largest automobile producer, has already taken control of the Czech Republic's Skoda works.[24] The single market is forcing the USA and Japan to develop new strategies regarding production, investment, marketing and exporting.[25]

Western Europe has become relatively more important to Japan than to the USA since the single market project was announced. Since 1985 the share of Japanese exports to the EU has grown from 15 to 20 per cent, while the share of exports to the USA has declined from 38 to 35 per cent. Imports from the EU to Japan have grown since 1985 from 15 per cent to 20 per cent, while imports from the USA have declined from 30 to 26 per cent.[26] At the same time, the USA may have a competitive advantage in exploiting opportunities in the single market, since there are more powerful ties – of history, trade, ethnicity, religion and language – between the EU and the

USA than between the EU and Japan. US and European companies are teaming up, for instance, to meet competition from Japan in the field of micro-electronics and high-definition television, with encouragement from the EU.

Europhoria has also led to difficulties for non-Europeans. The head of the European Bank for Reconstruction and Development, Jacques Attali, attempted to limit severely the US role in the reconstruction of Eastern Europe.[27] The West's victory in the Cold War has made both the EU and the USA more assertive and confrontational on trade issues, since the need for Atlantic harmony has appreciably diminished. The EU, in combination with its EFTA and Eastern European partners, will outperform both the USA and Japan in certain trade sectors, leading to rivalry among the three trading blocs and more frequent and intense trade conflict, with outright trade wars a possibility.[28]

There is undeniably an exclusive and discriminatory side to the achievement of a single European economy, which some fear will end in a 'Fortress Europe'. The EU has adopted rules favouring European manufacturers in sales to government-run utilities. The effect on such US companies as General Electric and American Telephone and Telegraph provoked retaliation against European products from the new administration of President Bill Clinton.[29] Monetary union could mean the end of the US dollar as the reference currency of trilateral trade among the Union, Japan and the USA, with the result that the EU and Japan would have greater bargaining power over US economic policy.[30] Neither the SEA nor the Maastricht treaty envisions the dismantling of the EU's Common Agricultural Policy (CAP), which consumes more than half of the EU's budget. The subsidies are provided primarily to French farmers and are a major source of trade friction between the USA and the EU. Japan, on the other hand, prior to the 1993 GATT agreement liberalizing agricultural trade tended to support the Europeans on this issue because of its desire to continue its own ban on the importation of rice.

Yet, on the whole, the advantages for the USA and Japan of the EC 92 initiative outweigh the drawbacks. All three types of liberalization included in the EC 92 programme – the removal of internal border formalities, the removal of obstacles to the flow of capital and skilled labour and the elimination of national public procurement policies and product standards – are trade-creating.[31] The completion of the internal market will also increase the wealth of the EU members, generating a greater demand for US and Japanese products and services.[32]

At the same time that the single market directives are stimulating growth in US and Japanese exports to and investments in Europe, the EU continues to support the multilateral trading system provided by GATT. GATT was created in 1947 to encourage international trade with a view to fostering growth in the world economy. Over the years, the number of contracting parties has swollen from 23 to 103. There have been eight rounds of trade negotiations, which have generated greater order, predictability and freedom in world trade. The ambitious eighth round of multilateral trade talks began in 1986 in Punta del Este, Uruguay. Its objectives were to gain greater protection for intellectual property rights, to enhance the operation of GATT and to attain freer trade in goods, services and investment. The USA used the Uruguay Round to shape the implementation of EC 92 in areas such as standards, sanitary requirements, film and broadcasting quotas, government procurement and rules of origin.[33] The USA also had success in using GATT to pressure the Europeans to reduce agricultural subsidies, the major trade irritant between the Atlantic trading partners. The USA blamed the breakdown of the GATT talks in December 1990 on the unwillingness of the EC to cut farm subsidies. In November 1992, however, Arthur Dunkel, GATT's Director-General, persuaded the EC to agree to a compromise on this thorny issue[34] and the round was successfully completed in December 1993.

THE CANADA–US FREE TRADE AGREEMENT

In 1985 Canadian Prime Minister Brian Mulroney initiated negotiations with the USA leading to a free trade agreement. This initiative represented a dramatic break from a long-standing Canadian policy of protectionism *vis-à-vis* its southern neighbour and a preference for multilateral efforts, such as GATT. In December 1985 President Ronald Reagan advised Congress of his intent to negotiate an agreement using the 'fast-track' procedure according to which Congress must approve or reject an agreement reached by the President without amending it. Negotiators agreed on a final draft in December 1987, and Prime Minister Mulroney and President Reagan signed it on 2 January 1988. It went into effect on 1 January 1989, immediately eliminating tariffs on some products and setting in motion the gradual abolition, over a ten-year period, of tariffs on remaining goods.

Chapter 2 in this volume analyses in detail the provisions and implications of the Canada–US Free Trade Agreement (FTA). This pact was the most comprehensive bilateral trade agreement ever negotiated and formed the world's largest common market. The USA ranks as the world's largest economy and Canada as the seventh largest in terms of gross domestic product (GDP). The USA and Canada rank first and second, respectively, in purchasing power parity, or the quantity of goods and services which can be purchased by the average pay packet. Canada is the leading trading partner of the USA, and US trade with Canada is only slightly less than its trade with the EC. In 1992 bilateral trade in goods and services totalled nearly $250 billion, the largest such relationship in the world. Approximately 33 per cent of US merchandise exports go to Canada. In the 1980s, the USA exported more to the province of Ontario than to Japan. Trade between the USA and Canada provides millions of jobs in each country. One in four Canadian jobs is dependent on US trade.[35]

Rationale for the FTA

Even before 1989, the US and Canadian economies were already largely integrated as a result of previous GATT rounds and the Automotive Products Trade Agreement of 1965. The Auto Pact provided for freer trade in motor vehicles and parts. The two countries had negotiated several other sector-specific agreements prior to the FTA, including one on military products in 1959 and softwood lumber in 1986. However, the 1989 FTA was in direct response to the SEA.[36] The USA and Canada were reacting to increasing competition from a reinvigorated EC. In the 1960s and 1970s, few US companies feared European competition. When Britain, France and Germany announced, for example, the formation of a consortium to build a wide-body passenger jet, US aerospace executives scoffed at the idea, calling it a 'camel', a horse designed by a committee, which would never sell. By 1990, however, Airbus Industrie had captured 52 per cent of the world's wide-body jet market and more than 26 per cent of the world's total commercial passenger jet market. These gains in market share were made completely at the expense of two US aerospace giants, Boeing and McDonnell Douglas. Western European governments had demonstrated an ability to pool resources and to work with private industry in order to compete effectively with the USA and Japan in high-technology products.[37]

The FTA was much more important to Canada than to the USA. One-quarter of Canada's wealth is generated by the export of goods and services, and the USA buys 79 per cent of all Canadian exports. Canada enjoys a trade surplus with the USA. While Canada imports about $105 billion in goods from the USA, it exports approximately US $120 billion (1992 figures). Still, prior to the FTA, the Canadian economy was beset by slow growth, declining competitiveness and heavy public indebtedness. Mulroney and his Progressive Conservative Party sought to transform Canada from a branch-plant into a world-class economy by providing incentives to the private sector to be entrepreneurial and to take risks.

The most compelling reason for Canada to request a free trade agreement was to secure access to the US market. The US market is the largest in the world, at $2.9 trillion. Canada's $263 billion market is roughly one-tenth that of its giant neighbour. Access to the US market is especially critical for the provinces of Alberta and Quebec, each of which has made substantial investments in the development of energy products for which the USA is the only feasible outlet. The growing burden of its public debt was also driving Canada into a trade deal with the USA. Canada owes more than $300 billion to foreigners, which amounts to 43.5 per cent of GDP. This is the highest debt-to-GDP ratio in the industrialized world, and the current figure represents a 20 per cent increase since 1985.[38]

The motive for US participation in the FTA was not short-term economic gain. The Canadian market is small, and the USA runs a trade deficit with Canada which amounted to $10.3 billion in 1992, up from $8 billion in 1991. Much of the bilateral trade consists of exchanges between US companies and their Canadian subsidiaries. Canada is the number one host nation for US FDI;[39] in fact, one in five of Canada's 500 largest industrial firms is owned by US proprietors. US interest was more in the multilateral trading system, and both Mulroney and Reagan hoped that the FTA would be a model of what could be achieved in the Uruguay Round of GATT, which was completed in 1993.

Dispute Resolution

The FTA's dispute resolution mechanism is the most elaborate between any two nations in the world. Each nation ceded a portion of its sovereignty to binational panels whose decisions constitute binding precedents and are enforceable. Previously, trade disputes could only be adjudicated in US or Canadian courts. Under the FTA, dispute settlement panels are established at the request of either country to determine if unfair dumping (that is, selling goods in a foreign country at less than cost) or subsidization has occurred. Most of the binational panels' decisions under the anti-dumping and countervailing duties provisions have been in favour of Canada, and all panel decisions under the FTA have been met with compliance. Much to the irritation of the Canadians, however, the USA has twice issued an 'extraordinary challenge' in a US federal court to a panel decision it alleged 'seriously departed from a fundamental rule of procedure or manifestly exceeded its powers'. The dispute resolution procedure tends to defuse conflict and to prevent trade disagreements from becoming political issues. Prepared to resolve their bilateral conflicts, Canada and the USA have found it easier to present a common front to Japan and the EC, as evident in their joint opposition to the EC's hefty wheat subsidies.[40]

The dispute resolution mechanism has not resolved all areas of trade friction between the USA and Canada, the reason being that FTA negotiators were unable to agree on the elimination of trade barriers in a number of sensitive sectors. In 1992, the USA and Canada skirmished over trade in softwood lumber, automobiles, beer, pork, beef, steel and magnesium.[41] Accusations of dumping have led to the placing of retaliatory duties on each nation's products.[42] The FTA set a target of 1995 to negotiate a code governing subsidies, but no progress was made in the first four years of the agreement. Canadians blame these constant US efforts to impose countervailing and anti-dumping duties on Canadian exports on the fragmented US political system, in which members of Congress and executive agencies are highly responsive to special interests. Probably only a new GATT agreement can render the US system less parochial.

Effects of the FTA

Studies of the effects of the FTA have concluded that the agreement in its first four years benefited the US economy only slightly and the Canadian economy moderately. The economic effects of the trade pact are difficult to measure, however, given the fact that it has only been in effect for a few years and it coincided with the onset of a deep recession in Canada. In 1990 the Canadian economy shrank by 0.5 per cent; in 1991 it shrank by 1.7 per cent and finally grew in 1992 by 0.9 per cent.[43]

Another reason for the limited stimulus of the FTA during its first three years was Canadian macroeconomic policy, including relatively high interest rates and an overvalued Canadian dollar propped up by the Bank of Canada. Critics argue that Canada will only reap the full fruits of the FTA once the Bank stops supporting the dollar and lets it fall to its natural level.[44] Devaluation of the Canadian dollar would also bring productivity and unit labour costs in line with their US competitors and make Canada more attractive to investors. The 13 per cent fall in the Canadian dollar in 1992, accompanied by replacement of the manufacturers' sales tax by a Goods and Services Tax (an indirect tax similar to the European Value Added Tax) made Canadian exports cheaper and spurred export growth in 1992.[45]

Trade between the USA and Canada climbed despite the recession from 1990 to 1992. A Statistics Canada study of Canadian exports to the USA over the period 1981–1991 found that Canada's share of the US import market increased significantly during the latter half of that decade, an increase which coincided with the FTA (see Table 1.1).[46] In 1992 exports accounted for 45 per cent of Canadian factory output, up from 33 per cent in 1988. Canadian exports totalled $157 billion in 1992, an 11 per cent increase from 1991 levels. Alberta was the biggest winner from the FTA: its

Table 1.1   Penetration of US and Canadian markets, 1981–83 and
1989–91 (%)

	US market		Canadian market	
	1981–83	1989–91	1981–83	1989–91
US share	90.7	85.4	24.4	27.4
Canadian share	1.9	2.6	66.9	59.3
All other countries' share	7.4	12.0	8.8	13.3
Total	100.0	100.0	100.1	100.0

Source: Bruce Little, 'Trade Report May Fuel Debate', *Trade Patterns: Canada–United States* (Ottawa: Statistics Canada, March 1993) p. B2.

trade with the USA jumped 48 per cent between 1989 and 1993, rising from $9.1 to $13.5 billion. As a result of the FTA and GATT, Canada has increased its penetration of the US market, while US companies have garnered a larger share of the much smaller Canadian market. Since 1989 nineteen of 22 industries in Canada report increasing their share of the US import market. The biggest gains were in those sectors most liberalized by the FTA.[47] The FTA has given Canadian businesses the economies of scale and experience with foreign markets needed to take full advantage of the opportunities opened up by the successful conclusion of the Uruguay Round of GATT.[48] After implementation of the FTA Canada attracted record levels of FDI.[49]

The greater openness of the economy has benefited other countries as well, including Japan, which now controls 12 per cent of the US and 13 per cent of the Canadian market. Freer trade is forcing US and Canadian producers to compete with the world's best to serve their domestic markets and making them more competitive in the global market.

Despite the benefits the FTA brought to Canada, the trade deal became unpopular and was blamed by the opposition Liberal and New Democratic Parties for the high unemployment rate of more than 11 per cent, and pilloried for not reducing trade friction with the USA. The free trade deal, coupled with the recession, is estimated to have wiped out as many as half a million jobs in Ontario alone.[50] Coupled with the even more unpopular Goods and Services Tax (GST), the FTA helped force the resignation of Mulroney as Prime Minister in June 1993 and ensure victory for the opposition Liberal Party in the October 1993 federal elections. A growing public debt and a record number of bankruptcies also undermined public confidence in the deal. Under the FTA, provincial and state governments continue to have power over international trade that local governments within the EC do not have. Ontario, for instance, was able to take action that had the effect of pricing US beer out of the market.[51]

NAFTA

The 1987 US–Mexico Framework Agreement liberalized bilateral trade in several sectors including steel, alcoholic beverages, agriculture, electronics, textiles and intellectual property. As an outgrowth of these discussions, the US Senate in February 1989 authorized negotiations towards a North American Free Trade Area.[52] In April 1990 both houses of Congress authorized the negotiation of a US–Mexico Free Trade Agreement. In August the Mexican President, Carlos Salinas de Gortari, in accordance with fast-track requirements, formally requested negotiation of a free trade agreement with the USA. In October 1990 the Canadian Government announced that it wished to be included in the negotiations. In February 1991 the three governments announced that, in keeping with Canadian wishes, the negotiations would be trilateral and move towards the establishment of a North American Free Trade Area. The formal negotiations commenced in June 1991 and resulted in an agreement in principle in August 1992. In October 1992 the external trade ministers of the three countries initialled NAFTA and on 17 December 1992, the three heads of government signed it. Before going into effect on 1 January 1994, however, it had to be ratified by the Canadian Parliament, the US Congress and the Mexican Senate. Under the fast-track procedure, the US Congress could not amend the agreement, and only a simple majority vote in the House and Senate was necessary to pass the implementing bill. The fast-track process is important because of the independence of Congress from the US President and the lack of party discipline comparable to that which prevails in the Canadian and Mexican legislatures. In Canada the socialist New Democratic Party and much of organized labour opposed NAFTA but could not stop the majority party, the Progressive Conservatives, from ratifying it.

President Clinton promised not to reopen the agreement for further talks but successfully negotiated side agreements on labour and environmental enforcement issues as a prerequisite to ratification of NAFTA. He also wanted a side deal which would protect US producers from 'surges' in imports as tariffs are lowered. Clinton wanted to set up three trilateral commissions: one on labour standards, one on environmental protection and one on import issues. In addition, he sought dispute settlement bodies with the power to investigate complaints of lax enforcement and to levy fines. These side negotiations began on 17 March 1993. By negotiating parallel agreements Clinton avoided the necessity of re-negotiating NAFTA, a process which probably would have killed the deal. Mexico and Canada did not object to pacts on the environment and labour as long as they were not enforced by trade sanctions. However, they successfully objected to a proposal on import surges on the grounds that the NAFTA text already covered this issue.[53] There was pressure from environmentalists and organized labour to authorize the use of trade sanctions to enforce violations of the supplemental environmental and labour agreements, but this effort came to nought. None of the three signatories was willing to surrender a portion of its sovereignty to the trinational panels of labour and environmental experts.

The US Congress received the final package in July 1993, and organized labour and environmental groups opposed it, as expected. Organized labour lobbied Congress against the deal for over a year, and two dozen environmental groups, the largest 'green' coalition ever assembled on Capitol Hill, joined in the effort to persuade Congress to reject it.[54] In order to gain approval in Congress, the Clinton Administration attempted to appease environmentalists (both inside and outside the administration) and organized labour by, for instance, supporting a bill to ban the hiring of non-union strike breakers.[55] The House of Representatives passed NAFTA by a narrow margin in October 1993 and the US Senate quickly followed suit.

Polls in 1993 revealed that a majority of Canadians did not like the free trade deal with the USA even though exports to the USA had increased by $5 billion since FTA's implementation in 1989. Leading up to the October 1993 federal elections in Canada, the opposition parties took different positions on NAFTA. The Liberal Party leader, Jean Chrétien, promised to renegotiate five points in the deal and threatened to abrogate the agreement if he did not receive sufficient satisfaction. By contrast, Audrey McLaughlin, leader of the New Democratic Party (NDP), did not waffle but made abrogation of the pact one of the central features of the NDP programme. Following his victory, Chretien was told firmly by Clinton and Salinas that no changes could be made in NAFTA, and the pact went into effect as scheduled on 1 January 1994.

NAFTA brought into being the largest and wealthiest free trade zone in the world. The North American Free Trade Area includes 363 million people, as compared to the EC's population of 340 million and Japan's population of 123 million. NAFTA encompasses a geographical area more than twice that of Europe and 50 times that of Japan. The combined GDP of the NAFTA members is $7 trillion, slightly larger than the combined GDP of the twelve members of the EC and twice the output of Japan. Three-way trade among the USA, Canada and Mexico is $300 billion.[57] What is particularly unusual about NAFTA is the pairing of two industrialized countries with a developing nation. This North–South, rich–poor combination is unprecedented in the history of post-war free trade arrangements.

Why Does the USA Need NAFTA?

The purpose of NAFTA is to eliminate or reduce all trade barriers in order to expand trade and investment opportunities and thereby promote employment and economic growth in Canada, the USA and Mexico. US interests are far less clear and more long-term than those of Mexico or Canada. The USA has changed from a largely self-sufficient economy in the 1950s and 1960s to one increasingly dependent upon exports to fuel economic growth. The US economy has become increasingly internationalized, with merchandise exports plus imports accounting for 16 per cent of GDP by 1989. The USA is already the world's largest exporting country, ahead of both Germany and Japan. It is estimated that every $1 billion increase in US exports generates from 19 000 to 25 000 jobs in the USA.[58] The number of Americans who produce goods for export increased from 5 million in 1986 to 7.2 million in 1990.[59] Export-related jobs, moreover, pay on average $3500 more a year.

Business and political leaders saw that the USA was becoming less and less competitive with Japan and the EC. The GATT was unable to eliminate the competitive advantage that Japan's industrial structure and distribution system and the EC's agricultural and high-technology subsidies provided. In the 1970s and 1980s US manufacturers lost their strong market positions in several key sectors, including consumer electronics, commercial aircraft, apparel, machine tools, semi-conductors and automobiles.[60] One of the many initiatives US companies have taken to regain both domestic and global market share is to establish a continental free-trade zone, comparable to that existing in Western Europe. By eliminating tariffs on Mexican imports, for example, US automobile firms expect to gain a competitive advantage over Japanese automakers through access to low cost Mexican labour and the burgeoning Mexican consumer market. US companies are facing increasing price competition as the EC teams up with Eastern Europe and Japan does likewise with the NICs of Asia. In order to have similar access to cheap labour and to remain competitive in the world market, the USA must establish stronger trading links with Mexico and the rest of Latin America. Mexico is the USA's third largest trading partner, after Canada and Japan. NAFTA, thus, is one US response to the current intensity of global competition.

The impetus for NAFTA came from Mexico, which badly needs access to the US market. Canada could not afford to stay out. The major benefit to the USA, however, is not secured access to the Canadian and Mexican markets but competition with Japan and the EC. As President Salinas put it, 'Europe and [Asia] are formidable competitors that are increasing their capacity to gain access to markets, day by day. It is in this context that the significance of the free-trade agreement should be viewed.'[61]

The USA sees NAFTA not only as an opportunity to boost exports but, probably more importantly, to support political stability and democratic reform in Mexico, betting that a more plural and open economy will lead to fewer abuses of human rights, a more independent judiciary and a competitive party system. The USA also hopes that the growth in economic opportunities in Mexico will reduce the high level of illegal migration into the USA. Although Mexico has legislated environmental and labour legislation comparable to that in Canada and the USA, it has lacked resources sufficient to enforce them. Higher levels of economic growth can supply these resources.

Why Does Mexico Need NAFTA?

Both Canada and Mexico have had difficult economic and political relations with the USA, but each wants NAFTA more than the USA itself. While the NAFTA partners, East Asia and the EU each account for about 30 per cent of US exports, the USA accounts for between 64 and 75 per cent of Canadian and Mexican imports and exports. Before long Mexico may replace Japan as the USA's second-largest trading partner.[62]

The initiative for a free trade arrangement with the USA came from Mexico and represented the culmination of a dramatic change of heart on the part of the Mexican Government. Since the Mexican Revolution of 1910–20, Mexico's economy had been relatively closed, marked by policies of import substitution and state ownership. This protectionist attitude reached a peak during the administration of Luis Echeverría (1970–6), when Mexico adopted highly restrictive laws governing direct foreign investment. As a result many firms, sheltered from both foreign and domestic competition, failed to reduce inefficiency and the costs of production.

Oil prices plummeted in 1981. By August 1982 Mexico was unable to pay its foreign debt, and capital fled the country. In 1984, under the leadership of President Miguel de la Madrid, the country decided to reverse its policy of economic self-sufficiency and to open the economy to foreign investment in order to revive economic growth, increase productivity and exports and pay the foreign debt. Another plunge in oil prices occurred in 1986. Adherence to GATT in 1986 was preceded by a relaxation of restrictions on foreign investments, privatization of a number of government enterprises, deregulation of most economic sectors, abolition of import licenses and a lowering of tariffs. By July 1992 the average tariffs in Mexico were 10.8 per cent, comparing favourably with average duties in Canada of 8.7 and in the USA of 6.7 per cent.[63] However, many non-tariff barriers (NTBs) remain in each country.

President Salinas, a Harvard-educated economist, continued the process of transforming Mexico into a nation with a market-oriented economy integrated into the global trading system. NAFTA is one component of President Salinas's National Development Plan 1989–94, which also includes liberalization of foreign investment regulations, continued privatization of government-owned enterprises and deregulation of industry.[64] Between 1988 and 1993 Mexico privatized $22 billion of state-owned companies, persuading local capitalists to repatriate billions of dollars they had invested in other countries during the debt crisis of the 1980s. Under the privatization programme, the number of government-owned enterprises in Mexico fell from 1155 in 1982 to 223 in 1992. Mexico wants a free trade agreement to help consolidate a series of domestic economic reforms and to stimulate much-needed foreign investment. It has the second largest external debt among developing countries and suffers from a large budget deficit. Currently, Mexico is building an interstate highway system which will eventually form a 4000-mile network. It has already spent $7 billion on the project and has completed 1300 miles of highway. A proposed North American highway linking the industrial heartlands of Canada, the USA and Mexico will connect with this network.

Since the reforms of 1986, Mexico has shown considerable stability and encouraging levels of economic growth. Mexico recorded a growth in GDP of 3.3 per cent in 1989, 4.4 per cent in 1990 and 3.6 per cent in 1991.[65] Mexico has been a net importer of capital since 1991. Imports from the USA grew to $30 billion by 1991 (6 per cent of total US exports and 62 per cent of Mexican imports), making Mexico the USA's third largest trading partner, after Canada and Japan. In 1989, 66 per cent of Mexican exports went to the USA. Another sign of investor confidence is that in 1991 two-thirds of capital expenditures in North America were made in Mexico, although Mexico accounts for only 4 per cent of North American GDP, in contrast to Canada (9 per cent) and the USA (87 per cent). For Mexico economic forecasters predict sustained growth in GDP, a moderate inflation rate and a decline in public debt.

Why Does Canada Need NAFTA?

Canada's stated goals in joining the NAFTA negotiations were to gain access to the fast-growing Mexican market on equal footing with the USA, to ensure continued access to the US market, to resolve irritants with the USA under the FTA and to attract domestic and foreign investors who are seeking access to the North American market.[66] There is a perception among many Canadians and Mexicans that a higher standard of living is dependent upon economic growth, which in turn is tied to free trade. In the words of Quebec's International Affairs Minister, John Ciaccia, 'Free trade is not a choice; it is a necessity.'[67]

Canada needs a free trade agreement with the USA more than does Mexico, since the volume of bilateral trade between Canada and the USA is very large and Canada is heavily dependent on the USA both for imports and exports. NAFTA meets the principal objectives set by Canada when the negotiations began: to preserve the advantages of the FTA, to maintain Canada's position in the US market, to strengthen Canada's comparative advantages for investors, to adapt to competition from Mexican products in Canada and to participate in opportunities in the Mexican market. Because Mexico is the gateway to Latin America, Canada's access to the Western hemisphere will be assured by joining NAFTA.

In 1991 Mexico signed a bilateral free trade agreement with Chile, in which customs duties will be lowered gradually until their elimination in 1996. Mexico negotiated similar deals with Venezuela and Colombia. Canadians feared that unless Canada were a part of NAFTA, the USA would negotiate bilateral agreements with each country in the hemisphere. By joining NAFTA, Canada remains attractive to investors because it will have access to the Mexican market, which has enjoyed impressive growth since Mexico acceded to GATT in 1986. If Canada concluded two bilateral agreements, one with the USA and one with Mexico, foreign investors would tend to select the USA, with its privileged position in the North American market.[68] Under NAFTA Canadian goods are on an equal basis with Mexican goods when they enter the USA. Although Canada already had a free trade deal with the USA, it had little choice but to join NAFTA otherwise a hub-and-spoke arrangement would have arisen, with only the USA enjoying privileged access to all three North American markets.

Although trade between Canada and Mexico is relatively small, Canada is positioning itself to take advantage of what it regards as new opportunities presented by Mexico. In December 1992, the government of Quebec launched a $3 million plan to position the province to take advantage of opportunities likely to be opened up by NAFTA in 1994. Quebec runs a trade deficit with Mexico. In 1991 it exported $88 million worth of goods to Mexico, but imported $440 million worth of Mexican goods.[69] From NAFTA Canada will gain elimination of Mexican customs duties on its leading export products as of 1 January 1994, progressive elimination of nearly all other Mexican customs duties over a five- to ten-year period, elimination of requirements for import licences, access to Mexican Government procurement, clarification of rules of origin in relation to the FTA and improvement of FTA's dispute settlement mechanism.

Mexico is Canada's largest Latin American trading partner. In 1991 trade between Canada and Mexico totalled more than $3 billion (Canada exported $543 million and imported $2.6 billion). In 1992 Canada exported $850 million in goods to Mexico, an astonishing 57 per cent increase. Canada and the USA are in a good position to benefit from the fact that Mexico is one of the fastest growing markets in the world, especially hungry for investment, technology and capital goods. Mexico has urgent needs in sectors such as infrastructure, transportation, telecommunications and electronics, which Canadian firms are well-placed to meet.

The federal government will spend $27 million over four years to help Canadian businesses seize opportunities opened up by NAFTA, the government announced in March 1993. Key elements of the programme, entitled Access North America, focus on enabling Canadian companies to gain a foothold in Mexico. The programme is targeted at industries which have the best potential for Canadian exports to Mexico, including environmental services, energy, telecommunications and transportation. Nevertheless, Mexico will remain a much more important market for the USA than for Canada. Trade between Canada and Mexico is only 1 per cent of trade between Canada and the USA.

Provisions of NAFTA

NAFTA is both an extension of the FTA and a further development. NAFTA will eliminate all tariffs over fifteen years. Two-thirds of US exports to Mexico will become duty-free within five years. NAFTA is not a customs union.[70] It is directed not only at the elimination of import tariffs but at the reduction of NTBs, including import quotas and licences, protection of intellectual property rights and the provision of dispute settlement procedures. Since the goal of the negotiations was to extend the FTA to Mexico, Mexico will have to make the most extensive changes to its laws and practices.

Neither the FTA nor NAFTA are, strictly speaking, free trade agreements. They are better described as efforts to manage trade among the USA,

Canada and Mexico, since tariffs are to be phased out only gradually, and many NTBs will remain. NAFTA fills three volumes, not including the side agreements on labour and environmental standards. It is, thus, more about government controlling North American trade than establishing a common market, which could be done in one short paragraph.[71] The main features of the pact are explained below.

1. *Mexican tariffs and trade restrictive import licensing requirements are eliminated.* US and Canadian firms will be able to participate in the previously closed sectors of automobiles and automobile parts, financial services, trucking, energy and fisheries. There are clearer rules of origin. Canada is allowed to continue quotas to support supply management for poultry, egg and dairy products, a concession which is particularly important to Quebec. Cultural industries continue to be exempt from open competition.

The rules of origin are of peculiar significance to Japan. As a result of the Plaza Accord of September 1985, the Japanese yen appreciated sharply. The appreciation, coupled with a fear of US and European protectionism, precipitated a surge of Japanese FDI as Japanese firms sought to lower their production costs and secure access to the US and EC markets. Japanese FDI reached $112 billion in 1986–89, divided among the financial, real estate and manufacturing sectors, including the US automobile industry. By 1989 30 per cent of all Japanese cars sold in the USA were produced there.[72] The rules of origin affect trade flows between Japan and the USA since a high North American content standard can force Japanese companies to buy more parts from local producers.

2. *Chapter 19 of the FTA, providing for bilateral review of countervailing and anti-dumping duties, was incorporated in NAFTA.* The dispute settlement chapter strengthens the FTA's mediation and conciliation provisions and assures a professional roster of panelists available to arbitrate disputes.

3. *NAFTA retains features of the FTA demanded by Canada, namely the exclusion of the entertainment industry – what the Canadians call 'culture' – from competition and protection for the agricultural marketing boards.* Article 71 of the trade agreement specifically excludes water. Some Canadians were concerned that NAFTA could give access by the relatively dry USA and Mexico to Canada's water. Also excluded from the agreement are air transportation, basic telecommunications, social services and intra-country transportation.

4. *NAFTA is more liberal than FTA with regard to such issues as the opening of the service sector*, especially financial services, transportation of passengers and freight, circulation of business persons and professionals and protection of intellectual property rights such as patents, trademarks and copyrights.

5. *On some products customs duties of all three countries were abolished on 1 January 1994.* Duties on most products subject to tariffs will be lowered to zero in equal instalments over five or ten years. In the case of certain products entering the USA from Mexico, the tariff abolition will be spread out over fifteen years. In the case of US–Canadian trade, the FTA timetable will continue to be observed.

6. *Members may resort to safeguard measures in the case of harmful import surges.*

7. *The rules of origin are precisely drawn.* For automobiles, the North American content requirement will rise from 50 per cent to 62.5 per cent. The North American content requirement will also increase for textile and apparel goods. The latter is offset somewhat by higher export tariff rate quotas.

8. *Foreign suppliers of services must be treated the same as domestic service suppliers.*

9. *It provides a dispute resolution mechanism just for the investment sector.*

10. *It restricts favouritism in government procurement.*

11. *It limits duties on imported goods that are re-exported, a practice known as 'drawback'.*

Likely Effects of NAFTA

The effect on the US economy of NAFTA will be slight: it is estimated to contribute 0.1 to 0.3 per cent to GDP. In the 1992 presidential election campaign, President George Bush defended NAFTA as having three aims: 'jobs, jobs, and jobs'. Yet, it is expected to generate only 171 000 net new jobs by 1995, $^1/_{100}$ of 1 per cent of the total workforce. The Institute for International Economics estimates that between 1990 and 1995 NAFTA will help generate 240 000 new jobs in the USA, while displacing 110 000 jobs, with a net increase of 130 000 new jobs. The effects of NAFTA on the USA will be small because of the changes the Mexican economy has already gone through. As we noted earlier, soon after his election in 1988 President Salinas privatized and deregulated much of industry and lowered tariffs from a maximum 100 per cent to 20 per cent.

NAFTA will provide overseas corporations with an incentive to invest for the first time or to increase current investments in North America.[73] Just the prospects of NAFTA led to a surge in FDI in Mexico.

US and Canadian companies are not likely to make a mass exodus for Mexico once NAFTA comes into effect, the reason being that wages by themselves mean relatively little to an industrial firm. The labour cost of production is a combination of wages and productivity. Mexican workers earn about one-seventh as much per hour as US and Canadian workers because they produce on average about one-seventh as much per hour. Canada and the USA, moreover, can always compete favourably with Mexico on price simply by depreciating their currencies.

The International Monetary Fund (IMF) predicts that Canada in 1990s will enjoy the highest rate of economic growth among the G-7 countries. Access to the expanding Mexican and recovering US economies will pay off handsomely for Canadian exporters. The Canadian industries most likely to compete effectively in the North American Free Trade zone are transportation, computer equipment, telecommunications and financial services.[74] Many trade disputes between Canada and the USA will remain. NAFTA negotiators, for instance, failed to resolve shortcomings in the Canadian-US pact regarding bilateral trade in steel.[75]

The economic effects of NAFTA will be muted because the economic integration of North America has proceeded already to a very great degree. Already integrated are energy supply, labour supply, cross-border media penetration and trading relations with Japan and the EC. The pact simply formalizes North-America-wide integration, driven by business interests and marked by relatively free cross-border trade. The major supporters of NAFTA in the USA were multinational corporations, such as Ford, Chrysler, Kodak, IBM and Texas Instruments. They see Mexico as a source of cheap labour and low-cost production. These corporations already produce a large volume and variety of goods in Mexican *maquiladora* factories near the US–Mexican frontier. In 1942 the USA allowed Mexican agricultural workers to migrate temporarily to the USA to replace US workers serving in the armed forces. After the USA terminated the programme in 1964, the Mexican Government inaugurated a Border Industrialization Program to provide jobs for the 400 000 Mexican citizens expected to return from the USA. Known as the *maquiladora* programme, the initiative allows products and materials to be shipped from the USA for assembly and processing in zones along the Mexican side of the border and then to be re-shipped to the USA. The importer only has to pay tariff on the value-added component. The *maquiladora* plants account for almost 25 per cent of Mexican–US trade.[76] Multinational corporations are also attracted by the long-term potential for the growth of the Mexican consumer market. With a population of 88 million, 47 per cent of whom are under the age of 15 and 70 per cent of whom are under the age of 30, Mexico represents substantial long-term opportunities for US exporters and investors. The Institute for International Economics has estimated that growth stimulus and efficiency benefits to the three countries from the trade pact will exceed $15 billion annually, with Mexico enjoying the largest gains.[77] Mexico will probably see real GDP growth of between 3 per cent and 4 per cent a year between 1994 and 2000.[78]

The primary benefits to Canada and the USA from NAFTA will accrue to high-wage, high-value-added industries. Hurt most will be industries which employ large numbers of low-wage unskilled and semi-skilled workers. Clinton is expected to retaliate against trade barriers in Japan, China and the EC and to take a harder line on trade than Bush or Reagan. One result under NAFTA of increasing protectionism in the USA is to force European and Asian manufacturers to locate plants within North America, most likely in Mexico. For instance, by reclassifying minivans as trucks, the Clinton Administration raised the tariff on Japanese and European minivans from 2 per cent to 25 per cent.[79] Canada's unit manpower cost exceeds Mexico's by 18 per cent, but the unit cost of capital in Canada is 50 per cent of what it is in Mexico. This means that under NAFTA Mexico will enjoy a competitive advantage in products whose manufacture is labour-intensive but which require little capital, while Canada will enjoy a substantial advantage in capital-intensive industries.

NAFTA will have the largest impact upon the automobile industry. By the turn of the century, most lower-price cars and parts sold in North America will be manufactured in northern Mexico. This includes European and Japanese cars destined for sale in North America as well. US and Canadian plants will specialize in the manufacture of vans, heavy trucks and luxury passenger vehicles. The *maquiladora* auto plants are already among the most efficient and defect-free plants in the world.

NAFTA will lead, over a ten-year period, to the elimination of all Mexican restrictions on the import of automotive goods from Canada and the USA. A new North American content rule of 62.5 per cent for automobiles will provide an incentive for European, Japanese, US and Canadian manufacturers to increase their sourcing of original equipment parts from within the NAFTA zone. The higher regional content standard will provide opportunities for Canadian and Mexican automotive parts makers at the expense of European and Asian parts producers.

Japanese and European investors will face new restrictions once NAFTA becomes law. Especially worrisome to those outside the region will be the rules of origin and preferential treatment for North American firms in government procurement contracts. The automotive rules of origin are more restrictive than either Mexico or Canada wanted but reflect the interests of Detroit's Big Three automakers. Rules of origin will also protect North American producers of textiles, clothing and electronics.[80]

Canada and the USA are not pursuing North American integration with a view to excluding Japan from their markets. They believe that NAFTA is consistent with GATT and with expanding world trade. Canada has even encouraged Japan to help build a regional framework, including a North Pacific security forum and a strengthened Asia-Pacific Economic Cooperation (APEC) forum.[81]

To qualify for duty-free treatment under NAFTA, a car maker will initially have to spend as much on North American as on imported parts, but over the ensuing eight years the proportion of parts of North American origin will rise to 62.5 per cent. Under NAFTA's simplified accounting rules, however, it will be easier for Honda and other Japanese auto makers to meet the North American content requirements which make cars made in Canada and Mexico eligible for duty free import into the USA.[83] All Japanese auto makers except Nissan, which is the only Japanese company currently assembling vehicles in Mexico, are likely to be effectively excluded from the booming Mexican car market, however, because of restrictions contained in NAFTA. By contrast, the American Big Three auto makers expect to do extremely well in Mexico.[84]

Canada and the USA are willing to accept the fact that a disproportionate share of the economic benefits of NAFTA will go to Mexico, because one of the hoped-for results of continental free trade is political stability in Mexico and the development of democratic and free market institutions. A stable, liberal democratic Mexico is in the long-term political and economic interests of both Canada and the USA. Job growth and shrinking of the rate of population growth, for instance, are expected to decrease the number of Mexicans seeking to enter the USA illegally, which is currently estimated at one million a year. Organizations such as the Montreal-based International Centre for Human Rights and Democratic Development advocated using NAFTA, a deal which Mexico desperately wanted, to pressure Mexico into improving its recognition of human rights, such as the right to form independent labour unions and to have free elections, and to reduce abuses such as torture and extra-judicial killing of prisoners.[85]

A number of observers foresee the USA and Canada as following a parallel path to the EC, where monetary and political union are succeeding economic integration.[86] Quebec separatism and Mexican autocracy, however, darken the prospects of political union.[87] If Quebec were to secede from Canada, a union of the English-speaking provinces with the USA would be feasible, presenting a formidable political challenge to Japan and the EC.[88] President Salinas, moreover, expects that trade liberalization will boost efforts to strengthen party competition and respect for human rights, making Mexico a more suitable North American political partner. Also impeding political union is NAFTA's accession clause (Article 2204), which could lead to the inclusion of several members from the Caribbean, Central America and South America, regions where neither capitalism nor liberal democracy have yet to be entrenched.

Free trade with the USA and the Uruguay Round of the GATT negotiations are bringing increasing pressure on Canada to abandon its unique
supply management system, a system which is specifically protected in the
text of NAFTA. Canadian processors, who must buy at high prices from
Canadian marketing boards, cannot compete with US processors. Processors, thus, have an incentive to locate in the USA, where they have access
to cheaper milk, eggs and poultry and can then export processed foods to
Canada under the FTA. Under these circumstances, many believe, it is
inevitable that supply management will wither away.[89] Canada was virtually
isolated in its defence of supply management in the GATT negotiations,
where Canada was under pressure to replace import restrictions with high
tariffs that would fall over time. It is also unclear whether the USA, in the
context of NAFTA, will continue to remain silent about Quebec's policy of
targeted government assistance for key and nascent industries.

On 26 October 1992, Canadians voted on a package of constitutional
reforms designed to satisfy Quebec's reservations stemming from the 1982
patriation of the Constitution to which it did not accede. The so-called
Charlottetown Accord was decisively rejected, both by Quebecers (55 per
cent opposed) and a majority of English Canadians (five of nine provinces).
Quebecers felt it did not go far enough to meet Quebec's legitimate claim
to provincial autonomy, while the rest of Canada believed that it went too
far in giving Quebec special treatment. Much depends on the outcome of
the 1994 Quebec provincial election. If the separatist Parti Québecois forms
the next provincial government, political uncertainty may hamper free trade
efforts. The Charlottetown Accord, for instance, put political considerations
ahead of economic, allowing more than 500 interprovincial trade barriers to
remain.[90] The value of trade among the Canadian provinces in 1988 was $90
billion, a 16 per cent increase since 1984.[91] Nevertheless, subsidies and
other non-tariff obstacles to interprovincial commerce are estimated to cost
Canadian consumers $6.5 billion a year. There are champions of North
American free trade who see it as an opportunity to overcome some of the
inherent inefficiencies in the federal principle.[92] The problem is particularly
acute in Canada where, first, the Judicial Committee of the Privy Council in
London and then the Supreme Court allocated political responsibility for
regulation of the economy to the provincial governments. In terms of the
regulatory burden, it is easier, for example, to drive a truck from Canada to
Mexico than across Canada.[93] Five billion dollars a year, moreover, could
be saved if provincial governments simply purchased from the lowest
bidder. A likely effect of NAFTA is to put pressure on the provinces to
lower these barriers.

The effort to establish a North American common market is producing
pressure similar to that felt in the European Union to harmonize and unify

US, Canadian and Mexican national policies in a variety of areas. One of the principal US and Canadian reservations about including a developing country in NAFTA is that firms will attempt to take advantage of the relatively lax enforcement of environmental and labour regulations in Mexico by moving manufacturing plants to NAFTA's Latin American partner. A likely development is that, due to competitive pressure and the side environmental and labour accords negotiated in 1993, US and Canadian enforcement of environmental protection and occupational safety legislation will be relaxed and that Mexican enforcement efforts will intensify, producing a convergence in both the content of regulation and levels of policing in the three regimes.[94] There are also demands for common patent and copyright rules in the three member states. Calls for a common North American currency are even being heard.[95]

Unlike the FTA, NAFTA contains an accession clause similar to the provisions for accession to the GATT. It allows countries to join NAFTA simply by agreeing to abide by its terms, and there is no need for the member states to reopen negotiations every time a new country seeks membership.

President George Bush regarded NAFTA as the first step in the establishment of a hemispheric free trade area. Bush announced the Enterprise for the Americas Initiative (EAI) in June 1990. EAI's three pillars are trade, investment and debt reduction. EAI envisages a huge free trade area of which NAFTA is a key stepping stone. Under EAI the US signed sixteen trade and investment agreements with 31 countries in Latin America and the Caribbean. The EAI is likely to bring first Chile and then Brazil into the free trade arrangement with Canada and Mexico. Argentina has also expressed interest in joining.

Independently of the USA, many Latin American nations are attempting to establish their own free trade zones. Existing and proposed trade groups include the Andean Pact (1969), MERCOSUR, consisting of Brazil, Argentina, Paraguay and Uruguay, and the Central American Common Market, or Caricom (1963). In 1991 Mexico signed free trade agreements with Chile, Colombia and Venezuela, giving those countries 'back-door' access to the US market under NAFTA. In 1993 twenty Caribbean and Central American countries formed a common market.

The Bush Administration considered the economic integration of the Western hemisphere to be the key to the entrenchment of democratic regimes in Latin America.[96] Thus, the Mulroney Government in Canada in 1993 talked of expanding its efforts to promote trade and other forms of economic cooperation in Latin America. There was a growing opinion among government officials in both Washington and Ottawa that opportunities to trade with the USA and Canada were more important in the economic development of Latin America than traditional foreign aid.[97]

The inclusion of Mexico in the free trade zone and the presence of the accession clause represent a change in the policy which the USA and Canada have taken towards the developing nations of Latin America. Whereas in the past Canada and the USA have given one-way preferential treatment to imports from developing countries, now Mexico and any future NAFTA signatories will have to provide reciprocity for any reduction in tariffs. Countries unwilling to provide reciprocity to US and Canadian exporters will find their exports to North America and their ability to attract foreign investment handicapped.[98] NAFTA provides a springboard for US and Canadian firms into Central and South America, where country after country is jettisoning its protectionist policies and adopting market reforms.

The USA feels pressure to finance its trade deficit with Japan by exporting more to Latin America. The US trade deficit with Latin America dropped from $11 billion in 1986 to less than $1 billion in 1991. Latin America's market is over three times larger than that of Central and Eastern Europe and larger than the entire South-east Asian market. In 1991 the Mexican economy grew by 4.5 per cent and Chile's by 5.5 per cent. Latin America's population of 450 million is 30 million more than the populations of Central and Eastern Europe and the former Soviet Union combined. The population of Latin America will exceed 700 million by 2020. In 1990 US exports to Latin America were $5 billion more than exports to Japan and 50 per cent of exports to Europe. The USA accounts for 57 per cent of exports to Latin America. In 1991 US exports to Mexico increased 18 per cent. US direct investment in Mexico doubled from 1986 to 1990, to $73 billion. The chief obstacle to further export growth is the low incomes and purchasing power of Latin Americans.[99]

An unanswered question is whether the 'widening' of NAFTA will be accompanied by its 'deepening'. The latter would involve, among other measures, harmonization of the laws of the member countries, coordination of fiscal and tax policies and limitations on exchange rate fluctuations.[100]

NAFTA is part of a trend in free trade and must be viewed in the context of the Uruguay Round of the GATT negotiations, Going Global, Pacific 2000 and EC 92. FTA helped move the stalled GATT negotiations forward because it facilitated US–Canada cooperation in trying to overcome European and Japanese resistance to ending agricultural subsidies, the major stumbling block to the completion of the Uruguay Round. Canadian grain farmers pinned their hopes of recovery on GATT negotiations, successfully completed in 1993, aimed at producing a truce in the subsidy war between the USA and the EC. Canada could not afford to provide export subsidies on the scale of the USA and the EC.[101]

Regional free trade deals do not contradict but rather complement the multilateral approach symbolized by GATT and help reinforce the latter.[102] GATT has never opposed regional trade agreements, as long as they do not interfere with the international obligations of the contracting parties. Such initiatives are authorized under Article XXIV of the GATT, which deals with free trade pacts and customs unions. That the three nations of North America could reach agreement on free trade was an encouraging sign for participants in the Uruguay Round. If agreement is not possible on a continental level, agreement on a global level is less likely.[103]

The proliferation in regional agreements is a response to the exigencies accompanying the globalization of production and markets. Other causes of regional integration are the need to provide wider outlets to domestic producers; to enhance competitiveness through greater specialization, economies of scale, development of business networks, more efficient use of resources and elimination of structural obstacles; to achieve greater stability and security of access to the markets of a country's main trading partners; and to improve procedures for settling disputes and remedying imbalances in bilateral trade.

There will also be pressures on Canada, Mexico and the USA to change their domestic policies in areas such as sales taxes, safety laws, environmental laws, oil and natural gas price subsidies, tax inducements, access to timber on government lands at below-market prices, labour rights and workers' compensation. Each of these policies could be characterized as 'trade-distorting' by its North American partners.[104]

As the accession clause makes clear, NAFTA does not form a 'Fortress North America', or an impenetrable trade bloc. It incorporates nearly all the clauses of GATT and goes even further in liberalizing investment and trade in services, provisions which were included in the 1993 GATT agreement. NAFTA was a model for the GATT in several respects. In order for the accord to be effective the GATT negotiators knew they had to cover trade in agricultural products and textiles, provide rules for protection of intellectual property, for investment and for services and deal effectively with dumping and subsidies. The final agreement touched on each of these critical areas for the first time.

CONCLUSION

There is a fundamental difference between NAFTA and SEA. For instance, when Spain, Portugal and Greece joined the EC, the EC's richer members provided generous assistance to help these countries raise their environmental and labour standards. Under NAFTA, by contrast, Canada and the USA offer no such direct aid to Mexico.

Europe is much closer to achieving free trade in goods, services, capital and investment than is North America. The reason is that Europe has supranational institutions which are supervising the economic union. The community project is the product of a political decision made after the Second World War. There is no equivalent will to establish a North American Community. The Maastricht's goal is an economic, monetary and political union. By contrast, NAFTA is a traditional free trade pact, which leaves each member state in control of its own policies. The collateral agreements on labour and the environment, for instance, do not establish commissions with power to force new standards on Mexico: they simply hear complaints of failure by Mexico to enforce its own standards. The essential difference between EC 92 and NAFTA is illustrated by the contrasting treatment of Poland and Mexico, both of which are economically underdeveloped regimes lacking democratic institutions. Whereas the EU demands that both economic and political reforms occur in Poland before it will be eligible for membership, the USA and Canada are making no explicit political demands on Mexico.[105]

Regional trade agreements such as NAFTA, although presented as complementary to GATT, carry the potential to be trade discriminatory and trade diverting. ASEAN, including Brunei, Indonesia, Malaysia, the Philippines, Singapore and Thailand, says that NAFTA will cost its members $2 billion a year in US business.[106] There is also the possibility that, as NAFTA grows to include more Latin American countries, it will be seen in the USA as a substitute for multilateralism. The result could be a world divided into three trading blocs dominated, respectively, by Germany, the USA and Japan. The evolution of the EC and the great difficulty in concluding the Uruguay Round make these developments all the more likely. Rivalry between the USA and the EC over wheat exports, for instance, had a negative impact on farmers outside the USA and Europe, as each rival provided export subsidies to its grain farmers causing Australian and Canadian wheat growers, for instance, to lose a portion of their export market.

In addition to diverting trade, NAFTA may also divert investment away from non-NAFTA countries. Automobile manufacturing in Mexico is expected to attract a great deal of FDI, and the ongoing economic reforms in Mexico will continue to attract overseas capital. The USA will have an advantage in exporting agricultural products to Mexico to the exclusion of traditional suppliers, such as New Zealand. On the other hand, the expected surge in Mexican incomes following NAFTA will generate new market demand, from which all of Mexico's trading partners will benefit.

NAFTA is likely to succeed for a number of reasons. According to one analyst, successful trading blocs have four characteristics: (1) political commitment to organize regionally; (2) similar laws and regulatory regimes; (3) geographic proximity; and (4) similar levels of per capitum GNP (gross national product).[107] The USA, Canada and Mexico are continental neighbours and are committed to the formation of a continental trade bloc. Mexico's per capitum GNP is far lower than that of its northern neighbours, and its legal and administrative systems are quite different. These deficiencies are probably offset, however, by the degree to which the three economies are already integrated and by Mexico's willingness to undergo political, legal and economic reform.[108] All three countries, of course, are afraid of being excluded from the Asian and especially the European markets as a result of the EC 92 process.

Although Mexico has a much lower per capitum GNP than the USA or Canada, and Mexico's legal and political systems are quite different, successive Mexican governments have displayed a readiness to accept major structural reforms in order to become more like their North American partners. The negative effect on the USA and Canada of bringing Mexico into a free trade area is limited by the small size of the Mexican economy, about the same size as that of the state of Indiana. Moreover, US industry recognizes the need to relocate some of its production to low-wage regions. The most important promise of success is the extent to which the three economies are already integrated and the need each country has in managing this three-way trade, which will continue to grow whether there is a NAFTA or not.[109]

Japan and other third parties have some legitimate concerns about the implications of NAFTA. In any common market arrangement, there is a potential for trade discrimination and trade diversion. These effects may be heightened because it is the intention of the North American members to extend NAFTA's trade preferences to Central and South America. NAFTA may be a sign that the USA is replacing multilateralism with regionalism, with the ultimate result being the division of the world into three major trading blocs, contrary to the spirit and letter of GATT. Finally, of concern to many is the managed trade nature of NAFTA, which seems inconsistent with the liberal features of GATT.

These fears, however, are largely groundless. First, all three countries view NAFTA as complementary to GATT. Each partner has a strong incentive to continue to support extension of the multilateral trading system. The sheer diversity of US trade around the globe deters efforts to replace a multilateral with a regional trade policy. Canada and Mexico, with relatively small and vulnerable economies, have a strong incentive to rely on GATT to protect them against punitive and protectionist US measures. The desire of many Latin American countries to expand NAFTA into a Western Hemisphere Free Trade Area, moreover, is forcing market reforms on a large scale in those countries with the consequence of freeing more and more world trade.[110]

The USA, viewed the FTA and NAFTA as attempts to move beyond the stalled Uruguay Round and spur on its completion. The longer-term effects on the multilateral trading system in the North American negotiations were more important to the USA than short-term gains. As it turned out, the completion of the Uruguay Round essentially depended on the EC's position on agricultural trade, a position which was not greatly affected by the existence of NAFTA.[111]

Sensitive that Japan might feel excluded by Canada's heightened interest in trade with the USA and Mexico, in May 1991 the prime minister of Canada joined the Japanese prime minister in launching an ambitious effort to strengthen investment and trade links between the two Pacific countries. President Clinton believed ratification of NAFTA gave him momentum in trade liberalization talks with Japan, at the APEC meeting in October 1993 and in bilateral negotiations during the following months.

The Japanese have no more to fear from NAFTA than from the SEA. Both agreements are compatible with GATT and helped to stimulate completion of the Uruguay Round and to provide examples of possible improvements in the international trade regime, including the areas of enforcement, dispute resolution, intellectual property, investment and services. On balance, we can say that both NAFTA and the SEA essentially are trade-generating, not trade-diverting, arrangements.

Notes

1. Michel Godet, 'A Quasi Certainty: Europtimism', *The Annals of the American Academy of Political and Social Sciences*, 522 (July 1992) p. 80.
2. Alan Tiller, *Doing Business in Today's Western Europe* (Lincolnwood, NJ: NTC Business Books, 1992) p. 8.
3. Commission of the European Communities, *Completing the Internal Market* (Brussels: European Community, 14 June 1985), COM (85) 310.
4. Commission of the European Communities, 'Single European Act', *Bulletin of the European Communities* (1986 EC Bulletin supplement N0. 2).
5. Shawn Tully, 'Europe 1992: More Unity Than You Think', *Fortune*, 24 August 1992, p. 139.
6. Tully, 'Europe 1992', p. 138.
7. Hartmut Elsenhans, 'Europe 89–92 and the Third World', *International Social Science Journal*, 44 (1992) pp. 135–6.
8. 'General Motors in Germany', *The Economist*, 26 September 1992, p. 77.
9. Joseph LaPalombara, 'A New Europe?', *The Yale Review*, 80 (July 1992) p. 9.
10. LaPalombara, 'A New Europe?', p. 4.

11. Craig R. Whitney, 'Europe's Muted Joy, and its Misgivings', *New York Times*, 21 September 1992, p. A1.
12. Whitney, 'Europe's Muted Joy', p. A1.
13. Werner J. Feld, 'The Struggle for Political Union', *National Forum*, Spring 1992, p. 41.
14. 'Europe in Pieces', *Newsweek*, 28 September 1992, p. 26.
15. Pierre-Henri Laurent, 'Europe 1992: From the Crossroads Toward Unity', *Phi Kappa Phi Journal*, Spring 1992, p. 36.
16. C. Bernard Meyers, 'Europe 1992 and Beyond', *Fortune*, 21 September 1992, p. 140.
17. Harry P. Bowen and David G. Mayes, *The European Challenge: Industry's Response to the 1992 Programme* (New York: Harvester Wheatsheaf, 1991) p. 26.
18. Tully, 'Europe 1992', p. 142.
19. Dave Skidmore, 'America's Trade Gap Gets Worse Without Much Hope for Gain', *The (Memphis) Commercial Appeal*, 2 March 1993, p. B4.
20. René Schwok, *US–EC Relations in the Post-Cold War Era: Conflict or Partnership?* (Boulder, CO: Westview Press, 1991) pp. 53–6.
21. Eugene J. McAllister, 'EC 1992 and US Business', *US Department of State Dispatch*, 15 June 1992, p. 467.
22. McAllister, 'EC 1992 and US Business', p. 466.
23. Laurent, 'Europe 1992', p. 36.
24. 'General Motors in Germany', *The Economist*, 26 September 1992, p. 78.
25. Laurent, 'Europe 1992', p. 38.
26. Robert Corker, 'The Changing Nature of Japanese Trade', *Finance and Development*, 28 (June 1991) p. 7.
27. John van Oudenaren, 'European Integration as Seen From the United States', *International Social Science Journal*, 44 (1992) p. 118.
28. Laurent, 'Europe 1992', p. 38.
29. Martin Crutsinger, 'US May Limit Purchases From EC', *The (Memphis) Commercial Appeal*, 2 February 1992, p. 1A.
30. Schwok, *US–EC Relations in the Post-Cold War Era*, p. 56.
31. Herbert Grubel, 'Effects on the Rest of the World: Trade Diversion, Creation and Wealth', in Silvio Borner and Herbert Grubel (eds), *The European Community After 1992: Perspectives from the Outside* (London: Macmillan, 1992) p. 35.
32. Grubel, 'Effects on the Rest of the World', p. 41.
33. McAllister, 'EC 1992 and US Business', p. 466.
34 Lindley H. Clark, Jr, 'The GATT Struggle Continues', *The Wall Street Journal*, 16 March 1993, p. A20.
35. Diane Francis, 'A Year for Change and a Chance to Sputter Ahead', *The Financial Post*, 2 January 1993.
36. *North American Free Trade Agreement: An Overview and Description* (Ottawa: Government of Canada, 1992) p. i.
37. Axel Krause, *Inside the New Europe* (New York: Cornelia & Michael Bessie Books, 1991) p. 105.
38. 'Canada World's No. 1 Debtor', *Ottawa Citizen*, 16 January 1993.
39. *Survey of Current Business*, May 1992, p. 61.
40. 'Mayer Stresses "Co-operation With US on Wheat"', *Newscan* (Washington, DC: Canadian Embassy) 19 February 1993.

41. Jerry Haar, 'Will Trade Pact Survive Mulroney Exit?', *The Miami Herald*, 14 March 1993.
42. 'Canada/US Steel Dispute Escalates', *Newscan* (Washington, DC: Canadian Embassy) 19 February 1993.
43. Canadian Press, 1 March 1993.
44. Francis, 'A Year for Change'.
45. Alan Toulin, 'Study Sheds Some Light on Wisdom of Trade Policy', *The Financial Post*, 6 March 1993.
46. Bruce Little, 'Trade Report May Fuel Debate', *The Globe and Mail*, 18 December 1992, p. B2.
47. *Québec and the North American Free Trade Agreement* (Quebec City: Government of Quebec, 1993) p. iii.
48. 'The boom that Dare Not Speak its Name', *The Globe and Mail*, 28 November 1992.
49. *Survey of Current Business*, August 1992, p. 125.
50. 'Riding Clinton's Coattails', *The Edmonton Journal*, 22 March 1993.
51. 'Ontario Proposal to Settle Beer War "Flawed": US', *The Financial Post*, 28 November 1992.
52. See Sidney Weintraub and Leigh Boske, *US–Mexico Free Trade Agreement: Economic Impact on Texas* (Austin, TX: University of Texas, 1992).
53. Canadian Press, 18 March 1993.
54. Rod McQueen, 'Debate over NAFTA has long way to go in US', *Financial Post*, 10 March 1993.
55. Rowland Evans and Robert Novak, 'Administration Environmentalists Get Warning on NAFTA', *The Commercial Appeal*, 25 March 1993, p. A13.
56. 'Ottawa Firm on Trade Deal, Wilson Insists', *Toronto Star*, 9 March 1993.
57. Earl H. Fry, 'Canada's Constitutional and Unity Crises: Implications for North American Economic Relations', unpublished paper presented at a conference in Wellington, New Zealand, 14–16 December 1992.
58. Robert G. Cushing, John Higley, Tain Tompkins, Michael Sutton, and Sidney Weintraub, *Australia and New Zealand: The Challenge of NAFTA*, (Austin, TX: Lyndon B. Johnson School of Public Affairs, 1992) p. 43.
59. Dan Goodgame, 'Trade Warrior', *Time*, 15 March 1993, p. 51.
60. David W. Cravens, H. Kirk Downey and Paul Lauritano, 'Global Competition in the Commercial Aircraft Industry: Positioning for Advantage by the Triad Nations', *Columbia Journal of World Business*, 26 (Winter 1992) p. 47.
61. Mark Lacter, 'NAFTA: Trade Accord Lacks Identity', *The (Memphis) Commercial Appeal*, 7 March 1993, p. B1.
62. Peter Morton, 'Canada the "Honest Broker" on NAFTA Side Deals', *The Financial Post*, 21 April 1993.
63. Organization for Economic Cooperation and Development, *Études économiques de l'OCDE; Mexique* (Paris: OECD, July 1992).
64. Arturo Carrillo, 'Note – The New Mexican Revolution: Economic Reform and the 1989 Regulations of the Law for the Promotion of Mexican Investment and the Regulation of Foreign Investment', *The George Washington Journal of International Law and Economics*, 24 (1991) p. 648.
65. OECD, *Études économiques de l'OCDE: Mexique*.
66. *North American Free Trade Agreement*, p. iv.
67. 'Study on North American Free Trade Agreement Unveiled', *Québec Update*, 14 March 1993, p. 1.

68. *Québec and the North American Free Trade Agreement*, p. iv.
69. 'Québec to Promote Trade with Mexico,' *Québec Update*, 13 December 1992, p. 1.
70. In a free trade area, all barriers are removed on trade among member countries. In a customs union, members allow for no tariffs or other barriers to trade among their economies. In a common market, there is free movement of labour and capital as well as goods and services among member nations.
71. 'Keep An Eye on the Side Deals,' *The Ottawa Citizen*, 15 March 1993.
72. Robert Corker, 'The Changing Nature of Japanese Trade', *Finance and Development*, 28 (June 1991) pp. 6–7.
73. *Quebec and the North American Free Trade Agreement*, p. 9.
74. Haar, 'Will Trade Pact Survive Mulroney Exit?'.
75. Joanne Chianello, 'Stelco Urges NAFTA Side Accord on Steel', *Financial Post*, 26 March 1993.
76. Khosrow Fatema (ed.), *The Maquiladora Industry: Economic Solution or Problem?* (New York: Praeger, 1990).
77. 'Talks Set for Next Month on "Parallel" NAFTA Deals', *Financial Post*, 18 February 1993.
78. Gayle MacDonald, 'Developers Explore Mexican Frontier', *The Financial Post*, 13 February 1993, p. S19.
79. *The Kiplinger Washington Letter*, 8 January 1993, p. 2.
80. David Crane, 'NAFTA Still Puzzles Canadians', *The Toronto Star*, 31 December 1992.
81. Canadian Press, 24 February 1993.
82. Keith Bradsher, 'Hondas' Nationality Proves Troublesome for Free-Trade Pact', *New York Times*, 9 October 1992, p. A1.
83. Lindsay Chappell, 'Honda has Big Incentive to Back New Trade Treaty', *Automotive News*, 14 September 1992, p. 33.
84. Lindsay Chappell, 'Japanese Seek Legal Trade with Mexico', *Automotive News*, 28 September 1992, p. 10.
85. 'Use NAFTA to Advance Rights', *The (Montreal) Gazette*, 15 February 1993.
86. Conrad Black, 'Renewed Federalism – With Washington?', *The Globe and Mail*, 23 June 1992, p. A15.
87. 'Analysts: US–Mexico Pact Requires Broad Thinking', *North American Report on Free Trade*, 4 February 1991, p. 6.
88. Black, 'Renewed Federalism – With Washington?', p. A15.
89. H.G. Grubel, 'Border-trade, Free Trade and Interest Groups', Economics Discussion Paper 90 (1990), Simon Fraser University, Department of Economics.
90. Diane Francis, 'The Dangers of a National Divorce', *Maclean's*, 19 October 1992, p. 13.
91. 'Interprovincial Trade Figures', *Québec Update*, June 1992, p. 1.
92. D.J. Markwell, 'The Federal States: Lessons from North American and European Experience', Ditchley Conference Report No. D91/11, p. 2.
93. *Financial Post*, 17 April 1991, p. 6; *Maclean's*, 7 September 1992, pp. 30–1.
94. Tim Golden, 'US Defends Pact on Mexico Trade; White House Sees No Exodus of Businesses to Escape Environmental Rules', *New York Times*, 18 October 1991, p. A4.

95. Sylvia Nasar, 'North American Currency Links?' *New York Times*, 18 December 1991, p. C2.
96. John H. Costello, 'Hemispheric Free Trade: The Key to the United States' Economic Future', *The Fact Sheet* (Clearinghouse on State International Policies, August–September 1992) p. 4.
97. Jeff Sallot, 'The Changing Face of Foreign Aid', *The (Ottawa) Globe and Mail*, 13 February 1993, p. A6.
98. Crane, 'NAFTA Still Puzzles Canadians'.
99. Costello, 'Hemispheric Free Trade', p. 3.
100. Peter Morici, *Trade Talks With Mexico: A Time for Realism* (Washington, DC: National Planning Association, 1991).
101. 'Glut the Issue, Not Subsidies', *The (Ottawa) Citizen*, 8 February 1993.
102. *The Liberalization of Trade Between Canada, the United States and Mexico: The Issues from a Quebec Perspective* (Quebec City: Foreign Ministry, 1992).
103. 'New Hazards for NAFTA', *The Financial Post*, 17 March 1993.
104. Crane, 'NAFTA Still Puzzles Canadians'.
105. Judith Gentleman and Voytek Zubek, 'International Integration and Democratic Development: The Cases of Poland and Mexico', *Journal of Interamerican Studies and World Affairs*, 34 (1992) p. 61.
106. 'Southeast Asia Fears American Trade Pact', *The (Memphis) Commercial Appeal*, 24 November 1992, p. B2.
107. Jeffrey J. Schott, 'Trading Blocs and the World Trading System', *The World Economy*, March 1991.
108. Cushing *et al.*, *Australia and New Zealand*, p. 13.
109. Ibid, p. 12.
110. C.A. Primo Braga, 'US Policies and the Prospects for Latin American Economic Integration', in Werner Baer and Donald V. Coes (eds), *United States Policies and the Latin American Economies* (New York: Praeger, 1990).
111. C.A Primo Braga, 'NAFTA and the Rest of the World', in Nora Lustig, Barry Bosworth and Robert Lawrence (eds), *North American Free Trade: Assessing the Impact* (Washington, DC: The Brookings Institution, 1992) p. 232.

2 The Canada–US Free Trade Agreement: Implications for the Global Trading Regime
William Dymond

Negotiations between Canada and the USA for a free trade agreement began in May 1986 and concluded in December 1987. Following approval of domestic implementing legislation in the Canadian Parliament and the US Congress, the Canada–US Free Trade Agreement[1] entered into effect on 1 January 1989. The FTA is the largest free trade agreement ever concluded between two countries.[2] It is, moreover, the first economically significant bilateral or multilateral trade agreement to be concluded since the end of the Tokyo Round in 1979.[3] The Agreement not only responds to the unique needs of Canada and the USA but it reverses the growing trend to protectionism in international trade by providing a tangible demonstration of the economic and political vitality and viability of trade liberalization.

The significance of the FTA for the multilateral trading system lies in the motivations of the two countries in departing from the GATT framework for the conduct of their bilateral trade relationship, in the unprecedented scope and coverage of the Agreement and in the impact it will have on multilateral trade negotiations.

The first part of this chapter analyses the different but compatible objectives that Canada and the USA brought to the negotiations. For Canada, such an agreement offered the means to accelerate the adjustment of the Canadian economy to a rapidly evolving and highly competitive world trading system. For the USA, the Agreement was an opportunity to resolve long-standing trade problems with Canada and to advance its multilateral trading objectives. The second part describes the scope of the FTA. The provisions governing trade in goods broadly follow the provisions of European free trade agreements. However, the provisions creating new rights and obligations for trade in services (including financial services) and for the treatment of investment and investors significantly advance the frontiers of international trade agreements. The provisions for further negotiations ensure the continual evolution of the FTA as a dynamic instrument of trade relations between Canada and the USA. The FTA makes a major contribution to international trade law through the imposition of more comprehensive limits upon the capacity of governments to interfere with international trade through the application of innovative principles and procedures for the settlement of disputes. The third part examines the consistency of the FTA with the GATT, discusses the issue of trade creation and trade diversion and analyses the impact of the Agreement upon multilateral trade negotiations.

For Canada, the FTA is a major step forward in securing and improving access to the US market, which absorbs some three-quarters of Canadian exports. The FTA establishes an institutional and statutory shield against either legislated or administrative US protectionism by transforming a patchwork of contractual rights and obligations, informal arrangements and *ad hoc* understandings into a treaty relationship. The FTA demonstrates that comprehensive trade liberalization can overcome deeply rooted protectionist sentiment in the US Congress. Because the Uruguay Round did not achieve all the major objectives on the US multilateral agenda, the USA, if it does not adopt a more protectionist posture, will continue to look to further bilateral agreements rather than leaving its trade policy objectives hostage to an unresponsive multilateral framework.

THE RATIONALE

The entry into force of the FTA was the culmination of 150 years of efforts to remove trade barriers between Canada and the USA. Previous efforts had fallen victim to indifference or hostility in one country or the other.[4] If the politics for negotiating a bilateral free trade agreement had usually been unaccommodating, the economic rationale was constant.

Canada's Motivations

A free trade agreement with the USA offered Canada the potential to remove the limits to economic growth inherent in a small, open, export-driven economy. Historically, Canada has always depended upon export markets to absorb a large part of the output of its resource-based and manufacturing industries. Much of Canadian infrastructure investment has been directed towards the development of transportation systems to move exports to world markets. More than half of the production of the mining, forestry and manufacturing sectors is exported.[5] In 1986, Canada traded over $165 billion of goods and $30 billion of services (excluding investment and other investment income), representing the equivalent of 53 per cent of national production.[6] Despite seven rounds of multilateral trade liberalization under GATT extending over 30 years, many sectors of Canadian industry remained characterized by fragmented and small-scale production, and faced growing threats to their competitive position in both export and domestic markets. Indeed, in the absence of secure and open terms of export market access, Canadian industry risked falling into a trap. On one hand, the levels of Canadian protection were no longer sufficient to prevent significant import penetration of the domestic market. On the other, access to world markets was impeded by tariff and non-tariff barriers, depriving Canadian industry of the opportunity to adjust out of inefficient production and achieve economies of scale and specialization.[7] Since some 75 per cent of Canadian exports are sold in the USA,[8] the terms and conditions of access to this market are critical to the domestic and international competitive position of Canadian industry.

From 1948 until 1989 when the FTA entered into force, Canada and the USA relied upon GATT as the principal contractual basis of their bilateral trade relationship. GATT provided a stable framework of trading rules and a productive negotiating forum for the rapid growth of international trade generally, and trade between Canada and the USA in particular. However, in the 1970s and 1980s the stability and security of this framework, erected on the principle of non-discrimination, began to erode, thereby undermining the confidence of investors and traders in the continued growth of international trade on a predictable and competitive basis.

Between 1974 and 1988, four major trade bills were enacted in the USA,[9] each adding to the arsenal of weapons available to US industry, Congress and the Administration to protect the US market. In the 1980s, the imposition of voluntary export restraint (VER) arrangements on steel, automobiles and shoes heralded the undisciplined application of measures outside the GATT to restrict the flow of imports in sensitive US industry sectors. Further, US industry began to make aggressive use of trade remedy legislation,[10] encouraged by an accommodating attitude on the part of the Reagan Administration that reflected and in part fuelled the rise of protectionist sentiment in the USA.

For Canada, it was the emergence of trade remedy legislation – countervailing and anti-dumping duties – to replace the tariff as the principal instrument of protection of domestic industry which signified the erosion of the principle and practice of non-discrimination. Such laws are inherently discriminatory in the treatment accorded to domestic products and imports. Countervailing duties may be applied to imported products judged (unilaterally) to benefit from an injurious subsidy, irrespective of subsidies granted to the domestic product or to the injury which such domestic subsidies cause other domestic producers. Anti-dumping duties may be applied to dumped imports, but domestic products dumped on the domestic market are subject only to competition laws operating under wholly different standards and procedures.

The GATT codes of 1967 and 1979, through the elaboration of detailed rules for the application of trade remedy laws, have in effect conferred multilateral blessing on the use of highly sophisticated and basically discriminatory instruments of protection.[11] Dependent upon the US market to absorb an ever-increasing share of its exports, Canada could not afford the luxury of indifference to steadily increasing threats to its access to that market. Hence, in September 1985 the Canadian Government decided to enter into negotiations for a comprehensive bilateral trade agreement to secure and enhance market access to the USA. Brian Mulroney, the Prime Minister defined Canadian objectives as follows: 'Such a [free trade] agreement should secure and enhance access to each other's markets by reducing and eliminating tariff and non-tariff barriers and result in a better and more predictable set of rules whereby our trade is conducted.'[12]

The USA had different motivations in entering into negotiations for a free trade agreement. Hitherto committed to a multilateral trade policy, the US had become increasingly impatient and frustrated with the capacity of the multilateral trading system to address its trade interests.[13] The 1979 Trade Agreements Act called for a study of trade agreements with countries of the northern portion of the Western hemisphere; the 1984 Trade Act provided for the negotiation of bilateral agreement with Israel and any other country which so requested.[14] In the wake of the 1985 Plaza Accord on exchange rates, the Reagan Administration issued a 'Trade Policy Statement' which declared both US interest in the early launch of a new round of multilateral trade negotiations and US willingness to consider the negotiation of bilateral trade agreements.[15] Accordingly, when Mulroney formally proposed the negotiation of a bilateral agreement in September 1985, President Reagan responded promptly and enthusiastically.[16]

The USA's Motivations

The USA approached the free trade negotiations as an opportunity to address long-standing bilateral trade problems and to advance its multilateral objectives.[17] Chief among the USA's bilateral objectives was the elimination of Canadian tariffs, which nominally averaged three times the US tariff levels. The USA also sought the elimination of a number of Canadian NTBs, notably the discriminatory restrictions maintained by Canadian provinces on the sale of US wine and spirits.

The multilateral objectives the USA brought to the negotiating table included intellectual property protection, services and investment. More importantly for the international trading environment, the USA perceived a free trade agreement with Canada as an opportunity to liberate its trade policy from exclusive reliance on the multilateral trading system, and the USA was willing and able to negotiate bilateral trade agreements to achieve this. No demonstration could be more credible than a comprehensive agreement with its largest trading partner.[18]

The negotiations were extraordinarily difficult, not only because of the magnitude of the issues at stake, but because of the historical baggage of indifference or hostility to a bilateral free trade agreement. On this occasion, the negotiations provoked an emotional national debate in Canada, terminating in an election where the FTA figured as the central issue.[19] In the USA, indifference reigned until the Secretary of the Treasury took control of the negotiations. The Agreement was approved in Congress[20] despite the passage of the highly protectionist Omnibus Trade and Competitiveness Act of 1988. Hence, the economic rationale by itself was not enough to ensure success; political vision and leadership in both countries played an indispensable role in the negotiation of the Agreement and its subsequent passage in the Canadian Parliament and the US Congress.

SCOPE AND COVERAGE OF THE FTA

The FTA[21] establishes a free trade area within the meaning of Article XXIV of the GATT.[22] The Agreement has eight parts. Part one, covering *objectives and scope*, and parts seven and eight, covering *miscellaneous and final provisions*, bracket the three central elements of the Agreement: *trade in goods* is covered in parts two and three, *services, business travel, investment, and financial services* are covered in parts four and five, and the *institutional and dispute-settlement provisions* are covered in part six.

Objectives and Scope[23]

The objectives and scope articles establish the principle of national treatment as the basic underpinning of the Agreement. While the Agreement explicitly affirms the parties' rights and obligations under other bilateral and multilateral agreements, the FTA is accorded precedence unless there is a specific provision to the contrary (as is the case for the Agreement on an International Energy Programme).[24] The Agreement requires the two federal governments, as the parties to the Agreement, to ensure compliance by subnational governments – the Canadian provinces and US states – respecting matters properly within their jurisdiction.[25]

Trade in Goods[26]

The articles governing trade in goods establish the rules of origin. They establish a tariff reduction schedule that provides for the elimination of all tariffs on all goods by 1998. These articles also specify the associated rules respecting duty drawbacks, duty remissions and waivers, customs procedures and customs cooperation. Finally, they spell out the rules respecting the application of emergency safeguard measures to deal with import surges and the general exceptions to these obligations based upon Article XX of the GATT. GATT Article III and its interpretative notes respecting national treatment are also incorporated into and made an integral part of the Agreement. Part three incorporates the GATT Government Procurement Code, elaborates its transparency procedures and provides for a modest expansion of government purchases open to bidders from the other country. It also requires both parties to provide a mechanism whereby dissatisfied bidders can appeal about procurement decisions to an independent agency.

The FTA contains significant new rights and obligations in the agriculture and energy sectors and in the application of trade restrictions to deal with import surges. These articles go beyond the provisions of the GATT and previous free trade agreements in their specificity and discipline.[27] The innovative elements in agriculture are the prohibition of direct export subsidies on bilateral trade (effectively replacing the 'best endeavours' commitment of the GATT),[28] and the obligation to remove restrictions on imports of wheat and other grains from the other country if the level of government support in the country maintaining the restrictions exceeds government support in the other country.[29] The energy articles[30] amplify the GATT provisions respecting export restrictions in situations of short supply or for reasons of national security. As regards short supply, export restrictions may not reduce the proportion of energy goods exported to the other party relative to total production, or disrupt normal supply patterns or alter the product mix of exports to the other country. Exceptions to any provision of the FTA on grounds of national security may only be allowed to supply a military establishment or fulfil a critical defence contract; to respond to situations of armed conflict; to implement national policies or international agreements respecting non-proliferation of nuclear weapons; or to respond to direct threats of disruption in the supply of nuclear materials for defence purposes.

The FTA establishes important new limitations on the right to impose temporary restrictions to deal with import surges.[31] No restriction may be imposed unless imports from the other party alone are the substantial cause of serious injury. No restriction can last longer than three years or extend beyond 1998, by which time all tariffs are to be eliminated. No restriction may reduce imports from the other country below their level in a representative period. Furthermore, Canada and the USA will exempt each other from global import restrictions taken under GATT Article XIX, unless imports from the other country are contributing substantially to serious injury to a domestic industry. Imports below 10 per cent of total imports will normally not be considered as substantial. Any disputes arising out of these provisions are subject to binding arbitration under the dispute settlement procedures of the Agreement.[32]

Services[33] and Business Travel[34]

The FTA extends the principle of national treatment to the regulation of most commercial services. The obligations are prospective. In other words, they do not require either government to change any existing laws and practices. The party making a change in existing regulations for covered services cannot make those regulations any more discriminatory than they already are. Any new regulations for covered services must fully conform to the principle of national treatment. While the FTA does not establish rules of origin with respect to services, either party remains free to deny the benefits of the Agreement to a service provider who is a national of a third party. Neither government is, however, obliged to discriminate against third-party providers of services. These general obligations are elaborated for three service sectors: architecture, tourism, and enhanced telecommunications and computer services.[35] The Agreement also provides that Canada and the USA will negotiate further sectoral annexes extending these obligations. In 1990, a bilateral working group was established to recommend sectors for further negotiations once the Uruguay Round of multilateral trade negotiations has concluded.

The FTA establishes a unique set of obligations to deal with an increasingly vexing problem in international trade: the cross-border movement of company personnel, individual entrepreneurs and investors, and professional and sales representatives. The FTA requires that cross-border movements be facilitated for business travellers, traders, investors, professionals and intra-company transferees.

Investment[36] and Financial Services Industry[37]

The FTA similarly extends national treatment to Canadian and US investors operating in the other country. This basic principle is translated into specific undertakings respecting the establishment of new businesses, the acquisition of existing businesses (including a higher Canadian threshold for the review of direct acquisitions and the gradual elimination of review of indirect acquisitions), and the conduct, operation and sale of businesses once established.

The FTA prohibits the imposition on investors of either party of performance requirements such as local content and import substitution. The Agreement, however, does not preclude the parties from negotiating with investors any requirements respecting product mandate, research and development (R&D) and technology transfers. Expropriation is subject to due process and requires the payment of fair and adequate compensation. No restrictions may be placed on the repatriation of profits or on the proceeds of a sale other than those necessary to implement domestic laws of general application, such as bankruptcy laws, the regulation of securities, or balance of payment measures. The above undertakings on investment apply only to future changes in laws and regulations. Existing laws, policies and practices are generally 'grandfathered'. The practical effect of grandfathering is to freeze the current exceptions to national treatment under Canadian and US law, such as the restrictions in both countries on foreign ownership in the communications and transportation industries.

The financial services sector is covered by a separate set of obligations that guarantees the access which Canadian and US financial institutions currently enjoy in the other country's market and assures them of the benefits of future liberalization. Prior to 1978, Canadian and other foreign banks were generally permitted to operate in more than one US state. These privileges, which were subject to review after ten years, have now been grandfathered indefinitely. Canadian banks in the USA will be able to underwrite and deal in securities of Canadian governments and their agents. Hitherto, under the US Glass–Steagall Act[38] only dealers unaffiliated with a bank were permitted to underwrite these securities in the USA. For the future, Canadian financial institutions are guaranteed the same treatment as that accorded to US financial institutions under any amendments to the Glass–Steagall Act.

The FTA exempts US companies from some aspects of Canadian laws restricting foreign ownership of financial institutions. Additionally, US bank subsidiaries are exempted from the 16 per cent ceiling on the size of the foreign bank sector.

Dispute Settlement[39]

The FTA provides for two types of dispute settlement. The general dispute settlement procedures are based upon GATT principles and procedures and used for all issues except the application of anti-dumping and countervailing duty laws. Any dispute which arises under both the FTA and the GATT may be referred to the dispute resolution procedures of either Agreement. Once a dispute has been so referred, the procedure initiated must be used to the exclusion of any other.

In the general provisions,[40] significant improvements to the GATT procedures have been incorporated, including greater automaticity through the requirement to meet strict time limits beginning with consultations through to the decision of a panel and action on its findings. The provisions for the suspension of benefits in the event of unresolved disputes follow the pattern of other agreements and the GATT.

The FTA's provisions dealing with anti-dumping and countervailing duty law[41] are among the most significant innovations in international trading rules in the Agreement, and they confirm its dynamic character. Either party may refer final anti-dumping and countervailing duty orders to a bilateral panel drawn from a roster of experts. Findings by a panel will be binding on both governments. Decisions of the panel must be rendered within strict time limits. In effect, binational review replaces judicial review by domestic courts.[42]

While existing Canadian and US anti-dumping and countervailing duty laws remain applicable, changes to those laws will apply to the other party only following consultations and only if the new legislation is made specifically applicable to that other party. Either party may refer such a legislative change to a panel for a declaratory opinion on its conformity with the GATT and with the object and purpose of the Agreement. In the event that the panel finds non-conformity and recommends modifications to the new law, and that consultations do not then lead to a mutually satisfactory solution (which may include remedial legislation) within 90 days of the issuance of the declaratory opinion, the party that requested the panel may take comparable legislative or administrative action or may terminate the Agreement upon 60 days' notice.

These provisions address a fundamental weakness in dispute-settlement procedures as currently provided for in the GATT. In such procedures, the ultimate decision of whether to change the measure determined to be contrary to the obligations of the Agreement lies with the party imposing the measure. That party has the options of changing the measure to conform with its obligations under the Agreement, of offering compensation advantages to the complaining party, or of accepting a retaliatory measure. The last two options both amount to rebalancing the rights and obligations of the Agreement at a lower level. The breakthrough achieved by the FTA procedures respecting anti-dumping and countervailing duties is the elimination of the choice of options for compliance with an arbitral ruling. The result of this major advance in international trade law should be greater security and predictability in the terms of market access, and this has always been one of the central objectives of international trade agreements.

Miscellaneous and Final Provisions[43]

The FTA's miscellaneous provisions cover a range of specific issues such as tax conventions, balance of payment problems, national security, intellectual property and cable retransmission rights, and the general exclusion of the cultural industry sector from the rights and obligations of the Agreement. The final provisions concern statistical and publication requirements, amendments to the Agreement, entry into force, duration and termination.

Further Consultations and Negotiations[44]

The specific provisions for further consultations and negotiations give the FTA a dynamic capacity for growth and adaptation. In addition to a general consultation clause, the Agreement provides for consultations on customs issues, grain support levels, energy regulatory issues, the application of investment provisions and financial services. The Agreement provides for further negotiations to accelerate the schedule of tariff elimination, to harmonize or render equivalent product standards (including health and sanitary requirements), to expand the provisions on government procurement, to develop further sectoral annexes on services, and to design a new set of rights and obligations respecting subsidies, dumping, countervailing and anti-dumping duties. These consultations and negotiations will be undertaken through a range of working groups specifically provided for in the Agreement.[45]

The FTA does not address intellectual property rights. Both Canada and the USA had specific objectives in this area. The USA sought principally to secure enhanced protection for patents, especially on pharmaceutical products. Canada for its part sought principally to eliminate a discriminatory provision (Section 337) of the US Tariff Act which offers domestic patent holders a recourse against imports that is not available against domestic products alleged to be infringing patents. Since a compromise could not be reached, intellectual property issues were dropped from the FTA.

ACHIEVEMENTS OF THE FTA

The FTA is a striking achievement as it stands. It brings under the discipline of agreed rules an economic and trade relationship of unique closeness and complexity. It gives the relationship a greater mutuality and defines a common object and purpose for the parties, and it provides Canada and the USA with the means to ensure the implementation of the Agreement and to manage the relationship more effectively, in particular by its pioneering system of dispute settlement and its provisions for further negotiations.

The FTA makes a major contribution to international trade law in several ways. First, the new limits on governmental trade-restrictive action permeate the whole Agreement. By incorporating the rules and precedents of the GATT and building upon these obligations, the Agreement imposes significant new constraints on the capacity of the two countries to interfere with bilateral trade in goods and services and investment flows. These limits are particularly apparent in the rules on emergency safeguards, the more stringent standards for the invocation of the national security exception to restrict energy trade, the obligation of the parties to ensure compliance by subnational levels of government, and the requirement to remove restrictions on trade in grains when support levels are determined to be equivalent. The obligations respecting services, investment and financial services are without precedent in international trade law. These amount to severe constraints on the ability of the two parties to favour nationals over citizens and corporations of the other country. The provisions in these areas not only demonstrate that national treatment standards may be applied to non-goods trade: they also liberate the fastest growing sector of international exchange from future mercantilism laws and regulations.

Second, the comprehensiveness of the Agreement is assured by the broad statement of objectives focused upon the removal of restrictions to trade. The notification provisions of the Agreement enable either party both to be informed of actions which directly or indirectly affect the operation of the Agreement and to submit such actions for consultations and dispute settlement. Hence, in responding to pressures for trade-restrictive action, the parties will need to be cognizant that any action, whether or not it is subject to specific rights and obligations of the FTA, is open to challenge. The effect is that the Agreement will become the principal instrument governing trade relations between Canada and the USA, against which all measures affecting bilateral trade should be measured.

Third, the principles and procedures of dispute settlement are a net improvement over those of the GATT in several important ways. The time limits are certain, whereas they are indeterminate under the GATT. In some matters, proceedings may be instituted at an earlier stage than is possible under GATT procedures. Panels may not be blocked from the adoption of their reports, as can happen in GATT disputes.[46] Remedies under the Agreement are more direct and more effective and, for some important matters, are binding upon the parties. The independence of panels is better assured since government officials are barred from participating, whereas GATT panels are almost always chosen from the representatives of Geneva diplomatic missions. Finally by limiting the choice of panelists to Canadian and US nationals, these procedures will ensure familiarity with the issues and North American legal principles and traditions.

Fourth, the provisions for continuous negotiations covering virtually the whole range of the agreement's rights and obligations ensure the dynamic evolution of the Agreement. It is this feature of the Agreement which most distinguishes it from the GATT and other free trade agreements, and confirms its character as a dynamic instrument of trade relations. These provisions are more than a pious hope or an attempt to mask the failure of the parties to achieve all their objectives in one negotiation. Indeed, in a number of areas, the US statute implementing the FTA[47] spells out in considerable detail the expectations of the Congress that the Administration will vigorously pursue US objectives in the further negotiations. The result is that the FTA will be in continual evolution, ensuring that it will evolve to serve the already complex and extensive bilateral trade and investment relationship between Canada and the USA.

THE IMPACT ON MULTILATERAL TRADE NEGOTIATIONS

As described by one commentator, 'A well functioning multilateral trading system [is] a multilateral non-discriminatory one based on negotiated general rules of behaviour providing for stability and predictability.'[48] It is the erosion of that system which, in large measure, accounts for the decision of Canada and the USA to negotiate a comprehensive bilateral free trade agreement. The FTA's entry into force has, accordingly, major implications for the multilateral trading system. In assessing whether the Agreement will weaken or strengthen the multilateral system, a number of factors are relevant.

One is the consistency of the FTA with Article XXIV of the GATT, which permits two or more contracting parties to conclude a free trade area (or a customs union).[49] The basic principle of Article XXIV is laid out in paragraphs 4 and 5: free trade areas and customs unions are desirable if they facilitate trade between the constituent territories and do not raise barriers to the trade of other contracting parties. Paragraphs 6–10 then spell out certain specific requirements as follows: the parties constituting the free trade area must remove duties and other restrictive regulations of commerce on substantially all trade between them. Some restrictive regulations may be maintained if they are permitted by specified articles of the GATT.[50] Where elimination of trade barriers is not achieved immediately, the Agreement should contain a plan and schedule for the completion of a free trade area within a reasonable length of time.

The consistency of the FTA with the requirements of Article XXIV is beyond dispute. There is no increase in trade barriers against other countries. The Agreement covers all bilateral trade, and all tariffs will be removed in ten years, meeting the requirement for coverage of substantially all trade and for a plan schedule. The remaining bilateral trade restrictions are generally those permitted by Article XI of the GATT or US rights pursuant to its 1955 GATT waiver to impose import restrictions to support agricultural programmes. Finally, the FTA has been duly notified to the GATT and the process for GATT review is well advanced.[51]

A second factor relevant to the multilateral system is whether the FTA is trade-creating or trade-diverting. In practice, a free trade agreement has both trade-creating and trade-diverting effects. Trade creation arises from more efficient patterns of production and higher incomes brought about by the elimination of trade barriers within the free trade area. Trade diversion results from the displacement of lower-cost imports from third countries caused by the elimination of barriers on goods traded within the area, while simultaneously maintaining existing barriers to trade from outside the area. This effect has made some economists hostile to regional arrangements on the grounds that they can result in a loss of economic welfare.[52] The losses due to trade diversion are mitigated, even though the lowest cost goods that hitherto were imported from non-parties are displaced by goods produced within the area. In sectors protected by high external barriers, there will be income gains for consumers who switch to the goods produced within the area that are made cheaper by the elimination of bilateral trade barriers. The dynamic effect of economies of scale arising from free access to the larger market will make goods produced within the area cheaper. The extent to which the Agreement encompasses NTBs will further mitigate the losses that might arise from trade diversion. If one party's exports have been restrained by the other's quantitative restrictions, economic gains will arise from each country's exclusion from the other's restrictions.[53]

Since Canadian tariffs are on average 50 per cent higher than US tariffs (calculated as the potential increase in domestic prices made possible by tariffs),[54] it is reasonable to expect a higher trade diversion effect in Canada than in the USA. However, the positive impact upon income in Canada should lead to more rapid economic growth in Canada[55] and greater imports from the world generally. It is, therefore, unlikely that the trade diversion effect will have a significant impact on the rate of imports from third countries.[56]

A third factor in assessing whether the FTA will weaken or strengthen the multilateral system is the impact of the FTA on multilateral trade negotiations. Here the issue is problematic. Multilateral negotiations permit countries such as Canada to obtain the benefits of trade liberalization on volumes of trade considerably exceeding the volume they liberalize themselves. They allow countries like the USA to deploy the bargaining power of a large market to maximum advantage. The advantages of multilateral negotiations can be realized only if such negotiations advance the objectives of those countries which might otherwise form a regional arrangement. Indeed, unless the appetite for trade liberalization is shared in roughly equal measure, multilateral negotiations can retard rather than advance the elimination of trade barriers.

The system has the inherent disadvantage of imposing convoy rules on trade negotiations: that is, progress is confined to the speed of the most reluctant participant. This means that the reduction of barriers, which two countries may be prepared to accept, may not materialize unless other participants reduce their own trade barriers. The efficiency gains which multilateral negotiations ought to induce may not occur, since the refusal of one or more countries to participate may mean that trade barriers are maintained for all.[57] While the EC and countries like the USA and Japan, with domestic markets exceeding 100 million consumers, can exploit economies of scale and specialization without trade liberalization, smaller countries like Canada pay heavy costs from the maintenance of barriers against their exports.

The growth of regional arrangements has effectively reduced the appetite for multilateral trade negotiations. During the Kennedy Round (1963–67), Britain, Ireland, the Nordics, Austria, Switzerland, Spain, Portugal, Australia and New Zealand (which were as dependent as Canada upon multilateral negotiations) formed a group of countries with which alliances could be forged in pursuit of common interests. By the time of the Tokyo Round, the European members of this group had become linked to the EC as full members, either through accession (as in the case of the Britain, Denmark and Ireland) or as a party to free trade agreements with the EC (as in the case of Sweden and the other EFTA countries). No longer independent participants in the multilateral process, these countries aligned their trade policies with their regional partners rather than form strategic alliances with others. The basis for participation in multilateral trade negotiations had changed not only for these countries, but also for countries like Canada which remained outside regional arrangements and discovered fewer and fewer prospective alliance partners.

Multilateral trade negotiations are difficult to launch and take many years to conclude. Six years elapsed between the Kennedy Round and the launch of the Tokyo Round, and a further six years went by before it concluded in 1979. The current negotiations, the Uruguay Round, began seven years later, in 1986, and were not concluded until late in 1993. In contrast, Canada proposed the negotiation of a comprehensive bilateral agreement to the USA in September 1985; negotiations began in May 1986 and concluded in December 1987. With the agreement's entry into force on 1 January 1989, a little more than three years elapsed from start to finish: a breath-taking pace for modern trade negotiations.

In light of these factors, the impact of the FTA upon multilateral negotiations will depend on whether Canada and the USA can successfully use the Uruguay Round to achieve the reduction and elimination of trade barriers with third countries. It would, of course, be possible for the governments of Canada and the USA to decide that their primary trade policy objective should be the preservation of the preferential advantages of the Agreement. However, the Uruguay Round negotiating objectives of both countries called for the broadest possible trade liberalization,[58] covering not only issues that were not addressed in the Canada–US FTA, such as intellectual property, but services, trade-related investment measures and trade in agriculture, among others. In the FTA, the two countries have pledged to work closely together to achieve their common objectives. Agricultural subsidies are one example; government procurement is another.[59]

In previous multilateral negotiations, Canada has had to deploy its bargaining leverage to purchase concessions with the USA. As a consequence, Canadian negotiators have had little scope to address Canadian objectives *vis-à-vis* Canada by 'piggybacking' on Canadian concessions granted to the USA. Since trade with the USA is covered by the FTA, the stakes for Canada in the Uruguay Round were lower. However, Canada now gained real negotiating coin to exchange with its non-US trading partners in multilateral negotiations.

Both countries are, however, hedging their bets. While reaffirming the importance of a successful and far-reaching conclusion of the Uruguay Round, Canada and the USA decided to enter negotiations for a comprehensive North American free trade agreement encompassing Mexico.[60] For Canada, the small volume of trade with Mexico will not add significantly in the short term to the volume of its trade governed by rules outside the multilateral system. For the USA, such an agreement will encompass its first and third largest trading partners, accounting for almost 40 per cent of US trade. Although the Uruguay Round delivered a major package of multilateral trade liberalization, there are still strong incentives for the USA to seek further bilateral and regional free trade agreements.

CONCLUSION

The capacity for Canada to lurch into protectionism without sustaining immediate economic damage is limited; the capacity of the USA to take that route, while diminished, is considerable and the internal constraints weak. For Canada, the FTA is a major step forward in securing and improving access to the US market, which accounts for some three-quarters of Canadian exports. Beyond the trade covered, the FTA creates an institutional and statutory shield against either legislated or administrative US protectionism by transforming a patchwork of contractual rights and obligations, informal arrangements and *ad hoc* understandings into a treaty relationship. It creates a permanent institutional mechanism to manage the relationship, both as regards individual problems and the negotiation of new rights and obligations. The FTA institutionalizes for Canada a liberal outward-looking US trade policy by restoring security and predictability of access to the US market and cementing the principle of national treatment into US trade policy *vis-à-vis* Canada.

The conditions for translating these developments into the broader multilateral framework have been created. Over many areas, notably trade in services, the FTA establishes a model for multilateral agreement. The FTA demonstrates that comprehensive trade liberalization can overcome deeply-rooted protectionist sentiment in the US Congress. Unless the Uruguay Round achieves the major objectives on the US multilateral agenda, the USA, if it does not adopt a more protectionist posture, will look to bilateral agreements rather than leaving its trade policy objectives hostage to an unresponsive multilateral framework. The success of the Round, and the potential that further bilateral trade agreements might emerge in the future, depends critically upon the readiness of other players in the system to seize the momentum towards trade liberalization re-established and reinforced by the Canada–US Free Trade Agreement.

Notes

1. *Canadian Treaty Series*, 3 (1989) and *International Legal Materials*, 27 (March, 1988) p. 281, American Society of International Law, concluded at Ottawa and Palm Springs (2 January 1988).
2. Canada and the USA enjoy the largest trading relationship of any two countries in the world. Their trade in goods amounted to US$132 billion in 1987,

considerably exceeding US trade with Japan ($82 billion) and bilateral trade between the Federal Republic of Germany and France ($55 billion), which is the largest in the EC. All figures are in US dollars. See US Bureau of the Census, *Highlights of U.S. Export and Import Trade* (Washington, DC: US Department of Commerce, 1988), and Ministry of Finance and the Budget, *Enchantés* (Paris: Government of France).

3. No multilateral trade agreement was concluded between 1979 and the conclusion of the Uruguay Round in 1993. In 1983, Australia and New Zealand concluded the 'Closer Economic Relations Agreement'; see *New Zealand Treaty Series*, 1 (Ministry of Foreign Affairs, 1988). In 1985, the USA and Israel entered into a free trade agreement; see *International Legal Materials*, 14, 3 (May 1985) pp. 63, 281. Both these agreements cover relatively small amounts of trade compared to the FTA.

4. The 1854–1866 Reciprocity Agreement was terminated by the USA. The 1911 Reciprocity Agreement was rejected by Canadian voters in the election of that year.

5. See *Canadian Trade Policy for the 1980s* (Ottawa: Minister of Supply and Services), Cat. No. E2-104/1983E, pp. 7–8.

6. See *The Canada–US Free Trade Agreement: An Economic Assessment* (Ottawa: Department of Finance, 1987) p. 3.

7. See Report of the *Royal Commission on the Economic Union and Development Prospects For Canada* (Ottawa: Minister of Supply and Services, 1985), Cat. No. Z1-1983/1-1E. The report notes on page 300, 'We [Canadian] manufacturers, are caught in a catch 22 situation. On one hand, the tariffs in Canada are no longer high enough to offset the higher costs of producing solely for the Canadian market. On the other hand, even modest tariffs in the U.S. can make it difficult, if not impossible to set up production in Canada to export into that market.' (Statement by J.E. Newall, Dupont Canada Limited.)

8. See *Export by Commodities* (Ottawa: Statistics Canada), Cat. No. 65-004.

9. Trade Act of 1974 (Public Law 93-618), Trade Agreements Act of 1979 (Public Law 96-39), Trade and Tariff Act of 1984 (Public Law 98-573), Omnibus Trade and Competitiveness Act of 1988 (Public Law 100-418).

10. See I.M. Destler, *American Trade Politics: System Under Stress* (Washington, DC: Institute For International Economics, 1986). To take one example, ten separate countervailing duty investigations were launched in 1980, 27 in 1981, 146 in 1982, 30 in 1983, 55 in 1984 and 43 in 1985. The value of trade covered by such investigations rose four-fold, from under $500 million prior to 1980 to over $2 billion in 1985.

11. For a fuller discussion, see M. Hart, 'The Mercantilist's Lament: National Treatment and Modern Trade Negotiations', *Journal of World Trade Law*, 21 (1987) pp. 317–56.

12. See *Report of the Minister of International Trade on Canadian Trade Negotiations*, and *Statement of Prime Minister Mulroney to the House of Commons* (Ottawa: Minister of Supply and Services), Cat. No. E74-8/1986E, pp. 65 and 73.

13. 'The failure of the [world trading system] to move has put the US in the position where we have to contemplate defending our own vital interests. One of the ways we can do that is to take one or more countries and setting up [*sic*] a complete process by which we remove all trade barriers.' Statement by

William Brock, United States Trade Representative in *Report of the Minister of International Trade*, p. 376.

14. Section 1104 of the Trade Agreements Act of 1979 (Public Law 96-39). Section 401 of the Trade and Tariff Act of 1984 (Public Law 98-573).
15. President Reagan in *Remarks to President's Export Council and the Advisory Committee for Trade Negotiations*, 23 September 1985.
16. The exchange of letters between Prime Minister Mulroney and President Reagan is published in *Canadian Treaty Series*, p. 77.
17. US negotiating objectives are set out in the *Report of the United States Trade Representative to the President on Bilateral Trade with Canada*, published in *Canadian Treaty Series*, p. 70.
18. See the Honourable James Baker, Secretary of the Treasury, 'Geopolitical Implications of The US–Canada Trade Pact', *International Economy*, 11 (January/February 1988) p. 34. See also Statement by Senator Lloyd Bentsen, Chairman of the Senate Finance Committee, *Congressional Record* 134, 129 (19 September 1988) pp. S12782–S12784. Referring to the significance of the FTA, Senator Bentsen observed during consideration of HR 5090, a bill to implement the United States–Canada Free Trade Agreement, that the USA could say to other countries in Geneva, 'If you won't work with us to open up world trade, then we can negotiate trade agreements with other countries on a bilateral basis and those two countries will have the advantage of it and you won't be sharing in it.'
19. The Canadian election of 21 November 1988, like that of 1911, focused on free trade with the USA. Mulroney's Government was returned to office with a majority of 35 members over the combined Opposition, assuring the necessary majority for the subsequent passage of the Canadian implementing legislation.
20. The House of Representatives passed the implementing legislation by a vote of 366–41 on 11 August 1988; the Senate passed it by a vote of 81–9 on 19 September 1988.
21. This part summarizes the principal provisions of the FTA. For more detailed analysis, see J.H. Bellow and A.F. Holmer, *Guide to the US–Canada FTA* (Englewood Cliffs, NJ: Prentice-Hall, 1990), and J. Johnson and J. Schachter, *The Free Trade Agreement: A Comprehensive Guide* (Aurora, Ontario: Canada Law Book, 1988).
22. See text accompanying note 51.
23. FTA: Articles 101–5.
24. FTA: Article 908.
25. This obligation is spelled out with respect to trade in wines and spirits in FTA Articles 801–8, requiring Canada and the USA to ensure the removal of discriminatory measures in the marketing practices of monopolies maintained by the Canadian provinces and a number of US states.
26. FTA: Chapters 4–13.
27. See, for example, the EC–Sweden Free Trade Agreements in the *Official Journal of the European Communities*, 19 December 1972.
28. FTA: Article 701 and GATT Article XVI:1.
29. The first action under this provision was taken in May 1989. Following a joint determination that Canadian support levels for barley exceeded those in the USA, Canadian import licensing requirements on barley and barley products

were removed. In May 1991, Canada removed import restrictions on wheat imports from the USA: see *News Release No. 109* (Ottawa: Minister for International Trade) 3 May 1991.

30. FTA: Articles 901–9.
31. FTA: Articles 1101–4.
32. See text accompanying note 41.
33. FTA: Articles 1401–7.
34. FTA: Articles 1501–6.
35. FTA: Annex 1404.
36. FTA: Articles 1601–11.
37. FTA: Articles 1701–6.
38. Public Law 73-66.
39. FTA: Articles 1801–8.
40. The procedure has been used twice since the FTA entered into effect. In the first case, a panel reviewed landing requirements for salmon and herring introduced by Canada (to replace GATT-inconsistent export controls) for consistency with the FTA. The panel report provided the basis for settlement. In the second case, a panel report found that US restrictions on the import of small lobsters were not inconsistent with the FTA. See *The United States–Canada Free Trade Agreement Biennial Report*, A Report from the President to the Congress under section 304 9F of The United States–Canada Free Trade Agreement Implementation Act (Washington, DC: United States Trade Representatives Office, January 1991).
41. FTA: Articles 1901–11.
42. Since the FTA entered into effect, sixteen cases are active or have been completed. See *Caseload Report for May 1991*, United States–Canada Free Trade Agreement, Binational Secretariat, US Section.
43. FTA: Articles 2001–12 and 2102–6.
44. The provisions for the specific consultations and negotiations are found within articles dealing with the substantive issue. Hence, Article 1907 sets out the mandate for a working group to negotiate new rights and obligations respecting subsidies, countervailing duties, dumping and anti-dumping duties.
45. Working Groups have been formed to harmonize or render equivalent agricultural standards, negotiate new service sectoral annexes and new rules on trade remedies. Bilateral government procurement negotiations are to commence within one year of the termination of the Uruguay Round. Two negotiations to accelerate the eliminations of tariffs have taken place covering $8 billion (US) in bilateral trade. See Minister for International Trade, *News Release No. 235*, 11 October 1990.
46. A GATT panel report on pork which found for Canada has been blocked from adoption by the USA since in September 1990. It is still in litigation.
47. The United States–Canada Free Trade Agreement Implementation Act of 1988, Public Law 100-449.
48. See G. Patterson, 'The European Community as a Threat to the System', in W.R. Cline (ed.), *Trade Policy in the 1980's* (Washington, DC: Institute for International Economics, 1983).
49. Some scholars have suggested that acceptance of free trade areas is a departure from the Most Favoured Nation (MFN) principle related to the secret free

trade negotiations between Canada and the USA in 1947. Such negotiations did take place but were terminated when the Canadian Prime Minister decided that a free trade agreement would be rejected by popular opinion in Canada. For a fuller discussion of the negotiation history of GATT Article XXIV and the relevance of the provisions of this article to the Canada–US FTA, see M. Hart, 'GATT Article XXIV and Canada–United States Free Trade Negotiations', *Review of International Business Law* (1987) pp. 317–56.

50.	Namely Articles XI and XIII (certain quantitative restrictions), Articles XII, XIV and XV (balance of payments and exchange restrictions) and Article XX (general exceptions).

51.	The GATT Working group examining the consistency of the FTA with the GATT was scheduled to report in July 1991.

52.	J. Viner, *The Customs Union Issue* (New York: Carnegie Endowment for International Peace, 1950).

53.	See P. Wonnacut and M. Lutz, 'Is There a Case for More Free Trade Areas?' in J.J. Schott (ed.), *Free Trade Areas and US Trade Policy* (Washington, DC: Institute for International Economics, 1989).

54.	*Canada–US Free Trade Agreement: Economic Assessment,* p. 18.

55.	The FTA is expected to generate an increase of 2.5 per cent in Canadian income over what would normally be recorded. See ibid, p. 35.

56.	In the first two years of the agreement, there was no significant change in the pattern of trade between Canada and the USA and between Canada and other countries. See *Export by Commodities* (Ottawa: Statistics Canada), Cat. No. 65-005.

57.	In the Tokyo Round, Canada sought major reductions in US petrochemical tariffs. Since the small Canadian market offered inadequate reciprocity for the USA, negotiators sought reductions in EC petrochemical tariffs. When the EC refused, the possibility of a Canada–US deal collapsed and Canadian petrochemical producers were left facing high US tariff barriers until the entry into force of the FTA. See Rodney de C. Grey, *Trade Policy in the 1980's,* Policy Commentary No. 3 (Montreal: C.D. Howe Institute, 1981).

58.	See Office of the Press Secretary, *Extension of Fast Track Authority* (Washington, DC: The White House, 19 March 1991), p. 6; and *Address by the Honourable John Crosbie, Minister of International Trade* (10 April 1991).

59.	Article 7011 commits Canada and the USA to work together in the Uruguay Round for the elimination of all trade-distorting agricultural subsidies. Article 1301 similarly commits the two countries to work for the widest possible liberalization of government procurement trade barriers.

60.	See Office of the Prime Minister, *News Release* Ottawa, 5 February 1991.

3 'Europe 1992' and Japan's Relations with Western Europe
John R. McIntyre

The enhanced economic integration of the member countries of the EC under the EC 1992 initiative is arguably one of the most important developments in the global political economy over the last several decades. It is also one of the most direct and dramatic reactions to the economic upsurge and dynamism of the Pacific Basin area generally and Japan specifically. This chapter presents an analysis of economic relations between the EC and Japan in the post-Second World War period in the area of trade and FDI. Its particular emphasis bears on the impact on EC–Japanese relations of what has come to be referred to as Europe 1992 or EC 92.

Relations between the EC and Japan have always been somewhat difficult. The relationship in recent years has been characterized by an increasing level of anxiety in the Community about the level of Japanese penetration of the EC economies and, as a direct corollary, about the 'unfair' obstacles with which EC firms seeking entry into Japan must contend. Japan is perceived in Europe as the most tangible threat to the competitive position of the EC and its individual member states' industries.[1] Many have come to regard the EC 92 programme as the building of a 'Europe Inc.' as a countermove to the 'Japan Inc.' syndrome: in short, a European strategy geared to recapturing its competitive position in trade, technology and the economic momentum primarily from Japan and, to a lesser extent, from the USA. Japan is often perceived as practising what Peter Drucker has called 'adversarial trade': it tends not to import any of the products it exports. In contrast, European countries and the US are seen as practising 'competitive trade': firms and consumers manufacture, sell and purchase a wide range of goods from all over the world, based mostly on consumer preference and comparative advantage.[2]

Japan, for its part, has reacted in a poised but concerned fashion to both the efforts to create an incipient North American Free Trade Area and to the EC 92 programme. The North American free trade agreements (including the existing USA–Canada FTA and NAFTA which includes the USA,

58

Canada and Mexico) are somewhat less threatening, largely because Japanese economic interests are already deeply implanted in manufacturing and distribution facilities in all three NAFTA countries. Moreover, the US open-door and national treatment policies have greatly facilitated Japanese FDI, roughly two-fifths of which is in the USA and Canada. But Europe has received less than 15 per cent of total Japanese investment.

The prevailing Japanese view of Western Europe, at least until the mid-1980s, had been one of mild condescension towards the 'English disease'.[3] Alfred Dienst, chairman of the Council of the European Business Community and of Hoechst Japan observed: 'Looking at the Triangle of Europe, the United States, and Japan, it is clear that the Japan–Europe side is the weakest link. I think people in Japan need to reassess this situation once more. There seems to be a feeling in Japan that Europe is over the hill.'[4] It is only in the most recent years that Japanese attitudes towards post-Second World War Europe shifted from one of mild condescension to one of acute concern. These attitudes have changed in Japan in part because of a shifting world political economy but also because of the pronounced trend towards regional trading blocs in world trade, with increasing emphasis on sectoral managed trade. The Europeans have indicated informally that the Community will be looking for ways to limit Japan's ability to reap the benefits of a more integrated regional market.[5]

REGIONAL BLOCS AND MANAGED TRADE THROUGH A TRILATERAL LENS

The decade of the 1980s was one of acute strain for the advanced industrialized democracies. The basic unity of the Western Alliance has so far survived the test of time, but other difficulties have emerged. The consensus among the industrialized nations has eroded as to goals, sometimes, and certainly as to means. The powerful thrust of multilateralism that had undergirded world trade in what the French often call the *trente glorieuses* (the 30 or so years of rapid economic growth and recovery in the post-Second World War period) has lost much of its compelling logic. Concurrently, enormous trade imbalances, engendered first by sharp rises in energy prices and then by rapidly shifting comparative advantages, have caused renewed strains in the world trading system.

By most indicators, the US economic position has eroded, at least in relative terms, although the myth of America's decline is a gross exaggeration.[6] The perception of decline has taken root, however, no matter what cold economic statistics may tell us. Therefore, the USA has responded to this perception by hardening its position in international negotiations and by insisting on a 'level playing field' for US exports, while it strayed some-what from its traditional liberal hegemonic commitment to free trade. This manifested itself by the increasingly acrimonious relations between the forces of protectionism and of free trade in US interest group politics, and by an increasing use of voluntary export agreements and other import restraints.[7]

Japan's growing economic strength is gradually dislodging the USA from its pre-eminent position. In spite of its gains, Japan remains unwilling and probably unable to assume the burdens traditionally associated with global leadership.[8] Takashi Inoguchi expressed the idea well when he stated that 'a large majority of responsible Japanese leaders have found it virtually impossible to think beyond a world where the United States is of primary importance to Japan and where the Japanese–US friendship is a major pillar of global stability'.[9]

Masahiro Sakimoto considers Japan's immediate task to be supporting the virtue of the *Pax Americana* that has made possible Japan's remarkable progress by continuing Japan's domestic demand-oriented growth and by cooperating with the USA in defence and monetary policies, consistent with Japanese national interests.[10] In fact, Japanese global policy is still largely predicated on the Yoshida doctrine whereby Japan is a virtual military protectorate of the USA in exchange for certain concessions, such as mili-tary bases, contribution towards US defence expenditures, and so on.

Yet it is precisely the military dimension of the Japanese–US relationship that gave pause to Western observers such as Paul Kennedy, who spoke of the USA running the risk of an 'imperial overstretch of military commit-ments' in Asia and Europe in view of its relatively declining economic capacity.[11] This situation has led some in the USA to suggest that Japan's new economic power, made manifest in the highly visible wave of Japanese direct investment, is a threat to the USA. James Fallows expressed the notion in a way that epitomizes the 'Japan-bashing' school of US–Japanese relations: 'America doesn't have a chance to stop declining if it must keep competing with both the Russians and the Japanese.'[12] Perhaps the prime exponent of this school of thought, which is gaining momentum in the USA in the wake of the Gulf War, is Clyde V. Prestowitz;[13] but paradoxically enough it is the American theorists of the 'Japan-bashing' school who proclaim the end of the American century and of hegemonic stability, while clinging nostalgically to a past order and refusing to accept the evolution in global trends.[14]

The European variety of 'Japan-bashing' has taken on a somewhat more directly economic form than the US variety, which tends to be more universal in its line. One of its primary exponents in Europe is none other than the first woman Prime Minister of France, Madame Edith Cresson, former Minister of Trade and Industry (1983–6). Her views are representative of many European industrialists. She is quoted as making the following pronouncements in the recent past:[15]

> Japan is an adversary who does not respect the rules of the game and whose overwhelming desire is to conquer the world ... Japanese investments are not like others. They destroy jobs. Those who can't see that must be blind ... We hear all too often that we must open up our markets, which really means first to the Japanese. In the name of what must we abandon France?

Changes are afoot in redefining the US–Japanese special relationship. These changes will eventually lead to a reassessment of the US relationship with the EC and, conversely, of the EC with Japan. Walter R. Mead has characterized the US–European relationship as a 'bad marriage' in which the USA provides the economic stimulus and suffers the deficits while Europe absorbs the dollars. This relationship, of late, has become a bad 'ménage à trois' with the addition of the Japanese trade surplus and dollar holdings.[16]

The concomitant rise in the American merchandise trade balance deficits and protectionist sentiment have resulted from the failure of the major economic powers – the USA, Japan and the EC – to coordinate macroeconomic policies. The troubles began in the early 1980s when economic policies on both sides of the Atlantic headed off in drastically different directions, while Japan pushed relentlessly into world markets. The USA followed a line of tight monetary control paired with an expansionary fiscal policy while Europe took exactly the opposite tack. The result has been steadily growing disequilibria which eventually led to the Wall Street crash of 19 October 1987 and which remain at the core of many of today's troubles. The macroeconomic imbalances have contributed to the erosion of the multilateral process embodied in GATT.[17] Robert Gilpin has noted that in the present context a 'highly ambiguous situation exists in which there is an ebb and flow from trade liberalization to economic protectionism rather than the continuously expanding trade liberalization of the 1950s and 1960s or a nationalism leading back to the chaos of the 1930s'.[18]

A new approach to trade problems has emerged in the 1980s. It has euphemistically been called 'organized free trade' in France or, more commonly in the USA, 'managed trade'. It entails the use of VERs and orderly marketing agreements on the part of governments to bypass the established GATT practices. The impact of managed trade is felt particularly in certain key industrial clusters such as textiles, electronics, steel and, above all, automobiles. This is rather a different approach from the use of NTBs which affected some 30 per cent of world trade in the mid- to late 1980s.

Yet another assault on the multilateral post-war trade regime is the rise in regional trade blocs. While these efforts to liberalize trade on a regional basis can indeed contribute to a liberal global trade regime, they should really operate within the parameters of the GATT. Gilpin, among others, is of the opinion that a related cause of 'rising protectionism has been the enlarged and increasing closure of the European Community', which had until recently been one of the driving forces of the 'overall expansion of world trade'.[19] These regional blocs, paradoxically, are arising at the very time when the world economy is becoming more global and interdependent. But global interdependencies are more a function of the activities of multinational corporations than of states because states still think in terms of national interests. As Kenichi Ohmae makes abundantly clear in his book *The Borderless World*, the defenders of the globalization of the world economy thesis view governments as little more than spoilers who disrupt markets with their interference and policy pronouncements.[20]

In fact, the formidable progress of large corporations in globalizing their business activities dwarfs the efforts and the accomplishments of national governments, for which regionalism is but an avatar.[21] At the corporate level, globalization requires a truly different way of thinking from the macroeconomic categories of government policy makers. A global company has no such thing as exports; it has investments, sales, and market shares but no exports or internal trade deficits. As national states seek to protect their fair share of world trade, global companies adapt with different legal, capital and financial structures for each local company around the world.

A caveat is in order regarding the concept of globalization: it should not modify macro-policy analysis. While 'globalization' has become a fashionable term these days, globalization is very much like Molière's *Le Bourgeois Gentilhomme*, in which the character discovers to his amazement that he has been speaking prose his whole life! Moreover, there are far more small and medium-sized companies dependent upon state economic policies than multinational corporations able to circumvent state-induced constraints. Additionally, some products and industries are amenable to globalization by their very nature while others are not; some resources (capital) are readily mobile across national boundaries while others (jobs) are not.

The notion of globalization is closely linked to that of 'triad', a concept first systematized by the Japanese business strategist, Kenichi Ohmae, though Molière's common sense dictum may apply yet again. The triad is characterized by a unique blend of cooperation and competition among American, European and Japanese counterpart multinationals. Ohmae favours a pragmatic alternative to competition: cross-national alliances which immunize their members to protectionism and state action and make for complementary global economies of scale.[22] This notion of a corporate triad must be distinguished from the triangularity of economic relations between Europe, Japan and the USA.

The Japanese inability to assume the mantle of global economic leadership, coupled with economic decline of a sort in the USA, leads one to the conclusion that the Western industrial world is again entering a rare period without a hegemonic power to provide the requisite regime stability. Three immediate consequences flow from this observation with identifiable impacts on European–Japanese economic relations.

1. The dollar and other major hard reserve currencies will continue to fluctuate into the twenty-first century, in part because the Group of Five cannot agree on fair exchange rates and the USA is unable to impose a currency standard.
2. Overcapacity in manufacturing will be aggravated as individual nations pursue a policy of developing a full set of industries, such that global output could not be absorbed and might lead to more frequent recessions.
3. A heightening of trade skirmishes escalating into fully-fledged 'beggar-thy-neighbour' wars becomes more likely.

These secular trends are easily illustrated. The USA and the EC have consistently complained that the Japanese makers of products such as automobiles, semi-conductors and other manufactured goods continue to churn out products in periods of oversupply and aggressively cut prices in order to build market share, even at the cost of short-term losses.

The combination of the scenarios outlined above implies rather strongly that regional blocs will eventually lose the efficiency and competitiveness they have sought to gain precisely through regional integration schemes.

EUROPE 1992: THE OBJECTIVES AND THE STAKES

The conjunction of three factors led the European to launch the 1992 initiatives, each acting as one of the proverbial three strokes before raising the curtain. First, there was heightened competition in high-technology areas from the Pacific region in general and from Japan in particular. Second, there was the paralysis of action in the EC institutions and the patent failure to resolve common European problems throughout the 1970s and early 1980s. Third, there was also the general economic stagnation characterized by high unemployment and little or no growth, a syndrome which the Japanese called the 'English disease'. The SEA, or EC 92 project, to reinforce the 'internal market' was designed to turn this situation around.

A truly economically united Europe with its 320 million consumers and its combined GNP projected to be US$6.5 trillion by 1992 represents a great potential market for Japan and other countries looking in from the outside. This can be compared to the USA's 245 million people and a 1992 projected GNP of US$6.4 trillion, or Japan's 124 million inhabitants and 1992 GNP of US$4.4 trillion.

Giovanni Agnelli, Fiat's Chairman, expressed the view that because '1992 has grown out of a recognition of the advantages of a free market, I believe its success will depend on strengthening Europe's traditional economic and political alliances rather than excluding the rest of the world'.[23] It is useful to bear in mind what some of the tacit objectives of this ongoing transformation might be, in the light of this optimistic and balanced statement by a European industrial leader of note. Stanley Hoffman, a seasoned observer of things European, finds that the EC 92 programme is aimed first at making penetration of external markets, through trade and investment, easier for European countries which are highly reliant on exports for economic growth and have excess capital for overseas investment. Additionally, the process seeks to 'minimize the penetration of the Community by forces deemed unfriendly'.[24]

In June of 1985 – under the leadership of the new European Commission President, Frenchman Jacques Delors – a landmark White Paper entitled 'Completing the Internal Market' was prepared by Lord Cockfield (a Briton), then commissioner for the internal market.[25] The document laid out a framework of specific measures to be adopted by the EC institutions and the member states in order to achieve the goals of a fully-fledged unified internal market before the arbitrary deadline of 31 December 1992. The White Paper divides the obstacles to a unified market into three broad classes – physical, technical and fiscal – and identifies timetables for about 280 measures.[26] It is noteworthy, however, that the detailed White Paper does not address the relationship between the great barrier-free single market in the making and the rest of the world.

In conjunction with the Cockfield White Paper, an amendment to the 1957 Treaty of Rome, known as the SEA of 1985, was ratified and entered into force in 1987, embodying the objectives of the report. This Act provides the means to untie the gordian knot of EC decision making which had often paralysed the Community in inactivity on several fronts throughout the 1970s. There is, however, no general agreement as to the meaning of 'completing the internal or single market'.[27] There are, therefore, no criteria against which to judge progress apart from the general open-ended standard of a market with 'no differential of economic significance attached to national frontiers or the residence and nationality of the economic agents of the member states'.[28]

The landmark Cecchini Report undertaken on behalf of the EC Commission details the impacts of completion of the internal market along four lines: reduction of operating costs in the EC, new forms of heightened competition, a surge in R&D and technological achievements, and a general improvement in economic efficiency. The report concludes that the process might yield, with a 30 per cent margin of error on either side, an EC GDP gain ranging from 4.5 per cent to 7 per cent with a concomitant increase of 2–5 million in employment and a reduction of some 4–6 per cent in retail prices.[29] The report, interestingly, does not seek to assess the trade-creating or trade-diverting effects for the EC and its trading partners, preferring a singular if not exclusive focus on internal dimensions.

A fuller understanding of the impact of the 1992 programme on EC–Japanese economic relations requires an appreciation of the development of relations in the post-war period. The next section provides a sense of perspective and seeks to establish the outlines of a context.

EC–JAPANESE ECONOMIC RELATIONS IN THE POST-WAR PERIOD[30]

In the immediate post-war period, Japanese interaction with Europe was minimal. With the end of the Korean conflict and of the boom it engendered regionally, Japan felt the need for foreign exchange earnings to cover essential raw material imports. The USA gave strong support to Japan's GATT membership application, but strong opposition was immediately felt by organized textile industry interests in Britain, France, Germany and Holland. By August 1955, Japan had become a member of GATT. Some European countries gave in to US pressures and did not oppose GATT membership. However, some invoked GATT Article 35 which made it possible for them to deny MFN status to Japan. Germany did extend MFN status but the German government acknowledged it had taken a risk.[31]

Rothacher has observed that 'it was in the context of continued discrimination in Europe – either legally via Article 35 or in violation of GATT standards by Germany and Italy – that Japan perceived the conclusion of the

Treaty of Rome in 1957'.[32] The Japanese eventually came around to the realization that a prosperous Europe would provide better market outlets. By the 1960s, the European economies were booming and Japanese exports benefited directly. This period saw Japan joining OECD (the Organization for Economic Cooperation and Development) and signing a number of treaties of commerce and navigation with European states.

The EC began to apply periodic pressures on Japan to liberalize its import policies. An early attempt was made by the EC Commission to develop a common (harmonized) commercial policy towards Japan in 1963. But member states, to Japan's relief, opted for national bilateral negotiations. The EC would seek to provide some degree of coordination among national policies. Japan was in fact 'horrified at the prospect of apparently doubled and parallelled safeguards and restrictions'.[33] Europe, at any rate, was beginning to rediscover Japan which, in the post-war period, had seemed geographically, economically and culturally far removed.

For this initial period of post-war relations, it is not unfair to say that Washington was guiding Euro–Japanese relations. The USA had been ready to offer its markets, as the hegemonic power, to Japan to guarantee stability, but it was intent on the Europeans doing likewise. In the 1960s, Japan traded with Europe mostly in light industry exports such as textiles, cutlery, sewing machines and so on. The eventual Japanese penetration in heavy industrial products (including steel, ships and ball bearings, for example) had not yet begun.

In the early 1970s, efforts were again made by the EC Commission to establish a common commercial policy to deal with Japan. These efforts came to naught. Neither the EC member states nor Japan proved willing and ready to negotiate in the framework of the EC.

European–Japanese economic relations began to change dramatically in the wake of a shifting global economy. Several factors led to Japan launching a major export drive targeted on the European area. In 1973, the Community experienced a major enlargement (Great Britain, Denmark and Ireland). Two years before came the devaluation of the US dollar and the Nixon Administration's imposition of a 10 per cent import surcharge, along with US pressures on Japan to restrain its exports to the USA. By 1974, the first oil shock had led to a recession and a sharp drop in Japanese consumer demand. The Community's exports to Japan fell drastically. As the US market seemed temporarily saturated, Japan focused on Europe which still held significant market opportunities and rich consumer markets. Between 1969 and 1975, Euro–Japanese trade grew from US$2 billion with a US$200 million European deficit to a US$8.7 billion with a US$3.2 billion European deficit!

Japan's 1975 export drive showed a degree of concentration higher than for any comparable advanced industrialized country. By the late 1970s, Japan's main exports to the EC remained in the form of high-technology, high-value-added goods while the EC's exports to Japan consisted mostly of semi-processed products for industrial use. The 1975 offensive emphasized cars but also ships, consumer electronics, textiles and ball bearings. Until then Japan had merely scratched the surface of the market, and no VERs were in force with European states. Rather, European diplomatic efforts had centred on opening the Japanese car market by removing NTBs. A British list of NTB complaints in the mid-1970s is illustrative and, to this day, some of them are still the subject of controversy and negotiations:[34]

- Japanese refused to test British-made cars on Japanese standards in the UK
- on trade marks, Japanese companies had registered with the Japanese Patent Office European product names and designs as being their own
- a delay of three years or more was required to process approvals for branches of foreign banks
- limitations were imposed on foreign investment in the retail sector

Most European governments had similar lists of complaints.

In the period before 1980, Japanese foreign investment in Europe was minimal. Japan invested in all the EC countries some US$3 billion for the period 1951–77. Most of these investments were in the British Isles, Germany, Ireland, Portugal and Spain, where the Japanese were clearly made welcome and found willing joint venture partners. In the same period, European investment in Japan was all but negligible. On the whole, until the mid-1970s Japan looked upon Europe as a ready target for their own merchandise surplus with which to balance its raw material imports and to cover a technology transfer and services deficit. Japan, thanks to the US cajoling, had success in obtaining access to European markets while Europe did not meet with much success in removing perceived Japanese NTBs.

The EC's institutions had not managed to craft a single credible EC-wide policy towards Japan. EC policy was therefore viewed by the Japanese as being in a state of confusion, not to say disarray. This gave Japan the necessary latitude in which to build its markets there. A status quo developed in which European states tried to protect their own markets, to the extent that GATT norms permitted, through the use of safeguard clauses. At the same time trade wars were effectively avoided.

Since the Carter Administration years, the consensus has been that EC–Japanese commercial relations have been in a state of continuing crisis. By 1976, the issues at stake were defined and centred on a chronic and ever-growing merchandise trade deficit with a typical concentration of Japanese exports in a few key sectors along with pricing practices which the Europeans deemed tantamount to dumping. European policy towards economic relations with Japan began to toughen up by late 1976. The global depression of the steel market, coupled with the European fear that Japan was about to wipe out Europe's ball bearing industry, led to the initiation of anti-dumping investigations and renewed demands for VERs. Japan did not oblige at this time. Negotiations stalled and in February 1977 the EC Commission fired the first salvo, announcing without prior consultation a 20 per cent anti-dumping duty on Japanese ball bearing imports. The Japanese proved unyielding save for a few concessions on emission standards testing of European car imports.

The then Vice-Minister for International Affairs of the Japanese Ministry of International Trade and Industry (MITI), Mr Matsuda, commented sharply: 'People who take life as easy as the Europeans [should not] condemn Japan for working hard. They close up their shops and factories for weeks on end in the summer and expect Japan to buy from them while they are on vacation.'[35]

By the end of the 1970s, the EC Commission had initiated a flood of anti-dumping investigations. It had also extended most of its member states' invocation of quotas on Japanese cars and motorcycles. In terms of the dynamics of the relationship, it is roughly at this time that both the Japanese and the Europeans begin to express a desire to bypass the USA as the intermediary of choice. This is perhaps best expressed by Mr Fukuda, a Japanese Minister, who said: 'Europe has not quite treated us as a true friend or a real partner, but rather as something alien to them. The days are past when Japan and Europe could be content with an indirect relationship through the US as an intermediary.'[36]

The Japanese also expressed disappointment and dismay at having to negotiate with the EC Commission when, in the words of Nabuhiko Ushiba, 'in fact the Commission cannot move at all without being given a mandate from the member countries': an old theme in Japanese perceptions of European affairs.[37]

Coming back from an unsuccessful trade negotiation mission to Tokyo to press for increase EC imports, Sir Roy Denman and other EC officials prepared an internal confidential document for the 19 March 1979 meeting of the Commission. The document considered selective import controls and gave a harsh analysis of Tokyo's international trade policy. The portrait of Japan it painted was symptomatic of European impatience with Japan and Japanese trade policy. Leaked to the British press, the document included the following revealing passage:[38]

[Japan's trade expansion was due to] hard work, discipline, corporate loyalties, and management skills of a crowded, highly competitive island people only recently emerged from a feudal past, a country of workaholics who live in what Westerners regard as little more than rabbit hutches ... [There is] as much propensity to import as there would be carnival spirit on a rainy Sunday morning in Glasgow ... Competition from a country such as this is not easy to face by a Europe where the Protestant work ethic has been substantially eroded by egalitarianism, social compassion, environmentalism, state interventionism and a wide-spread belief that working hard and making money are anti-social ... [Japanese exporters operate] like soldiers venturing out from a fortress, [and] create havoc in concentrated areas of industry in the Community with major regional employment problems.

Publication of this excerpt in the media had an electrifying effect in Japan. The rash references touched the raw nerve of unpleasant and negative cultural stereotypes and biases. Japan, now a fully-fledged member of the advanced industrialized democracies, deeply resented this tongue lashing in print and its racial overtones. EC–Japanese relations were dominated by this incident for the better part of the year.

As a tactical ploy to shock the Japanese, it failed to elicit concessions. The hostility evoked by Sir Roy Denman's comments in 1979 is not unique to Europeans and found a surprisingly similar thematic echo in the late 1980s in the USA.[39] The fact remains that Westerners have a profound difficulty understanding Japan much as the Japanese have in understanding the proverbial *gaijin* (non-Japanese).

By early 1980, Japan planned another export offensive emphasizing cars and electronics which was primarily targeted at Germany. This came at a time of high unemployment and elections in Europe. A worse time could not have been chosen by the Japanese. The balance in the motor industry was already well in the red at the of the 1970s. In 1979, over 630 000 Japanese vehicles were sold in Europe, compared to 1.5 million in the USA. Clearly a triangular relationship existed already. US protectionist measures, where Japan controlled over 20 per cent of the market share, yielded a strategy of diversion of vehicles to Europe. In response, the French government immediately reinstated its 3 per cent import limit on cars from Japan. Italy had a Treaty quota of 20 000 vehicles from Japan per year. Germany informally set the bar at below 10 per cent of the market, and the UK did likewise.

Responding to these limits and seeking to improve market share, Japanese car manufacturers began the search process for joint ventures with

European partners. Spain, which at the time was not yet an EC member, was the target of the first Japanese automotive joint venture effort, as Nissan joined forces with Motor Iberia, SA. The French Government indicated to Spain that large-scale Japanese manufacturing investment might prejudice Spain's application for admission into the EC. In Italy, Fiat opposed all Japanese overtures as 'Trojan horse' measures, and the French did the same. Similar Japanese overtures were emerging in other sectors such as television and electronics.

The EC Commission in November 1980 tried to pre-empt separate policies by individual member states by crafting a four-point common comprehensive policy which eventually was approved by the European Council with minor modifications. The policy called for the following.

1. Japanese VERs on cars and electronics should be as uniform as possible throughout the Community.
2. A stronger yen truly reflective of the strength of the Japanese economy was required.
3. A great opening of the Japanese market through the removal of NTBs was essential.
4. Equal treatment of US and EC demands by Japan should be pursued.[40]

The third demand had special resonance in the view of the fact that in 1979 only 42 000 European-made cars were sold in Japan, at prices 200 to 300 per cent above comparable Japanese models. This November 1980 EC policy declaration marks the beginning of a more unified, if not effective, EC trade policy towards Japan. It foreshadowed a prominent role for the EC institutions in all their future dealings.

A number of conclusions must be highlighted when considering the record of the first three decades of EC–Japanese economic (*qua* trade) relations. First, the Europeans belatedly and reluctantly recognized the significance of the Japanese economic presence and its potential influence for the balance of the century. This tardiness in facing the new global economic reality was perhaps indicative of a certain European bias towards things Asian, with the possible exception of the British. In fact, neither the Japanese nor the Europeans evince much of an understanding for each other's politics, cultures and economic cycles. It is not inaccurate to speak of a bilateral 'perception gap'.

Second, a common EC policy towards Japan was slow and haphazard in developing.[41] In this industrial pre-White Paper period, individual national states were unwilling to delegate much of their sovereignty over trade to the Brussels-based Commission. The Commission could have developed uniform Community positions on such issues as the use of import quotas, anti-dumping duties, the use of GATT-sanctioned safeguard clause provisions, and the negotiation of VERs with Japan. The European Council slowed the hand of the Commission on Japanese negotiations throughout the 1970s in the light of the proliferation of unilateral state measures.

Third, Japanese concessions on NTBs, quotas and other trade barriers requested by European states were met, for the most part, with largely symbolic moves. Japan, all the while, made significant market share gains in Europe but quickly reached a ceiling imposed by formal and informal import quotas. The Japanese markets remained relatively hermetic to European exporters owing to the nature of the Japanese economic system, and perhaps to the European lack of dedicated efforts to penetrate it.

Fourth, with few exceptions, Japanese manufacturing and marketing infrastructure investments in Europe were perceived by the Europeans in that period as so many 'Trojan horses'. Over the same period, Europe invested very little in Japan. The Japanese were extremely cautious in choosing European countries where they would be made welcome. Their investment had not reached a level of economic significance by the end of the 1970s. This situation changed dramatically in the late 1980s.[42]

Fifth, while tensions were mounting between the EC and Japan, the trade and investment issues were never escalated to the level of 'high' politics, remaining mostly in the hands of technocrats as opposed to elected leaders as is typical of 'low' politics. This was to change subsequently. Beginning in 1976–77, EC–Japanese relations gradually became politicized as a direct function of chronic and rising Japanese trade surpluses concentrated in key industrial sectors. The political significance of these surpluses was magnified in a Europe, with unemployment rates above the 10 per cent level. A cyclical pattern of politicization of the EC–Japan trade and economic relationship began to emerge, driven by the Japanese economy's reaction to global factors such as oil prices and protectionist pressures in the USA.

Finally, EC–Japanese economic relations for that period cannot be characterized by trilateral (US–Japan–EC) joint efforts, aside from the regular functioning of GATT, OECD and other multilateral bodies where the three partners met. Rothacher has observed that, if anything, the relations between the three 'were really a shifting 2:1 alliance' during that period:[43] that is, both the EC and Japan were opposed to unilateral US moves, while the USA and Japan sought to prevent the EC from resorting outright to import controls and instead pressured Europe to conform to the letter and spirit of the GATT regime.[44]

We now turn to the most recent period in EC–Japan relations in the specific context of the ongoing '1992' reforms and their impacts.

EC–JAPANESE ECONOMIC RELATIONS IN THE SINGLE EUROPEAN MARKET ERA[45]

In order properly to frame the issues as we enter the era of EC 92, we must first review patterns of trade and investment flows between the EC and Japan during the 1980s. There are no significant discontinuities between the somewhat acrimonious pre-1980 period and the current era of trade and investment relations, other than an aggravation of the underlying trends identified in the preceding section. What changes the stakes drastically, in the context of existing trends, is the EC's '1992' accelerated programme to achieve a single unified market with a coherent common external commercial policy towards the rest of the world in general, and towards Japan in particular. As internal barriers disappear, the EC wants rules that clearly distinguish between insiders and outsiders.

Moreover, the shifts in the global economy, identified in previous sections, and the apparent lack of a liberal global hegemonic power willing and able to enforce a benevolent set of economic norms does signify that there is potential for previously contained trade disputes to get out of hand. The fundamental proposition that free and fair trade yields gains for all trading partners has been the basis for the US-led post-war trade regime. This position is coming under increasing challenge.

The EC's 1992 reforms have caused the utmost concern in Japan because policies affecting non-EC members are not fully articulated and also because the EC has expressed the desire to 'minimize penetration of the Community' by forces deemed unfriendly.[46] Japan's fears are founded on the fact that until very recently EC–Japanese relations were narrowly focused on trade with little related foreign investment. This new focus, which characterized the 1980s, deserves special attention.

At the global level, the EC accounts for some 17 per cent of world trade, compared to the USA with 11 per cent and Japan with 10 per cent. There is, therefore, a greater dependence on trade on the part of the EC than on the part of Japan (or the USA for that matter). A review of bilateral EC–Japan trade flows cannot fail to surprise since one would expect the EC countries to do as well in the Japanese market as they do in most other markets.

Table 3.1 provides a comparison of the evolution of Japan's export and import shares in the US economy and the EC markets. The data indicate that the USA still remains Japan's primary export market, while the EC has absorbed a steadily increasing share of Japanese exports since 1985. It also shows that since 1986 Japan has become an important market for EC products, although Japan does not have the same importance to the EC as

Table 3.1   Japan's trade with the USA and the EC
(percentage share of Japan's total exports or imports in yen)

Year	USA		EC	
	Exports	Imports	Exports	Imports
1980	24.2	17.4	12.8	5.6
1981	25.5	17.6	12.4	6.0
1982	26.2	18.3	12.3	5.7
1983	29.2	19.5	12.6	6.4
1984	35.3	19.7	11.4	6.8
1985	37.1	20.0	11.4	6.8
1986	38.4	22.8	14.7	10.9
1987	36.5	21.1	16.5	11.8
1988 (I–III)	33.5	22.4	18.1	12.8

Source: Japanese Ministry of Finance, Tokyo, Japan.

they have for Japan. But Japanese exports far exceed EC sales to Japan, as has always been the case, and it is this imbalance that has been largely responsible for EC–Japan disputes. The Community has pressed Japan considerably 'to reduce its dependence on exports and move towards an economy led by domestic demand'.[47]

Table 3.2 presents the Japanese merchandise trade balance with its major developed country trading partners for the years 1984–88 inclusive. Japan's surplus with the EC for the latest year is close to US$23 billion, compared to a surplus of some US$57 billion with the USA for the same period. What is noteworthy is that the EC-generated surplus more than doubled, even in current dollars. It appears that the EC may be absorbing market shares losses sustained by Japan in the USA as Japan redirects some of its exports to Europe.[48] The year 1989, after all, marks the twenty-first anniversary of American trade deficits with Japan. The Federal Republic of Germany, the UK, the Netherlands, Belgium and Spain all ran deficits with Japan in the billion dollar range for the year 1988.

Looking at the actual composition of the Japanese exports to the EC (using 1987 figures as a base), the transportation equipment area (including motor vehicles, parts and motorcycles) accounts for 25.6 per cent, non-electric machinery (such as office machinery, power generation and construction/mining) comprises 2.3 per cent, and electrical machinery and equipment (including telecommunications and electric power machinery)

Table 3.2   Japan's trade balance with major trading partners, 1984–88 (millions of dollars; exports f.o.b., imports c.i.f.)

	1984	1985	1986	1987	1988
Developed Countries	*41 680*	*49 347*	*68 917*	*71 273*	*67 062*
USA	33 075	39 485	51 401	52 090	57 597
Canada	–648	–253	631	–462	–1884
Western Europe	*10 908*	*12 843*	*19 365*	*22 806*	*25 445*
Denmark	59	176	209	–27	–350
UK	2 408	2 906	3 073	5 343	6 439
Netherlands	1 381	1 632	2 684	3 314	4 059
Belgium	870	995	1 521	1 837	2 265
France	700	759	1 297	1 143	672
West Germany	3 937	4 010	6 180	6 682	7 692
Spain	108	256	779	987	1 324
Italy	–17	67	228	–32	–108
EC	*10 071*	*11 124*	*46 687*	*20 024*	*22 802*
Sweden	537	653	864	1 250	1 343
Switzerland	–876	–597	–684	–835	–790
Austria	227	293	517	658	964
Australia	–2 112	–2 073	–1 754	–2 743	–3 604
New Zealand	228	169	147	–41	–605
South Africa	229	–824	–874	–396	114

Source: Japanese Ministry of Finance, Tokyo, Japan.

contributes 19.2 per cent. Conversely, total Japanese imports from the EC were composed of 31 per cent machinery and equipment, 22 per cent chemicals (pharmaceuticals and organic chemicals) and 10.2 per cent food-stuffs. What is in fact the major worry for the Europeans is not so much the existence of a deficit or its size, but rather its composition. In essence, Japan sells high-value-added goods to Europe while the Europeans tend to sell to Japan a wider range of items such as objets d'arts, diamonds, woollens and other low-value-added goods. A September 1990 export promotion placed the emphasis again on the same type of consumer products.

Most forecasts indicate that there is a growing concentration of Japanese exports in the Community because exchange rate movements have meant a partial recovery of the competitiveness of Japan's exports in the EC. As Andreas van Agt, Head of the Delegation of the European Communities in Japan, noted in an October 1988 address: 'the Europe/Japan trade is conspicuously out of step. After the Yen revolution Japan has turned to Europe, to a much larger extent than before, for our currencies, on balance, have not devalued dramatically and our purchasing power has remained largely unaffected'.[49]

This situation of economic interdependence is somewhat new and will probably make Europe far more assertive with Japan in the wake of ongoing regional integration. German businessmen frequently complain that Japan's trade success is one-sided. The Federal Republic of Germany absorbs 4.5 per cent of Japan's global exports, whereas Japan purchases only about 1.7 per cent of Germany's global exports. As a result, in 1988 Germany had a trade deficit with Japan of DM15 billion, which amounted to fully one-third of Europe's deficit with Japan. The observation made by the French daily *Le Monde* in 1978, at the height of one of the many mini-crises in trade negotiations, that 'les Japonais savaient que les Européens faisaient beaucoup de bruit sans avoir les moyens de pression que supposaient leur fermeté' ('the Japanese knew full well that the Europeans made a lot of noise but did not possess the wherewithal to back up their demands') will most likely never be repeated in the new EC context of higher bilateral stakes.[50]

The counterpart to Japan's surplus in merchandise trade has been the massive increase in Japanese overseas investment, in Europe in particular.[51] Table 3.3 shows the evolution of these investments in the EC and North America. Total Japanese investment in Europe was over US$30 billion as of 31 March 1989, compared to some US$75 billion in North America. The Japanese Government is advising its firms to be careful not to cause a worsening of economic relations with the USA in their drive to 'Europeanize' their investment strategy.[52] As of 1988, a significant amount of these European investments were in high-technology industries (for instance, US$704 million in electronics, US$797 million in motor vehicles, US$347 million in pharmaceutical and chemicals). Significant Japanese investment in the USA is an old issue;[53] it is a relatively new one for the Europeans.

Japanese direct investment is now having a measurable effect on the European economy and has engendered a debate about its contribution.[54] Much doubt has been expressed about the added value of Japanese assembly operations ('turnscrew factories') and the inefficiencies flowing from the competition among regional authorities in, say, Scotland or Saarland or elsewhere, to attract Japanese investment at all cost, in a fashion reminiscent of the aggressive investment incentive programmes of individual states in the USA. The Thatcher Government, unlike other EC governments, went on record as being of the opinion that such investments will do more good than harm.[55] Britain has in fact been spectacularly successful in attracting Japanese car manufacturing investment. This has generated much envy and

Table 3.3   Japan's FDI by country, financial years 1984–88
(millions of dollars)

	1984	1985	1986	1987	1988	Total*
USA	3 360	5 395	10 165	14 704	21 704	71 860
Canada	184	100	276	653	624	3 231
North America	*3 544*	*5 495*	*10 441*	*15 357*	*22 328*	*75 091*
UK	318	375	984	2 473	3 956	10 544
Netherlands	452	613	651	829	2 359	5 525
Luxembourg	315	300	1 092	1 764	657	4 729
West Germany	245	172	210	403	409	2 364
France	117	67	152	330	463	1 764
Switzerland	229	60	91	224	454	1 432
Spain	140	91	86	283	161	1 045
Belgium	71	84	50	70	164	1 027
Others	50	168	153	200	493	1 727
Europe	*1 937*	*1 930*	*3 469*	*6 576*	*9 116*	*30 167*

*Total to 31 March 1989.
Source: Japanese Ministry of Finance, Tokyo, Japan.

anger on the continent.[56] The British position is that Japanese capital and know-how can help rebuild British industry.

It is generally conceded by the Japanese themselves that Britain is the likely battlefield for car wars in the EC in the 1990s, with Britain challenging German automotive leadership in Europe as a result.[57] Nissan, Toyota and Honda have all invested in manufacturing plants in the UK and have pledged to invest a total of US$2.7 billion by the late 1990s. The Japanese will therefore have the capacity, because of their manufacturing investment, to increase their share of the European market in the 1990s from 10 or 11 per cent to some 25 per cent. European car makers are alarmed. Jacques Calvet, Chairman of the French car manufacturers, Peugeot, has called outright for temporary measures restricting Japanese car makers until the Europeans gain equal access to Japan.[58]

In contrast, investment by EC firms in Japan has remained on a relatively small scale. Foreign investment in Japan grew some 16 per cent annually in the 1980s, according to a 1987 Booz & Allen Hamilton study of foreign investment in Japan.[59] But such investments have a long way to go to catch up with Japanese overseas investments. By 1987, for example, EC firms had invested some US$1.2 billion in Japan, and the USA had invested ten

times more. The strong yen has had the effect of discouraging many potential foreign investors.

We now turn to the specific areas of debate that plague the EC–Japan
trade relations in the new context.

EC–JAPANESE DISPUTES IN THE SINGLE MARKET ERA

The EC has all the while sought to address its policy towards Japan to three
interrelated problems:

* protecting its markets from Japan's continued export-led growth
* addressing its concerns over the high sectoral concentration of Japanese
  exports in the EC
* dealing with lack of access to Japanese markets

The margin of manoeuvre available to the EC in dealing with these
related problems has for a long time been limited by a set of constraints
which have emerged in the past 30 years. First there is the disunity among
the EC member states which the ongoing 1992 reforms may have tempered.
The greater policy coordination among EC members in the single market
era was made amply evident in the previous section's analysis. It is now
becoming harder for Japan to play one member state against another.
Second is the ever-present protectionist sentiment among EC member states'
electorates. This sentiment can easily be mobilized through the manipula-
tion of public opinion or during periods of poor economic performance.
When these sentiments are aroused, they often impede serious negotiations
on trade and investment issues. Third is the similarity of US and EC trade
interests *vis-à-vis* Japan. US gains in its economic relations with the Japanese in fact often translate into an EC loss. Fourth is the greater leverage the
USA enjoys with Japan because of its importance to Japan as a defence
partner and as its major market outlet. The significance of this factor was
made evident in the Structural Impediments Talks between the USA and
Japan, which excluded the Europeans even though it is not at all obvious the
EC would have wanted to negotiate with Japan on the same basis.

One of Japan's main concerns with the EC 1992 programme has been
how to deal with the rising protectionist sentiment there. Japanese appre-
hension about EC protectionism is justified by historical evidence and
current trends. The EC's most developed set of regulations, the CAP, is an
abyss of protectionism. The European continent's postal and telecommunication service industries have little or no domestic competition, and Europe's car market is always viewed as a special case. The EC member

countries fear that, when the single market is fully established, many industries will be threatened by foreign competition before they can attain the necessary economies of scale to compete effectively on a continental scale (or on a global scale for that matter). It is also often claimed that the resulting unemployment would have political consequences for the prospects of a united Europe itself.[60] This view is a bit reminiscent of the nineteenth-century claim of exception to the principles of comparative advantage and the rules of free trade. In effect it amounts to the infant industry argument by reason of scale and scope!

We next turn to a number of specific trade issues.

A Common External Tariff

EC 92 should not have any impact on the EC external tariff level. All tariff levels have already been negotiated within the framework of GATT's rounds and, with a few exceptions, the customs union has been in place for a long time in the EC. The EC legally cannot raise its tariff unilaterally under the pretence of new hidden benefits for third countries as a way to offset these benefits flowing from greater economic integration. The EC's common external tariff, moreover, has evolved over a long period and is well established.

The EC's Use of VERs and Quotas Against Japan's Exports

As of the end of 1988, over a dozen Japanese exports were being monitored by agreement between the EC and Japan and were limited by mutually agreed VERs. Such restraints do not technically violate the GATT norms and are allowed under the provision of the 'safeguard clause' that GATT members may invoke in defined circumstances (see Articles 19–23 of the GATT for 'severely endangered national industries'). Cars, videocassette recorders and other consumer and industrial goods are covered.

Additionally individual EC member states, with the approval of the EC Commission under the Treaty of Rome, also imposed individual quota restrictions. In fact, it is estimated that as many as 1000 EC country-specific measures restraining imports (that is, import quotas, 'voluntary' export restraints, industry-to-industry orderly marketing agreements and so on) currently exist. Most of them are targeted at Japan and the NICs of Asia. A classic example is France's limit on its motor vehicle market to 3 per cent of total annual sales. For the UK, the figures stand significantly higher at 11 per cent of the domestic market. Italy's quantitative restrictions are far tighter, though the Italian case is a special one. A reciprocal trade treaty between Italy and Japan, ironically initiated by the Japanese in the 1950s, restricted exports to each other's car market to 2200 units annually. This quota approach with a mix of VERs, whether treaty-defined or informally negotiated, has been the EC member states' chosen strategy thus far to deal with Japan's concentrated export strategy.

EC 92 should have the impact of gradually erasing the various and differing national policies on VERs. A uniform system of EC-wide voluntary quotas would presumably spread the burden of Japan's competitive exports more evenly throughout the EC. European opponents naturally argue that you cannot compare the Italian Mezzogiorno with Saarland and, consequently, national and regional differences should be tolerated. A truly open internal market would, however, make such national differentials impractical, if not impossible, because they do require stringent border controls. The dismantling of internal borders is at the root of the 1992 single market programme.

Tokyo's concern is somewhat different: EC-wide VER may be far stricter than what currently exists at the national level. There can be no doubt that no matter what the outcome of the debate in the EC over the use of VERs and associated quotas, there will be some transitional measures imposed to soften the impact of too rapid an opening of the single market. At issue will be whose quotas to use – the French, the Italian, the German – or whether it would be simpler to devise a new set of norms.

The Europeans will seek to extract reciprocal concession from Japan to lower these quotas. The EC will probably demand a certain level of penetration of the Japanese market in exchange for the existing 11 per cent share of the EC car market controlled by Japan. The French, for instance, argued for the export of 500 000 EC cars to Japan annually, a figure that represented five times the then current levels. Carl H. Hahn, VW Ag Chairman, summed it up when he said that Europe has 'never been protectionist but in view of different structures in [some] neighboring countries, it won't be possible to open [markets] by January 1, 1993', adding that 'the Japanese' car 'market [only] opened up after it was fully developed'.[61]

Willy de Clerq, then EC's External Trade Commissioner, noted that Europeans 'will have to ... open their own markets on equivalent terms'.[62] But a US official presented a somewhat different view, arguing that the EC always attempts to pass along its costs of integration to its trading partners.[63] But, in fact, it is unlikely that moving to a single EC set of import quotas would lower existing protectionist levels. One must consider that a single EC level would take in EC member states that do not currently have any VERs.

Obviously no one import quota or VER will be harder to handle than the one on cars applied to Japanese exports to Europe.[64] It is most unlikely that the EC will forgo both its import quotas and VERs. In fact, by the beginning of 1990 the European Commission had come up with a miraculous though fragile compromise on this very issue. The open market philosophy defended by Commissioners Andriessen and Martin Bangemann prevailed, at least in principle if not in implementation. The EC Commission decided to push for the gradual removal of all internal EC trade barriers on cars by the end of 1992 but to seek voluntary agreements from Japanese producers to restrain their imports, both from within and without the Community, for an undetermined and reviewable 'transition period' after 1992. Such a decision makes possible a process of continuous negotiations with the Japanese producers. This issue is far from being a closed one, given that the motor industry is the largest employer in Europe and has intimate ties with the key EC member governments.

The proposed removal of national car quotas by countries such as Britain, France, Italy, Spain and Portugal will therefore prove problematic, lengthy and subject to untold delays and negotiations. It will also lead to a restructuring of the motor industry in Europe. Such a restructuring is one of the presumptive objectives of EC 92 and, in this sense, it can be said that the Japanese are helping to make the EC automobile sector more competitive. But it remains a gamble of some magnitude on the part of the Commission to push for a restructuring of this industry sector both from within and from without. To fight the Japanese, US and European car makers are now indeed forming new strategic alliances that will create fewer and, it is hoped, stronger companies. Examples abound: Ford bought Jaguar in Britain in 1989; General Motors purchased 50 per cent of the motor division of Saab-Scania.

The European car market is doubtless the world's most attractive market for the 1990s. Sales have soared in Europe throughout the 1980s. So far the Japanese have been held back by national quotas to about 11 per cent of total EC market; by comparison, Japanese car manufacturers control 25 per cent share of the US market. It is obvious that, without national quotas or an equivalent mechanism to restrain imports, the Japanese will rapidly reach a 20 per cent market share in Europe.[65]

EC's Use of Anti-Dumping Countervailing Duties Against Japan

For European manufacturers, anti-dumping complaints with the EC Commission have become a favourite way of protecting domestic industries against imports from Japan as well as a number of Asian exporters. The American experience has taught the Europeans a lesson in the use of anti-dumping procedures. Sixty-two such cases were investigated by the Commission in 1987, and in 1988 the Commission imposed anti-dumping countervailing duties on US$1 billion worth of Japanese photocopiers, and US$1.3 billion of Japanese printers and videocassette recorders. It must be noted that Japan's share of the EC printer market went from 49 per cent in 1985 to 73 per cent in 1988.

The aim of such duties is laudable: to protect competition by forbidding a foreign firm or firms from taking advantage of predatory pricing to gain market share. But recent changes in EC law have stretched the definition of what is permissible under GATT by recently imposing such duties on products from Japanese firms using European or US plants to assemble largely low-priced, imported components as a way to circumvent anti-dumping countervailing duties.[66] This prompted Japan to take the unprecedented action of asking the GATT to hear a formal complaint charging that the EC's anti-dumping policy is in violation of GATT Articles 11 and 13, among others.[67] This step marked a more aggressive turn in Japan's approach to trade disputes with the EC, much in line with the philosophy inherent in the headline-making book, *The Japan That Can Say No* by Akio Morita and Shintaro Ishihara.[68]

An example of the EC approach stands out and bears noting. In February 1989, the EC ruled that imported photocopiers made at Ricoh's California plant, and therefore 'Made in USA', contained too many below-price Japanese parts. A 20 per cent levy was imposed.

Japan has contended that local subsidiaries of foreign companies must be treated the same as their domestic counterparts under the well-established principles of national treatment. Takae Negishi, a spokesman for the Electronics Association of Japan, called the EC action 'deplorable' and 'contradictory' in the sense that the Europeans are inviting companies in and 'restricting the use of vital components' difficult to procure within the Community.[69]

At the beginning of 1991 the EC Directorate General on Information Technology produced a landmark policy paper arguing that Europe's computer and electronics industry deserves special help because of its 'strategic' nature. It appears that two schools of thought may be confronting each other in this policy pronouncement: the free marketeers versus the Japanophobist.[70] The Japanophobists argue that foreign, and particularly Japanese, ownership of computer manufacturers is a risk, and that the Commission should not only be harder on Japan's trade barriers but should also consider resorting to more anti-dumping measures against Japanese computer exports. The free marketeers argue that the logic of competition and the forces of the market will ensure that a truly unified Europe can stand up to Japan and the USA. They argue, moreover, that prolonging protectionism can only weaken European industries in the medium to long term.

The debate on the use of anti-dumping duties appears to be far from over, even in the context of the 1992 reforms.

This EC crackdown has implications going beyond trade in parts and subassemblies since it could well have a chilling effect on certain investments in the Community, if the policy were to be implemented aggressively.

Rules of Origin and Local Content

A related question which partakes both of trade and investment is that of rules of origin and the nature of what is local content in finished products. The EC contends that Japan and some other countries are circumventing anti-dumping duties and quantitative import controls by opening 'screwdriver' assembly plants on the continent. Such assembly plants add little value, and key components are manufactured in Japan or elsewhere. The argument is thus made that such 'screwdriver' plant products are really imports in disguise and should be counted as such.

The French Government has argued that Bluebird cars manufactured in Great Britain by a Nissan subsidiary and shipped to France had less than the 80 per cent of local content required under French regulations and therefore should be included in the 3 per cent quota on imports of Japanese cars to France. The British Government did not accept this argument. It counters that the cars already have a 60 per cent local content and that Nissan will raise it to 70 per cent. The EC Commission has informally accepted the 70 per cent criterion for domestic content.

Until 1988, EC rules considered that the 'country of origin' was where the 'last significant economic transformation' had taken place.[71] The February 1989 EC decision changes this line of reason. The change is primarily directed at Japan but will affect all major trading partners of the EC as well. It appears that the EC, in preparing for 1992, is applying new local content rules to a wide range of products, from semi-conductors to television programmes. The implications are far reaching for Japanese plants in the USA which sell their production in the EC.

The so-called 'screwdriver plant' regulation (or anti-circumvention of anti-dumping duties laws) was originally passed in June 1987 by the EC. Under the provisions when a product is subject to an EC dumping finding, duties are then also assessed on the product assembled in the EC by corporate entities which are related to the foreign manufacturer, if the EC assembly plant was started or substantially augmented after the dumping investigation began. Sixty per cent of the parts used in the assembly must come from the foreign country subject to the dumping finding. If the content from third countries (including the EC) is increased to 40 per cent, then anti-dumping duties are not applied.

Tokyo's reaction has been two-fold. First, Japanese firms are gearing up to locate major production facilities within the EC, as clearly reflected in the Japanese investment patterns in Europe. Parenthetically, American firms are doing likewise. A Toshiba spokesman stated unequivocally that 'our basic position is that we want full production in the [EC] by 1992'.[72] Second, Tokyo has taken the initiative with other Asian nations to propose new uniform international rules of origin for manufactured products. Japan has challenged the legality of the so-called 'screwdriver plant' regulation before GATT. It has also pushed GATT during the bulk of the Uruguay Round negotiations to address the issue of national rules of origin regarding their level of hindrance of trade-related foreign investment with a view to evolving a GATT code of conduct. The USA has so far been supportive of the Japanese démarche in GATT.

Clearly, the Ricoh decision hit a raw nerve in the USA as well. US officials expect cars, among other products, made in the USA by Japanese companies 'eventually to be exported to the EC'; 'any rules that would redefine them as Japanese, based on the origin of their parts, could turn into a trade dispute.'[73] In fact, the logic of this decision would lead not only Japanese firms but also American firms to open up chip plants in Europe to satisfy the EC requirements and rules aimed at 'screwdriver' assembly plants.[74]

The USA is in fact beginning to feel that the EC is erecting new external rules as it removes internal trade barriers. EC business and government leaders retort that these new rules are targeted at Japan, not the USA. Umberto Agnelli, Fiat Chairman, states that 'we will let American goods in but we are not going to allow America to become a transshipment point for Japan'.[75] This approach does smack of the 'divide and reign' school which Japan has long practised with individual European countries. So far, the USA has remained true to the free trade principles on this issue and has not accepted the EC's argument. The US attitude can probably be credited partially for the early 1990 EC Commission decision (the Bangemann–Andriessen approach noted above regarding automobile quotas) to avoid setting minimum local content requirements to apply to cars made in EC factories. This decision, however, provides that locally made Japanese cars (whether made in the EC or outside as in the USA, for example) could indeed be treated differently during a defined and reviewable transition period.

The Ubiquitous Problem of Reciprocity

Lord Cockfield's 1985 White Paper took a position on the issue of EC reciprocity. The EC should require similarity of treatment in third (non-member) countries if they wish their firms to enjoy the benefits of the EC's integrated market. It clearly implies that foreign firms' access or operations in the EC would be limited to the extent that foreign governments did not provide EC firms with the same freedom of action in their markets. It is an extremely difficult concept to define with precision.[76]

Reciprocity and its practical applications have serious implications for Japanese and US financial service providers, the only area in which applying the EC rule has been proposed so far. Both US and Japanese laws separate investment banking from commercial banking, but the EC does not; does this mean that Japan and the USA will be forced to deregulate hastily?

The reciprocity provision contained in the EC Second Banking Directive remains vague and has aroused the concern of many governments. Both Britain and Germany have expressed a desire to make this directive compatible with GATT negotiations on financial services. Shipping and insurance companies will also be affected. Reciprocity has prompted many such companies to examine options for setting up shop in Europe. The second directive was aimed also at Japan's restrictive approach to licensing foreign banks.[77] It was designed to ease the entry of EC banks into Japan and, at the same time, to make it somewhat more difficult for Japanese banks to grow in Europe.

The EC has so far not expressed its intention as to the breadth of the principles of reciprocity. Frans Andriessen, then Vice-President of the EC Commission, stated in a formal speech on 27 September 1989 that the objective was 'comparable levels of market access', but since there was 'as yet no binding multinational obligations on trade in financial services ... it was reasonable for us to reserve the right to impose a reciprocity test as a possible condition of access for new banks from third countries to the unified EC market'.[78] Clearly such a test would not apply to foreign banks 'already established in the Community'.

It looks as if the test that the Commission will impose revolves around two conditions in the banking area: first, the nation has to treat European banks the same way it treats domestic banks and, second, it has to give European banks 'effective market access'. The European position remains ambiguous. It appears the Commission will retain a case-by-case right of review of national banking authorities' decisions.

So far, insurance remains untouched, but stock-exchange-related services are being examined. GATT has been silent on issues of services reciprocity, save in the area of trade where it clearly prohibits it. It may be an area of disagreement so serious that the USA may well act as 'Japan's battering ram into Europe' on the issue of services.[79]

Japanese NTBs and Structural Impediments

Japanese barriers to market entry are still numerous. It is true that Japan, as a global economic power, has set an example in lowering most of its tariffs and removing quite a few of its quotas and NTBs.[80] The Japanese tend to blame lack of foreign penetration of their markets on poor product quality, inability to adjust to the requirements of the Japanese consumer, lack of staying power on the part of salespersons, and plain lack of effort on Europeans' part. In fact, Katsuo Seiki, director of the West Europe Division of MITI's International Trade Policy Bureau, stated in an interview in 1989 that 'we like to think ... that there are already fewer institutional barriers – tariffs, quotas and what have you – in Japan than in the Europe and the United States'.[81]

Notwithstanding such blanket disclaimers, there are still quite a few significant Japanese impediments in the way of accessing Japanese domestic markets. Japan's barriers against free trade in rice readily come to mind. They are a clear violation of Article XI of the GATT instrument. A host of high tariffs persist on items such as imported beef.

Foremost in the minds of Europeans are the peculiarities of the Japanese economic and political system which make the Japanese business environment essentially different. This is not necessarily an unpleasant proposition for Japanese officials since they can then make a pleading for special treatment in the international community precisely because they are different. Karel van Wolferen, a Dutch journalist and Japan expert, has become one of the main critical exponents of this school of presumed uniqueness and has demonstrated how Japan has used this argument to best advantage in its relations with the West.[82]

Fundamentally what is at issue between Japan and its trading partners is the uniqueness of Japanese economic institutions and the comparative advantages they confer upon Japan in international markets and in its own domestic market. These systemic issues deserve special attention as relates to EC–Japan relations. We have chosen two to illustrate the point.

First there is the existence of large industrial conglomerates which belong to the *keiretsu* system, formerly known as *zaibatsu* in the pre-Second World War period. These conglomerates are endowed with commitments from large financial institutions which are members of their group. They represent a network of interlocking directorates and, additionally, create significant opportunities for lateral membership across industry *keiretsus*.

The Europeans do have a large state-owned sector but it can in no way be compared to Japan's unique *keiretsu* system.

Such conglomerates are able to engage in very far-sighted strategic planning because of the readily available capital and because of comparatively lower costs. They can withstand the vagaries of business cycles far better than their competitors and are able to launch strategic alliances with ease to penetrate overseas markets. Nothing matches *keiretsu* in the West, and the concept clearly runs counter to the anti-monopoly (anti-trust) practices of the West as well as the presumption of the free operation of markets forces in microeconomic decision-making. *Keiretsus* are especially adept at protecting their domestic market and at practising the dictum of Baron von Clausewitz in overseas ventures.

Second there is the Japanese distribution system, which is considered to be extremely complicated and forbidding. Many Europeans, van Wolferen among them, consider that it really is not all that complicated but rather that it is 'rigged'.[83] They argue that wholesalers and retailers are tied, through a *keiretsu*, to a particular manufacturer and cannot consequently be considered as independent competitors. This type of distribution promotes what many Europeans and Americans consider price-fixing and denies market access to outsiders. The argument is made that since tariffs and foreign exchange controls were removed, it is the distribution system which has had the functional task of excluding non-Japanese sellers from the home market. In other words, products not produced and distributed by members of a *keiretsu* are essentially barred from the regular Japanese market which imposes high margins over and beyond the original value of the product.[84]

It is interesting to note that all of the structural issues reviewed above were the subject of a protracted and very open-ended US–Japanese negotiations, known as the Structural Impediments Talks, to which the EC was not a party but merely a bystander. Clearly, the EC hoped to benefit from any Japanese reforms in the wake of the talks but did not wish to bind itself through reciprocal commitments as the USA had done. Moreover, it is not at all obvious that Japan would have wished to engage in such a systematic dialogue with the EC at this point.

CONCLUSIONS: FREE MARKETEERS VERSUS JAPANOPHOBISTS

The external impact of the internal market directives have been the 'missing link' in EC Commission's gigantic effort to detail and anticipate both intended and unintended consequences flowing from the SEA of 1987. This virtual silence, save for occasional brief press releases, short position papers and statements by the Commission, has naturally increased speculation and concern outside the Communities.

Two clearly contrasting polar visions of Europe are confronting each other as we enter 1993 and as politicians and industrialists are realizing that the road yet to travel is long and arduous. On the one hand, there is a vision of Europe which is overregulated by parallel bureaucracies at both the national and EC levels and highly protectionist. This implies that outsiders are kept at arm's length and that competition is seen as a threat rather than as an opportunity to create greater efficiency. This is a view closely aligned on the canons of managed trade and economic neo-nationalism. Regional integration, in this state-centred vision of the future, is only a tool or an avatar of protectionism. The other view is that of a deregulated, free market-oriented and open Europe. It is the view espoused by the initial promoters and theorists of the 1992 programme. It is the 'free-market' philosophy that was defended by Andriessen and Bangemann in the Commission in 1990. Such a view considers competition as the key to improving economic performance and stresses consumer preference as the ultimate form of sovereignty instead of the state or the Brussels institutions.

Japan and what it stands for in Europe has had a truly polarizing effect on EC trade politics. The liberal free trade-oriented political centre considers that Japan represents a possible model for European economic growth and industrial renewal. Japanese exports can be a positive stimulus to make European industries more competitive, while Japanese investment may create needed jobs and push the technological frontier forward. The nationalist right and the more left-oriented parties are wary of Japanese exports and industrial practices. Their reasons may vary but their analysis does not. Paradoxically, they decry the very type of Japanese protectionist practices that they would use against Japan in the EC. Moreover, they consider that the Japanese twin export and investment drives pose a real threat to their political objectives and to the existing European domestic industrial order. This is clearly demonstrated in the case of the motor industry. In this sense, they tend to be Japanophobists, willingly or unknowingly confusing effects for causes when it comes to Japanese competition in Europe.

To their credit, the Japanese have made a plea for sensitivity, sensibility and statesmanship in handling the relationship. Typical of the Japanese response is the statement by a seasoned Japanese diplomat and expert on European affairs, Ambassador Kazuo Chiba:[85]

To the EC, I'd like to say this: You might not like what we do and what we are. But please try to understand us, because we were not in the Europe concert of nations in the 19th century. One hundred and twenty years is very short for us to acquire the long habits of the traditional European concert of nations ... I do hope you will not to be too moralistic with us. We know that when the Commission talks about the 'balance of benefits', we are targeted.

It is useful to remind oneself when seeking an understanding of Japanese policy that Japan's international trade dependency is grossly overestimated: it is about 10 per cent of its GNP, while for most large EC member countries it is in the range of 20–30 per cent. Japan's primary source of economic growth is and remains its domestic demand.

Clearly, the Europeans are of two minds when it comes to dealing with the Japanese challenge and the 'balance of benefits'. The new uses of local content regulations, anti-dumping laws and rules of origin in the 1980s and early 1990s are evidence of a schizophrenic policy attitude. On the one hand, the Europeans are seeking to attract Japanese foreign investment in the Community while, at the very same time, many European government and business leaders favour restrictions on trade-related foreign investment.

To their credit, most Japanese observers of Europe do not believe in the emergence of a 'Fortress Europe'.[86] Most view EC 92 as an opportunity. The Japanese are the first to recognize that the Europeans will be fierce negotiators on a very long and detailed trade agenda with outsiders as they have been within their own internal area with each other. The danger therefore may be that the Europeans, in negotiating a fair 'balance of benefits' in the Japanese–EC relationship, 'may lose sight of the forest for the trees'.[87]

Notes

1.   Illustratively, see Jenny Corbett, *The European Community's Trade with Japan – Issues and Implications*, Australia–Japan Economics Research Project, Research Paper No. 48 (Canberra, Australia: Australia National University, 1978); see also *Public Opinion Survey Concerning Five European Community Countries Towards Japan* (Tokyo: Kahuhodo, 1978); Herman Kahn and Thomas Pepper, *The Japanese Challenge* (London: Harper & Row, 1979); Hanabusa Masamichi, *Trade Problems Between Japan and Western Europe* (Farnborough, Hants, England: Saxon House, 1979); Tibor Mende, *Soleils Levants (Rising Suns)* (Paris: Editions du Seuil, 1975); Jean-Jacques Servan Schreiber, *Le Défi Mondial (The Defiance of the World)* (Paris: Fayard, 1980); Isao Abe, 'La Communauté Européenne vue par un Japonais' (The EC seen by a Japanese), *Chronique de la Politique Étrangère*, 26 (1973)

pp. 21–7; Martin Beresford, 'And now, Le Défi Japonais', *The Atlantic Community Quarterly*, 13 (1975) pp. 204–19; H. Cheynel, 'Japon: Sourires et Grimaces' (Japan: Smiles and Frowns) *Le Moniteur du Commerce International*, 240 (2 May 1977) pp. 12–28.

2. Peter Drucker, Editorial, *Wall Street Journal*, 1 April 1986.
3. 'Eikokubyo' refers to the economics of decline and Great Power decadence that is marked by labour troubles, productivity lags, and economic rigidities which had characterized the UK and Europe more generally in the 1970s.
4. 'Europe Inc.', *Journal of Japanese Trade and Industry*, 2 (March/April 1989).
5. 'Japan May Make Biggest Gains From Single Market', *Financial Times*, 27 June 1988; 'EEC–Japan Trade: Japan-Bashing Catches On', *The Economist*, 25 July 1987.
6. Henry Nau, *The Myth of America's Decline* (New York: Oxford University Press, 1990).
7. I.M. Destler and J.S. Odell, *Anti Protection: Changing Forces in US Trade Politics* (Washington, DC: Institution for International Economics, 1987).
8. John H. Makin and Donald C. Hellman (eds), *Sharing World Leadership: A New Era for America and Japan* (Washington, DC: American Enterprise Institution for Public Policy Research, 1989).
9. Takashi Inoguchi, 'Four Japanese Scenarios for the Future', *International Affairs*, 65, 1 (Winter 1989).
10. Makin and Hellman, *Sharing World Leadership*, pp. 175–202.
11. Paul Kennedy, *The Rise and Fall of Great Powers* (New York: Random House, 1987) p. 515.
12. James Fallows, 'The White Peril', *Atlantic Monthly*, May 1987, p. 20.
13. Clyde V. Prestowitz Jr, *Trading Places* (New York: Basic Books, 1988).
14. David Brock, 'The Theory and Practice of Japan-Bashing', *The National Interest*, 17 (Autumn 1989) pp. 29–40.
15. 'Edith the First', *The Economist*, 18 May 1991, p. 52.
16. Walter R. Mead, 'American Economic Policy in the Antemillenial Era', *World Policy Journal*, VI (Summer 1989) p. 398.
17. Robert G. Gilpin, 'Implications of the Changing Trade Regime for US–Japanese Relations', pp. 173–224 in T. Inoguchi and D.I. Okimoto (eds), *The Political Economy of Japan: The Changing International Context*, vol. 2 (Stanford, CA: Stanford University Press, 1988). See also Ernest H. Preeg, 'The GATT Trading System in Transition: An Analytical Survey of Recent Literature', *The Washington Quarterly*, 12 (Autumn 1989) pp. 201–13.
18. Ibid, p. 170.
19. Ibid, p. 141.
20. Kenichi Ohmae, *The Borderless World* (New York: Harper Business, 1990).
21. DeAnne Julius, *Global Companies and Public Policy: The Growing Challenge of Foreign Direct Investment* (New York: Council on Foreign Relations Press, 1990). See also Richard W. Moxon, 'Multinational Consortia in Manufacturing', *Research in International Business and International Relations*, 3 (1989) pp. 11–28.
22. Kenichi Ohmae, *Triad Power: The Coming Shape of Global Competition* (New York: The Free Press, 1985); and Ohmae, *The Borderless World*.
23. Giovanni Agnelli, 'The Europe of 1992', *Foreign Affairs*, 68 (Autumn 1989) p. 63.

24.   Stanley Hoffman, 'The European Community and 1992', *Foreign Affairs*, 68 (Autumn 1989) p. 43.
25.   *White Paper from the Commission to the European Council*, Milan, 28–9 June 1985); COM (85) 310.
26.   For a detailed review of the genesis, politics and policy regarding the internal market, see Jeffrey Harrop, *The Political Economy of Integration in the European Community* (Brookfield, VT: Gower, 1989); see also for a US viewpoint, Michael Calingaert, *The 1992 Challenge from Europe: Development of the European Community's Internal Market* (Washington, DC: National Planning Association, 1988); see also for a French perspective Jean François Poncert and Bernard Barier, *Une Stratégie pour la France: l'Europe* (*A Strategy for France: Europe*) (Paris: Economica, 1988); for a Japanese perspective of the process, see Toshiro Tanaka, 'EC Integration Process: A Japanese View', *Hogaku Kenkyu*, 161 (May 1988).
27.   See the excellent special issue 'Europe's Internal Market: After the Fireworks', *The Economist*, 9 July 1988, pp. 5–44.
28.   Jacques Pelkmans and Alan Winter, *Europe's Domestic Market*, Chatham House Papers No. 43 (London: Royal Institute of International Affairs, 1988) p. 4.
29.   Paolo Cecchini with M. Catinant and A. Jacquemin, *1992: The European Challenge: The Benefits of a Single Market* (Brookfield. VT: Gower, 1989).
30.   This section draws from Albrecht Rothacher, *Economic Diplomacy Between the European Community and Japan, 1959–1981* (Aldershot, Hants, UK: Gower, 1983).
31.   Ibid, p. 86.
32.   Ibid, p. 90.
33.   Ibid, p. 110.
34.   Ibid.
35.   *International Herald Tribune*, 16 March 1977.
36.   *International Herald Tribune*, 20 July 1978.
37.   *International Herald Tribune*, 10 February 1978.
38.   Rothacher, *Economic Diplomacy*, p. 259.
39.   David Boaz, 'Yellow Peril Reinfects America', *The Wall Street Journal*, 7 April 1989.
40.   *Financial Times*, 11 November 1980.
41.   Seamus O'Cleireacain, 'European 1992 and Gaps in the EC's Common Commercial Policy', *Journal of Common Market Studies*, 28 (March 1990) pp. 201–18.
42.   Bernhard Heitgar and Jurgen Stehn, 'Japanese Direct Investments in the EC – Response to the Internal Market 1993?' *Journal of Common Market Studies*, 29 (September 1990) pp. 1–16.
43.   Rothacher, *Economic Diplomacy*, p. 318.
44.   Professor Chichiro Hosoya of International University at Nigata launched a multi-year project in 1988 on economic conflicts between Japan, the USA, and the EC.
45.   This section draws from the Japan External Trade Organization's (JETRO) November 1989 White Paper and the Commission of the European Community's Report, *Relations Between the Community and Japan: Recent Developments*, COM (88) 136, Final-II (Brussels, Belgium: EC 1988), as well as interviews with EC and JETRO officials in the USA.

46. Hoffman, 'The European Community and 1992', p. 43.
47. Commission of the European Community, *Relations Between the Community and Japan*, p. 1.
48. P. Rezvin, 'As Trade Gap Closes Partners of US Face End of Gravy Train', *The Wall Street Journal*, 17 March 1988, p. 1.
49. Address by Ambassador Andres Van Agt, Head of the EC Delegation in Japan, American Chamber of Commerce in Tokyo, 'EC–Japan: Moving Beyond Trade Friction', 12 October 1988, p. 16.
50. *Le Monde*, 26 and 27 March 1978.
51. Heitgar and Stehn, 'Japanese Direct Investments'.
52. A.E. Cullison, 'Tokyo Warns Manufacturers Investing in EC to be Cautious', *The Journal of Commerce*, 14 February 1989.
53. Kozo Yamamura (ed.), *Japanese Investments in the United States: Should We Be Concerned?* (Seattle, WA: Society for Japanese Studies, University of Washington, 1989).
54. See V. Pope, 'Japan's Investments Flood Germany . . .', *The Wall Street Journal*, 7 October 1987, p. 30; see also N. Bray, 'Spain is Flooded by Japanese Investment', *The Wall Street Journal*, 24 May 1988, p. 24; E.S. Browning, 'France Now Tries to Offer Welcome to Japanese Firms', *The Wall Street Journal*, 20 April 1989.
55. 'The Japanese Are Coming', *Business Week*, 20 February 1989, p. 46.
56. Steven Greenhouse, 'Europe's Agonizing Over Japan', *New York Times*, 30 April 1989.
57. 'Britain will be Likely Battlefield for Car Wars of the 1990s', *The Japan Times Weekly*, International Edition, 4–10 June 1990, p. 18.
58. Mark M. Nelson, 'Protectionism Looms as Europeans Unify', *The Wall Street Journal*, 10 May 1988, p. 34.
59. D. Darlin, 'Foreign Firms Thrive in Japan, Study Indicates', *The Wall Street Journal*, 29 September 1987.
60. T. Carrington, 'Europe's Left Fears 1992 Will Cost Jobs', *The Wall Street Journal*, 16 March 1989, p. A12.
61. D.C. Smith, 'A Fennig for your Thoughts', *Wards Auto World*, October 1989, p. 5.
62. Nelson, 'Protectionism Looms', p. 34.
63. Ibid, p. 34.
64. H. Landis Gabel and Anthony E. Hall, 'The EEC and the Automobile Industry', *Journal of Management Case Studies*, 1 (1985) pp. 191–5; and also H. Landis Gabel and Anthony E. Hall, 'Ford of Europe and Local Content Regulations', *Journal of Management Case Studies*, 1 (1984) pp. 38–59.
65. Shaw Tully, 'How Japan's Autos Push into Europe', *Fortune*, 29 January 1990, pp. 96–106.
66. 'The Anti-Dumping Dodge', *The Economist*, 10 September 1988, pp. 77–8.
67. Cullison, 'Tokyo Warns Manufacturers'.
68. Akio Morita and Shintaro Ishihara, *The Japan That Can Say No* (Tokyo: Kobunsha, 1989). On the subject of this book, see Lawrence H. Summers, 'The Ishihara–Morita Brouhaha', *The International Economy*, December–January 1989/90, pp. 49–54.
69. J. Wolf, 'EC May Fine Japanese Firms for Dumping', *The Wall Street Journal*, 8 March 1988.

70. 'Europe's Computer Industry: The Planners Strike Back', *The Economist*, 16 February 1991, p. 57.
71. Article 5 of Council Regulation (EEC) No. 802/68, adopted in 1968, defines a product's country of origin as that in which the last substantial process that is economically justified was performed, having been carried out in an undertaking equipped for the purpose, and resulting in the manufacture of a new product or representing an important stage of manufacture. This definition basically incorporates one of the origin standards listed by the Kyoto Convention of 1965.
72. R.L. Hudson, 'Europe Girds for Invasion by the Japanese', *The Wall Street Journal*, 3 February 1989, p. A12.
73. 'EC's Auto Plan Would Keep Japan at Bay', *The Wall Street Journal*, 27 October 1988.
74. Robert E. Ruggeri, 'EC Begins Taking Apart 'Screwdriver' Plants', *The Journal of European Business*, 1 (1989) pp. 35–40.
75. K.E. House, 'Europe's Clout is Limited by Divisions 1992 Can't Paper Over', *The Wall Street Journal*, 13 February 1989, p. A10.
76. B. Free, 'The EC Single Market: Implications for US Service Industries', *Business American*, 1 August 1988, pp. 10–11.
77. 'Fending Off the Foreigners – Foreign Banks in Japan', *Euromoney*, February 1988, pp. 34–43.
78. Presentation by Mr Frans Andriessen, Vice-President, Commission of the European Communities, 'Implications of European Integration for US and Japanese Financial Institutions', 27 September 1989, New York, NY.
79. House, 'Europe's Clout is Limited', p. A10.
80. Béla Balassa and Marcus Noland, *Japan and the World Economy* (Washington, DC: Institute for International Economics, 1988).
81. Interview with Katsuo Seiki, *Journal of Japanese Trade and Industry*, March/April 1989.
82. Karel van Wolferen, *The Enigma of Japanese Power* (New York: Vintage Books, 1990).
83. Ibid, p. 393.
84. Ishida Hideto, 'Anti-Competitive Practices in the Distribution of Goods and Services in Japan', *Journal of Japanese Studies* (Summer 1983), pp. 319–34.
85. Ambassador Kazuo Chiba, 'A Time for Statesmanship: Toward a Higher Level of Diplomacy in Japan–EC Relations', *Speaking of Japan*, 8 (January 1988) pp. 4–5.
86. Matoko Kuroda, 'Le Triangle Nippon–Americano–Européen', *Politique Internationale*, Dossier Special: Interdependence économique: le défi des années 90, 46 (Winter 1989–1990) p. 49.
87. Ibid, p. 50.

4 The Impact of 'Europe 1992' on Japan's Relations with Europe: A German View

Klaus W. Grewlich

There cannot be the slightest doubt that Europe owes its revitalization to a large extent to Japan. By the middle of the 1980s leaders in Europe had become fully cognizant of the bad performance of European economies. These were lagging behind in terms of output, growth and job creation and did not keep up with main competitors in the rejuvenation of their industrial base. Europe witnessed the decline of many of its traditional industries such as steel and shipbuilding, and discovered that in key areas of high technology it was being outpaced by the USA and notably Japan. The result was a sense of failure and the recognition that national economic policies in Europe had had only limited success. European leaders finally acknowledged that, in order to remedy the structural deficiencies, they had to do away with the unhealthy fragmentation of the European community's territory into twelve packets: they had to establish '*one* fully integrated market'.

EC 92 is a development of historic proportions, a process that for the next three to five years will primarily be an economic matter but which will establish the basis for greater European political unity and a more clearly pronounced European voice in international affairs. A century ago the fate of people in many parts of the world was greatly influenced by conferences in Berlin, London and Paris. Forty years ago, after two disastrous wars which left Europe in ruins, the destiny of Europeans was in the hands of policy makers in Washington and Moscow. The division of Europe has ended with the dismantling of the iron curtain and German unification. The historic meaning of EC 92 is that Europe regains its political self-confidence and that Europeans are determined to shape their own future.[1]

Parallel to the integrative process in Europe there is a trend in the Pacific towards closer partnership and a more clearly defined common framework among the nations of that region. This involves Japan, the Asian NICs, and ASEAN, and partly the USA and Oceania. There are also visions of Pacific integration which go much further than this. 'Nichibei' – a compound of Nihon (Japan) and Beikoku (USA) – is a new expression which stands for the vision of a combination of Japanese and American economic forces. The combination, or at least mutual penetration of forces, may lead to the establishment of a free trade area. In terms of economic policy it refers to the mutual dependence of Japan, which needs the open American market, and the USA, which sees Japan as a centre of financial power. It also entails the interdependence of large corporations, especially those involved in key technologies that are the basis of the information age. Today the Japanese and American GNPs together exceed the combined GNPs of all other market economy countries. Moreover, Japan as an economic superpower would be prepared to enter into closer relations with the USA, which continues to be the leading superpower in both the economic and technological fields and at the same time the greatest military power in the world. Nichibei would be a political and economic giant next to which even EC 92 would look relatively small.[2]

However, one could contrast the vision of Nichibei with the other based on the emergence of EC 92. That is to say, as one huge single market of continental dimensions, a European superpower, instead of becoming an economic colony of Nichibei by the year 2000, will not passively endure economic and technological developments in world markets but play a constructive part in shaping them. In other words, a continental Europe which could link the Eastern European countries with a genuinely open market, a common currency, and a common foreign and security policy, together with the overall cultural appeal, would be one of the principal actors on the world stage alongside the USA, Japan, China and whatever sovereign entity or entities emerge from the former Soviet Union.

What would be Japan's attitude towards such a European grand design? What is the impact of the sudden European burst of activity upon Japan? What are the implications of EC 92 for Japan's relations with Western Europe?

EC 92

EC 92 is a massive deregulation offensive[3] designed to loosen up ossified structures and infuse more competition into national European markets. Formerly the members of the EC often had to dampen the regulatory zeal of the European Commission. Today the deregulation proposals coming from Brussels are almost too progressive for some member states. The EC 92 deregulation offensive has created a mood of anticipation everywhere in

Western Europe which has already built up its own momentum. Experts say that about a third of the average annual growth in the EC is attributable to this feeling of expectancy. Thus the internal European market is already proving beneficial before it has even been completed.

In its efforts to liberalize the European market the Commission has adopted a pragmatic approach which also makes it easier to find solutions even for the Community's complex problems. For instance, harmonization will no longer be pursued if market homogeneity can be achieved through the mutual recognition of standards, certificates or health regulations. The Commission's general policy is to proceed as unbureaucratically as possible and to respect the principle of 'subsidiarity', which means leaving decisions to be taken at the lowest possible level.

The transition to majority decision making in the European Council has proved to be a catalyst for the completion of the internal market. Majority decisions have become an important instrument in this process. There can be no Europe *à la carte*, with every member just picking out the things it likes. Many governments have in fact only regained their sovereignty over national group interests after finding that they could not hold up the progress of European integration with their vote alone. The old right of veto all too often served narrow national interests. Now the internal market is pushing those vested interests back and helping reason to prevail.[4]

Not only politicians and diplomats, but also businessmen, workers and ordinary citizens have come to understand the degree to which the ambitious project in which the Community is now engaged will shape the world of today. This is apparent in Brussels in the urgency with which the Council of Ministers is addressing the approximately 300 proposals set out in the 1985 White Paper on completing the internal market, more than 70 per cent of which have now been approved at the time of writing. It is apparent in the constructive manner in which these proposals are scrutinized by the member states and by the European Parliament in Strasbourg, which has become a vital part of the Community's law-making process and a guarantor of its democratic legitimacy.

The completed internal market comprises over 330 million people, which makes it the second largest single market in the world, surpassed only by NAFTA and exceeding those in Japan or the former Soviet Union. More competitive, cost-effective production in a market of this size, together with cost-savings from the elimination of red tape, will provide an unprecedented boost to employment and income. This internal market, according to the most complete study which has been carried out, will increase national income in the Community by more than 5 per cent and create more than two million new jobs.[5]

These 300 measures, which are the yardstick for achieving the EC internal market,[6] were classified under three headings, spanning the whole range of Community activities.

1. The removal of *physical barriers*: internal frontier controls for goods and people such as customs, immigration controls, and so on.
2. The removal of *technical barriers:* obstacles inside the member states to the free movement of goods, services, people and capital. This includes not only public procurement, standards, rights of establishment and provision of services such as transport, financial services, and telecommunications, but also other services ranging from the traditional services – furnished by liberal profession to advertising, television and other 'culture' – to information services such as data banks.
3. The removal of *fiscal barriers*: this implies some harmonization of particular national economic policies and also indirect taxation.

Replacing twelve divergent sets of national rules with one transparent one, that of the Community, is in itself a major step towards liberalization. But the Community rules being established will, in addition, allow more competition than the national rules they are replacing. For instance, the EC is creating single markets for financial services, for telecommunications and for transport that are more liberal than those the member states now allow.

To some extent there may, on the other hand, indeed be a need for '(Euro)-re-regulation' and flanking policies, particularly in the fields of fair labour standards, immigration policies and company law, including co-determination. In addition, the internal market will require a common approach to the fight against terrorism and drugs and a revision of COCOM-type export controls closely linked with the non-binding foreign policy coordination mechanism of the EC known as 'political cooperation'.

What are the external implications of EC 92? The Community has been accused of planning to restrict imports and limit foreign investment so that the single market benefits only European firms. These worries are to a large extent the result of misunderstandings, both of the Community's external relations and of the whole nature of the 1992 programme. Indeed, it is striking that in Europe one hears exactly the opposite: that the Community will open its doors wide to third countries without their doing the same so that foreign companies will be the main beneficiaries of the single market. The latter view of 1992 is also mistaken as the Community intends that its internal liberalization will already be accompanied by external liberalization.

The Community is the largest trading power in the world and is keenly interested in strengthening and extending the multilateral trade system. It would be among the first to suffer from a spread of protectionism or from a failure to update and extend GATT. In fact, the completion of the single market is expected to give an impulse to the expansion and liberalization of world trade in goods and services. The Community, by completing its single market, will at the same time encourage growth and stable prices elsewhere in the world.

These are the general reasons why the Community is most unlikely to turn in on itself and become protectionist after 1992. But there is an even more pertinent one: the EC's international obligations, in particular those under GATT. One of these obligations is to give 'national treatment' to imported goods. This means that foreign goods will benefit from the elimination of border controls and the replacement of twelve different sets of standards and regulations by a single one. In other words, the advantages of the single market will be available to non-Community countries automatically without the Community asking for anything in return. Thus the notion of 'reciprocity' does not apply here. What does reciprocity really mean? Reciprocity does not pertain to the sectors covered by international rules, which mainly means the manufacturing sector. Reciprocity does come in, however, where international rules do not exist, primarily the service sector and public procurement. Here the EC Commission in charge of European trade policy does not see why the benefits of internal liberalization should be extended unilaterally and automatically to third countries. The Community, however, wishes to negotiate changes in concessions with third countries, preferably in a multilateral context, but also bilaterally as necessary. Thus, the Community has to negotiate such changes in pertinent fields in a mutually advantageous way.

Having explained what the EC means by reciprocity, it should now be made clear what it does not mean. The Community is not looking for reciprocity in the sense of sectoral balances of trade, and neither does it believe that the liberalization of trade in one sector should lead to any predetermined result. This would contradict the principle of specialization and comparative advantage. Indeed, the EC opposes the idea of sectoral balances and so-called 'mirror-image' concessions. What the Community is looking for is roughly equivalent conditions of access on an overall basis, taking into consideration a number of sectors together.

Now we turn to the issue of investment by third countries in Europe. There are fears that after 1992 the Community will restrict or impose conditions on foreign investment. There is much talk of local content, European origin and so on. While there are guidelines concerning national treatment and multinational enterprises agreed upon in the framework of the OECD,[7] the Treaty of Rome does not in fact give the Community competence in this field; it contains no articles on investment policy. This means the Community cannot and does not restrict investment, whether from Europe, America or Japan. What the Treaty does is to give the Community responsibility for trade policy, including investment measures related to trade, such as local content requirements. But this does not mean that the Community now sets such requirements, or that it should do so. That would be inconsistent with open policies on trade and capital flows, and the Community as a major exporter of goods, services and capital has a strong interest in being able to invest and trade freely.

Moreover, local content requirements would be a clear violation of GATT rules which contain the obligation of national treatment for imports. But what, then, of the origin rules and the references to 40, 50 or 60 per cent local content and so on? It is advisable to clarify this as there is a tendency to generalize from quite specific measures and to suppose that these represent a general policy and apply to investment in the EC as a whole. Agreement has been reached on 'rules of origin' for semi-conductors. Procedures for establishing rules for photocopiers and videos followed. These rules are simply an interpretation of the Community's general regulation on origin which merely says that origin is where the last substantial process or operation took place. But what do these rules of origin mean? They do not mean that a product has to have Community origin to circulate freely in the Community. The general rule is that if manufactured outside the Community goods can enter the European market freely once duties are paid and import formalities are completed. They can, of course, do this even if it has no EC content at all. But equally, origin rules for products do *not* mean that, if produced *in* the Community, they have to have a certain European content.

The purpose of origin rules is more simple and limited. If the Community gives tariff concessions to a country, as it does to those of EFTA and the Mediterranean Basin, it has to be sure that a particular import really comes from that country if it is to benefit from the concession. Similarly, if the Community limits imports of a certain product from a certain country (for instance, textiles from Hong Kong), it has to determine whether an import was really made there. When it applies its anti-dumping regulation, it may need to know the product's origin. So origin rules are simply set for the implementation of trade measures.

In addition, there is another piece of Community legislation that has given rise to many misunderstandings. In the summer of 1987, the anti-dumping legislation was extended to prevent anti-dumping measures being circumvented by companies assembling like products within the Community on the basis of imported parts. Under the new legislation the Community is able to extend duties to like products assembled in the EC if various conditions are met. One of these conditions is that at least 60 per cent of the parts used come from the same country as the product originally found to be dumped. If more than 40 per cent of the parts come from elsewhere, then there is no possibility of applying this special duty. Thus, this 40–60 split is not a limitation on investment or even a rule of origin. It is a specific measure of limited scope and subject to tight conditions and not part of a general policy on investment.[8] Mr Andriessen, the EC Commissioner for External Relations and Trade Policy, who was participating in trade talks in Hakone, Japan, between representatives of Japan, the USA, Canada and the EC, stated that the EC Commission was willing to drop the regulations on local content with respect to foreign manufacturers with production facilities within the Community. Nevertheless, there is a growing general feeling in the EC that Japanese investment should be better integrated into the economy and enhance the creation of employment and the transfer of technology.

This policy is, on the other hand, complicated by the fact that the EC-member states still retain national quotas. It is one of the objectives of 1992 to develop a genuinely integrated trade policy and to eliminate a wide range of national restrictions. This does not, of course, mean replacing national import quotas and local content requirements with a common EC quota and local content regulations.

Another matter of concern for the partners of the Community is industrial policy. The fear of exclusion relates as much to industrial policy as to trade. European R&D schemes are most important in this respect. R&D schemes have multiple implications for foreign trade and investment. At their simplest, they are intended as import substituting programmes (like ESPRIT, JESSI) and export promoting policies. ESPRIT (European Strategic Programme for Research and Information Technologies) and RACE (Research in Advanced Communications Technologies in Europe), but also JESSI (Joint European Submicron Silicon Initiative) and other EUREKA projects are designed to achieve technological breakthroughs and to develop technical standards through which to exercise countervailing power against proprietary standards developed by US and Japanese firms as part of their strategies. The perception giving rise to potential friction is that there exists a grey area of industrial trade policy combining standard setting, collective product differentiation strategies and preferential procurement. These issues will have to be addressed openly. Sunday speeches of enthusiastic support for free markets should not be allowed to replace constructive consultations designed to solve the real issues. The OECD has developed a framework ('positive adjustment policies') which might be helpful for addressing the problem of competing economic and technology policies.

IMPLICATIONS FOR JAPAN'S RELATIONS WITH WESTERN EUROPE

Relations between the EC and Japan have developed considerably over the last ten years both from the trade standpoint and through cooperation in other spheres. There are frequent contacts between the two sides. In addition to high-level contacts between representatives of EC member countries and Japan, regular meetings are held between members of the EC Commission and Japanese ministers. To date, most of these contacts have been dominated by the question of Japan's growing trade surplus with the Community. The Community and Japan alone account for some 25 per cent of world trade. No general agreement has been concluded between these two. Trade between them is based on GATT rules including the MFN clause, under which each side undertakes to grant equally favourable tariff conditions to its GATT partners, and these constitute the basis of trade between the parties.

Japan is the Community's second biggest supplier, in 1987 accounting for 10 per cent of its imports, and its fifth largest customer, taking 4 per cent of the Community's total exports. Trade between the two sides is mainly in industrial products, although the EC also exports meat and alcoholic beverages to Japan. The main Community exports are organic chemicals, pharmaceuticals, textiles, manufactured mineral products, non-ferrous metals, machinery, road vehicles and clothing. Japan exports mainly office machinery, electronic consumer goods and telecommunications equipment, electrical goods, road vehicles and photographic equipment. However, it also exports significant quantities of chemicals, manufactured rubber products, paper, textiles, manufactured mineral goods, steel products, machinery and precision instruments.

Over the last 15 years, trade between Japan and the Community has increased spectacularly, but largely in Japan's favour. EC statistics show its trade deficit with Japan rose from $0.5 billion in 1970 to $7 billion in 1978, $13.7 billion in 1985, $21.4 billion in 1986 and $24.2 billion in 1987, to around $27 billion in 1988.

The imbalance which exists in trade is also to be found in the investment sector. Direct Japanese investment (in aggregate terms) in the Community is around 15 times greater than Community investment in Japan. In the financial year 1988 (1 April–31 March) Japanese direct investments worldwide rose by 40.9 per cent to $47 billion. Europe accounted for $9.1 billion, and Germany's proportion of this was $409 million. According to a JETRO survey, local content of goods produced by Japanese-owned firms in Europe has risen from an average of 44 per cent to 55.9 per cent in 1987, which shows Japanese companies are successfully raising the level of locally-sourced components. In the case of 'simpler' products, the proportion is higher, whereas with those of high-technology firms it was only 51.7 per cent in 1987. The survey found that about 50 per cent of the Japanese producers in Europe are satisfied and the other half dissatisfied with local deliveries.[9] It is to be expected that, in view of the EC anti-dumping customs tariffs on components affecting several Japanese products, Japanese firms will continue their efforts to increase the local content still further. It is clear, however, that Japanese investors have also attracted, and will continue to attract, Japanese parts manufacturers to Europe.

The employment effect of Japanese investments in Europe is rather negligible. Probably one reason is that investments in the high-technology sector, such as the production of electronic equipment, is not very labour intensive.

As regards regional distribution, MITI statistics indicate that Europe has been able to increase its share of Japanese investments worldwide from 15.1 per cent in the period 1951–87 to 19.4 per cent in financial year 1988. The figures in the global context are: North America, 47.5 per cent; Europe, 19.4 per cent; Latin America, 10.7 per cent; South-east Asia, 11.8 per cent; Australia and New Zealand, 5.3 per cent.

The JETRO survey indicates that at the end of 1988 there were 411 Japanese subsidiaries or affiliates manufacturing in Europe. Ninety-two of these companies are in the UK, 85 in France, 67 in the Federal Republic of Germany, 41 in Spain, 27 in the Netherlands, 24 in Italy, 22 in Belgium and 19 in Ireland. Japan's considerable interest in the UK is no doubt due to the attraction of London as a major banking centre, the advantage of English as the language of commerce, and perhaps also certain deficiencies in the British economy (such as the weakness of the domestic car sector). Above all, however, Great Britain is attractive to Japanese investors because of the fear of protectionist and restrictive measures in other EC member states. Although the Federal Republic of Germany also has a liberal business climate, the Japanese have not given it priority consideration, no doubt because of high wages, the considerable cost of fringe benefits, the cost of shorter working hours and the relatively high taxes.

Thus, Japan is showing a greater interest in Europe. Ten years ago, when West European industries were becoming less competitive on world markets and the international press was talking about 'Eurosclerosis', 'a decadent pleasure resort' and the 'German disease', Japan was taking little notice of Europe as far as direct investments were concerned. EC 92 has swung the pendulum the other way.

Tokyo is today one of the most powerful financial metropolises in the capitalist world. It derives its power from a symbiosis of big industry and government bureaucracy – at least that is the European view of Japan – as symbolized by MITI.

For Japan, the late 1980s turned into an economic golden age, in which the country, after learning to cope with the disadvantages of a sudden rise in the value of its currency, revelled in the benefits of a 5.1 per cent growth in GNP for the 1988 financial year. The economy has shown signs of slowing down in subsequent years. Private analysts forecast that it will continue to expand at a rate above the government's official target of 4 per cent. The unemployment rate is projected to fall. The current external surplus is projected to remain.[10] Car sales have been particularly strong and so have sales of household appliances and consumer electronics, especially video recorders. Capital spending by industry remains very high: there was an increase of 12.9 per cent in 1989 following a 15 per cent hike in 1988. There is a strong propensity to invest. Some of the investment is improving the output of existing products. The car makers are installing so much new capacity that MITI has urged them to slow down. The problem is that Fiat and Volkswagen, for instance, have robot halls as modern as those of the Japanese, but in the face of overcapacities they cannot invest at no risk for themselves in other European countries.

In Japan funds are now pouring heavily into factory and office automation. The proportion of investment for developing and making new products has never been higher, especially in the electronics industry which has taken over from vehicles as the engine of the manufacturing economy. For example, virtually every leading electronics combine has now established production lines for 4 megabyte DRAM chips, the new generation of memory devices which are replacing 1 megabyte DRAM which were themselves launched only in late 1987.[11] Some observers explain that Japanese companies are now on the verge of another industrial revolution, one which would see the locus of industrial innovation moving increasingly from Western countries to Japan.

What does Japan's 'golden age' mean for Japan's relations with Western Europe? The Europeans, and the Federal Republic of Germany in particular, do not feel that the Japanese success poses a fatal threat to Europe. They tend to say, 'The Japanese are successful, but we are pretty good, too!' This view is no doubt partly due to the favourable world economic situation in the late 1980s. In both Japan and the Federal Republic of Germany, for instance, the economic indicators were pointing upwards for years. German industry enjoyed a boom in the 1980s, with production running to near capacity, falling unemployment and fairly stable prices. The Europeans were getting in trim for the post-1992 era. For example, prior to 1992 the Federal Republic's exports to Japan increased far more than its imports from that country, though the deficit is still running at a high level. Finally, the successful conclusion of the Uruguay Round improved the trade climate and eased relations between Western Europe and Japan.

These optimistic comments are not intended to play down the problems besetting economic relations between Western Europe and Japan, however. According to an internal study prepared by the EC Commission, the Japanese attack with military precision, causing chaos in the Community's industry. Indeed, observers (especially companies affected by the Japanese export drive) very often use military vocabulary. The Japanese are said to be behaving as if they had studied the campaign strategies of Carl von Clausewitz. Clausewitz argued that a sure recipe for success was to be strong at the right time in the right place. Japan's strategy is described as laser beam marketing directed at a few countries with the necessary purchasing power. By this method the Japanese have conquered profitable consumer goods markets, such as watches, cameras, cassette recorders, television sets, motorcycles, video recorders, office machines and precision instruments. The laser beam is said to have pierced all obstacles, with several Japanese firms usually entering target markets at about the same time. While it is true that they end up competing with one another, their motto is that internal competition makes them stronger, and they eventually take over the market.

It is said that in launching these attacks, the Japanese usually sell their goods cheaper abroad than at home. The European Commission has therefore frequently investigated allegations of dumping and has imposed tariffs and compensatory payments on Japanese firms found guilty of this practice. Since 1980 the Commission has looked into between 60 and 104 such allegations against Japanese firms a year. In two-thirds of these cases it has found evidence of unfair pricing for such products as compact disk players, outboard motors, excavators, ball bearings and zippers. The most serious cases of dumping have involved cross-country vehicles, computer printers, video recorders, electronic typewriters, scales and photocopiers.

Japan's critics, especially those in the EC, maintain that with their predatory pricing the Japanese accept initial losses but in this way ruin competitors. Once competition has been eliminated, the Japanese manufacturers dominate the market and can then raise their prices. There is also the charge that they 'assimilate ideas', and it is true that the trademark of successful Japanese companies is that they can market inventions faster and better than anyone else. As examples, one might consider the transistor, the quartz watch, or the compact disk player.

The Japanese take a different view of their relationship with the EC, whose growing strength they accept but of which they are not necessarily enamoured.[12] Many leading Japanese businessmen concerned with European affairs still fear the much-cited 'Fortress Europe', as borne out by the long dispute between the UK and France over acceptance of the Nissan Bluebird, for instance. The treatment of cars in the EC is considered by the Japanese to be a test of the sincerity of the EC's promise genuinely to open its market to the outside world in conformity with GATT rules.

Japanese companies have come to recognize that business can often be conducted better and with more assurance and stability by producing inside the EC rather than by exporting finished products to the EC. The Europeans should grasp that tax advantages and other incentives, such as cheap land, have much less influence on Japanese decisions to acquire production facilities in Europe than is generally believed. Much more important to the Japanese are such long-term location advantages as favourable wage costs, tolerable fringe benefits and, above all, maximum entrepreneurial freedom of movement. In other words, they prefer production sites with as few statutory restrictions as regards working hours and as little government intervention as possible. Japanese companies wishing to move a plant from Japan argue that it is imperative that they can manufacture products equal in quality to those produced in Japan. The newly-coined term, the 'screw-driver' assembly plant, would not do justice to hard working Japanese entrepreneurs.

The Japanese point out that, with the exception of Britain and Ireland, all the other ten countries of the EC maintain in various degrees quantitative restrictions against products imported from Japan. One particular country, it is alleged, has as many as 41 such discriminatory restrictions against Japanese goods. The Japanese show little understanding for charges of dumping. They point out that they are now producing even cheaper than they themselves thought possible.

An important issue for Japanese businessmen is that of reciprocity. The example normally cited by Japanese representatives in this context is the Nippon Telegraph and Telephone Corporation. When this was privatized and liberalized, Japan's telecommunication services market was opened to all countries equally, whereas in the Federal Republic of Germany and France this market is still controlled by government monopolies. The UK's market was already opened. How could one have dealt with this situation on the basis of reciprocity? Another case for Japanese anxiety is the *Green Paper on Copyright and the Challenge of Technology.*[13] Japanese businessmen fear that there will be suspension or withdrawal of concessions, the raising of customs duties or the introduction of quantitative restrictions if it is recognized that EC industries have been hurt by counterfeit imports, and this by unilateral measures without the establishment of international procedures.

Thus, the Japanese attitude[14] towards EC 92 may be summarized as follows. On the whole Japan takes a positive view of the EC's efforts to complete the internal market. At first the Japanese did not believe that such a market could be established, perhaps because the surrender of some elements of national sovereignty – borders without any controls, companies able to establish branches and persons able to exercise their profession in other countries without hindrance – are phenomena that are not easily understood in Japan. But now the Japanese are taking EC 92 very seriously.

Japan is also aware of Europe's growing political significance. There are signs that the Japanese establishment is considering whether cooperation with this new actor on the world stage might not widen Japan's own international political scope. This is one of the main reasons that Japan is currently intensifying contacts with all major EC institutions, with a view to building up the flow of information and strengthening its links at the Community level.

In the current multilateral negotiations, Japan is increasing pressure for the establishment of an open European market in conformity with GATT. Japan is expected to take more regular recourse to dispute settlement procedures instead of being pressured into restraints through questionable threats of safeguarding or anti-dumping. In addition, one cannot rule out the possibility that in the final round of the GATT negotiations and the ensuing implementation, where the question of lifting restrictions is concerned, Japan will, as a matter of enlightened self-interest, in future take the first steps, just as the USA has done in previous GATT rounds. In addition, it might be possible that Japan will actively promote the consequent application of pertinent OECD instruments, such as the 'Codes for Liberalization of Capital Movements and Invisibles' as well as the 'Positive Adjustment Politics'.[15]

Japanese companies will double (if not triple) their direct investments in the Common Market in the next few years. Apart from establishing commercial branches and production companies, they might also attract more R&D centres as well as Japanese suppliers to Europe. The standardization process in connection with EC 92 will bring even further advantages for Japanese companies operating in the European market. At the same time, Japanese companies will ask to participate in strategic European R&D efforts.

Japanese companies will strive to occupy key positions in the economies of EC member states. They might be inclined to build up clusters or 'verticals', although they increasingly understand that, as a matter of good corporate citizenship, they will have to integrate into the economic tissue.

Locations for direct investments will be carefully selected. Japanese companies will focus above all on regions where liberal conditions already prevail. But they may in any case concentrate certain products in certain regions, such as chemicals in the Federal Republic of Germany and foodstuffs in France. The number of joint ventures or technical cooperation agreements with European countries is likely to increase.

CONCLUSION

In view of the anticipated developments and attitudes described above, one cannot completely rule out the possibility of a more comprehensive bilateral European–Japanese basic agreement dealing with trade and investment, designed to optimize cooperation and minimize conflicts, that would also allow the Europeans improved access to the Japanese market. This agreement would, of course, not be an arrangement for self-restraint but for improving competition and the opening of markets. There is a dual political challenge of strengthening the cooperative framework of economic and trade relations, while at the same time creating the preconditions for qualitative growth and economic adjustment. Such a positive-sum policy[16] requires a further intensification of the relationship between Europe and Japan. The more Europe exposes itself to the Japanese challenge, the more successfully it will mobilize its dynamic forces.

Notes

1.   Martin E. Weinstein, 'Washington and EC 92' (to be published by Japanese–German Centre, Berlin).
2.   Gunter Nonnenmacher, 'Auf dem Weg nach Nichibei?' (on the way to Nichibei), *Frankfurter Allgemeine Zeitung*, 17 October 1989, p. 1.
3.   Andreas A.M. Van Agt, 'Neither Fortress nor Sieve', *Speaking of Japan*, 95 (9 November 1988) p. 19; Stanley Hoffmann, 'The European Community in 1992', *Foreign Affairs*, Autumn 1989, pp. 27–48; Alexander Von Rom, 'Europa – nur ein Binnenmarkt?', *epd-TOKUMENT*, number 45/89.
4.   Martin Bangemann, 'Einstellung und Umstellung auf 1993' (Discontinuity and Adjustments for 1993), unpublished speech at the EC Commission's Information Bureau, Bonn, 17 April 1989.
5.   Paolo Cecchini, *Europa 1992 – Der Vorteil des Binnenmarkts Nomos*, (Europe 1992–Prelude to the Single Market), (Baden-Baden: 1988).
6.   The EC Commission, *Completing the Internal Market*, White Paper from the Commission to the European Council (14 June 1985), COM (85) 310.

7. OECD, *International Investment and Multinational Enterprises* (Paris: OECD, 1976). See also OECD, *International Investment and Multinational Enterprises – Review of the 1976 Declarations and Decisions* (Paris: OECD, 1979).

8. J.F.B. Wilson, *Aims and Implementation of the Single Market: Consequences for Inter-regional Co-operation* (Berlin: Japanese-German Centre, 1989).

9. JETRO, *Current Management Situation of Japanese Manufacturing in Europe* (Tokyo: JETRO, March 1988).

10. OECD, *Economic Outlook* (Paris: OECD, June 1989), p. 65 *et seq.*; OECD, *Economic Surveys – Japan* (Paris: OECD, 1988).

11. Stefan Wagstyl, 'A Golden Age for Japan', *Financial Times*, 26 September 1989, p. v.

12. Michihiko Kunihiro, 'The External Implications of 1992: A Japanese View', *The World Today*, February 1989, p. 29.

13. EC Commission, *Green Paper on Copyright and the Challenge of Technology – Copyright Issues Requiring Immediate Action* (7 June 1988), COM (88) 172 final.

14. Peter Odrich, 'Japan blickt nach Europa' (Japan looks towards Europe), *Frankfurter Allgemeine Zeitung*, 26 May 1989; Karl-Rudolf Korte, 'Japan and the Single European Market', *Außenpolitik*, 4 (1989) p. 397 *et seq.*

15. OECD, *Positive Adjustment Policies – Managing Structural Change* (Paris: OECD, 1983).

16. Klaus W. Grewlich, 'Positive-Sum-Game U.S.–Japan–Europe', *Außenpolitik*, 3 (1988) pp. 217–36.

5 'Europe 1992' and Japan: A British Perspective

Frank Cassell

Obviously the thought in the minds of the editors of this volume is that a British perspective on the emergence of trade blocs may be different from a European perspective; I wonder if that is correct. I shall present one Briton's perspective and leave the reader to judge whether it is different.

I must admit at the outset that I share one very common European attitude towards Japan: ambivalence. I look at Japan with a mixture of admiration, consternation and incomprehension. I also look at it from afar: not the least paradox is that the yen is plainly too cheap but Tokyo is a very expensive place.

If we were asked to rank the G-7 economies not by the cost of a lunch or a night out but by the openness of their domestic markets, probably almost everyone would put Japan nearest the closed end of the list, and perhaps they would put Britain as the most open. Certainly, in its trading relationships, Britain is traditionally liberal internationalist. Its imports and exports, as a proportion of GDP, are both more than double those of the USA. It has made enormous investments in overseas countries, and it has also always welcomed foreign investment to its shores. In its trade policies it has followed the precepts of Adam Smith, not Friederich List. The question is whether the unified European market will be imbued with that same spirit. I believe it will: that is to say, the EC will develop into a market that is not only free from internal barriers to trade but that is also outward looking in its trading relations with the rest of the world.

I also believe that this will be true of NAFTA. Both Europe and North America recognize their dependence on trade for their prosperity, as also does Japan. The trouble is that there seems to be a greater awareness across the Atlantic than across the Pacific that trade is essentially a two-way business.

In the West, trade is driven by profit. If the profits are not there the trade will not flow. This is one reason why it is important to prevent exchange rates from getting out of line with domestic costs. In Japan, as I understand it, corporate strategy is driven more by concern about market share and economic control than by profit. This seems to reflect a feeling by the

Japanese that they live in a hostile world. In fact, the rest of the world is only too happy to trade with them, but mercantilism could in the end make Japan's fears a reality if the frustration it provokes leads to a protectionist backlash.

Japan's quest for market share has taken many forms. Some – like the 1 yen bids for computer contracts – seem to carry aggressive marketing strategy to the ultimate degree. One more familiar method that has become increasingly important has been to establish manufacturing capacity in overseas markets. This has provoked differing reactions in the countries selected for this investment. Perhaps Britain's perspective here has differed from that of its Continental partners. We have welcomed such investment and seen it as a means of injecting Japanese technology and management methods into British industry. As of 1989 there were 105 Japanese companies with plants in Britain, and we have taken a strong line within the EC to ensure that a Nissan car manufactured in Sunderland is of European and not Japanese origin.

It is now conventional wisdom to see the world developing into three regional trade blocs. One is centred in Western Europe but also effectively includes much of Africa and, very importantly at the moment, the emerging economies of Eastern Europe. The second is centred on the USA and includes not only Canada but also Mexico and possibly eventually the rest of Latin America. The third is centred on Japan and includes large parts of East Asia and the Pacific Islands. These blocs may be thought of as extended home markets. In themselves, they are to be welcomed. They widen the market within which trading can flow unimpeded and so increase the scope for reaping the benefits of specialization and economies of scale. The danger, of course, is that they will become inward-looking and protectionist against the rest of the world: in other words, that they will be trade-diverting rather than trade-creating.

The risk of this happening is reduced by the fact that so many of the companies engaged in international trading are now transnational. Is IBM any more really an American company? Is Unilever really a British company? More interestingly, are Nissan and Sony any longer merely Japanese? Or are they all now world companies, willing not only to locate production wherever the costs or taxes are lowest but to internationalize their management and ownership?

Nonetheless, the danger of the world trading system disintegrating is not one that we can lightly dismiss. If multilateralism is to prevail there must be a balance of opportunities and competitiveness. This not only means that real exchange rates must not get out of line, but also that there must be fair competition in domestic markets between home and foreign suppliers.

At the moment, of course, there are large imbalances in world trade, notably between the USA and Britain on the one side and Germany and Japan on the other. Behind these deficits and surpluses lie marked differences in savings and investment in these countries. With free capital movements such imbalances can be financed for a long time, but they would not be sustainable forever.

Japan's propensity to save is prodigious. It regularly saves about 20 per cent of its net national income. In the same league table, Germany stands quite high at about 11 per cent. The USA and Britain, by contrast, are well down the table, saving just over 4 per cent and 6 per cent respectively of their national incomes.[1]

These big differences in saving are reflected in the cost of capital in these countries and in the level of their investment. Some recent studies put the cost of capital in Japan at less than half the cost in the USA.[2] This gives Japanese companies a great advantage over their competitors but one that has been earned mainly by sound management of the economy. The resulting high levels of investment mean that the Japanese capital stock is growing much faster and embodying more of the latest technology than the capital stock of its competitors, a fact that also makes the Japanese economy highly adaptable to changing circumstances.

However, Japan's huge saving is greater than can be absorbed by domestic investment, so it is also reflected in a large external trade surplus, the counterpart of which is seen in Japanese purchases of overseas assets. So long as these asset purchases took the form of financial transactions – buying US Treasury Bills or bonds – they attracted little comment. Perhaps they should have, because without this ready source of financing it is doubtful if the US budget deficit would have been allowed to grow so high for so long. But increasingly, Japanese investors have moved into purchases of real America – the Rockefeller Center and Columbia Pictures, for instance – and have thus become much more evident and worrying to the American public. This is producing a protectionist reaction in the US Congress.[3]

The real cause for worry, however, is not the high level of Japan's savings but the low level of America's. If the USA wishes to spend more than it produces, it is hardly surprising that it has to sell off some of its assets. The days when it could pay for its excess imports simply by running up dollar liabilities are past. Japan, by contrast, seems much more intent on accumulating assets, both domestic and overseas, than on consuming the fruits of its wealth. When one looks at the incredibly inflated land values and stock market prices in Japan one feels that this cannot continue; but it does.

One currently popular view sees Japan as a unique and basically immutable society controlled by a cabal of bureaucrats and business leaders who force ordinary Japanese into lives of regimented drudgery in the service of ever higher and better output and asset prices.[4] This, of course, is a caricature. Some close Japan-watchers now see forces at work that will change all this. As Japan's population gets older its savings will fall,[5] and the Japanese consumer of any age will insist on having a greater share of the country's prosperity. So the enormous saving that has characterized Japan in recent decades may wane in the 1990s, but we cannot be sure.

The Japanese consumer does seem to have rather a raw deal. Restrictions on large retailers and the linking of many shops with particular suppliers stifle competition and severely limit the choice of goods, particularly imported goods, available to the public. In addition, the highly protectionist agricultural system means that the price of basic foods is several times the world market price. Yet even so it seems that three-quarters of the income of Japanese farmers comes from subsidies.

These structural restrictions are intolerable in a country that seeks to play a leading role in the world economy. If they are not broken down under the force of domestic reform, they will be subjected to increasing pressure, economic and political, from Japan's trading partners. The first wave of this pressure can be seen in Super 301 and the Structural Impediments Initiative. One can rightly deplore these unilateral actions, but one must also recognize the frustrations that have given rise to them.

So long as Japan maintains such restrictiveness, its relations with the other main trading areas are likely to be marked increasingly by confrontation rather than cooperation. Reciprocity could become the main instrument in trade negotiations, and reciprocity is not a good rule for optimizing trade. It can all too easily be negative, imposing restrictions on what Japanese firms can do in America and Europe, whereas what we want to ensure is that American and European firms can do what Japanese producers themselves can do in the Japanese market.

'Japan bashing' is said to be a popular pastime nowadays in Washington and Brussels. It is rather a silly phrase, not the least because it suggests the strong belabouring the weak. But if Japan is to be bashed, it should be for the right reasons and not the wrong ones. It would, in my view, be totally wrong to seek to address the problem of Japan's trade surplus by pressing for faster expansion of its economy. One can legitimately ask that the Japanese generate that expansion domestically, but they have in fact done just that in recent years. The management of their economy over the past four or five years has been very good both by domestic and external standards.

The structural rigidities in the Japanese economy, and the restrictions that enforce them, are another matter altogether. They deserve the censure that is increasingly directed at them. They restrict the choice of Japanese consumers in a way that is not defensible in a country at this stage of development, and they are incompatible with the type of open world trading system that we all say we seek.

Structural impediments, however, are not the monopoly of Japan. The test of post-1992 Europe will be the extent to which it sweeps away the complex of regulations and subsidies that distort, in varying degrees, the economies of the present twelve national markets. Likewise in the USA, there is no longer room for voluntary export restraints or for bizarre interventions like the semi-conductor agreement. Double standards will not do.

Free trade is impossible without free markets, and that applies to agriculture and services as much as it does to manufactures. My British perspective that 1992 will be a step toward freer trading is of course fortified by Mrs Thatcher's pledge that 'We have not successfully rolled back the frontiers of the state in Britain only to see them reimposed at a European level.' That is the negation of Fortress Europe. And if one surveys the record of the one trading bloc that has attempted to repress market forces and to look unblinkingly inwards the lesson is now surely as clear as any economic lesson can be; it does not work. That is what the dismantling of the Soviet Union and the liberalizing ferment in Eastern Europe has told us, in no uncertain manner.

Removing restrictions, especially where they benefit particular interests in a country, is seldom easy. The repeal of the Corn Laws is almost as memorable in English history as the Battle of Hastings, not only because its effects were in their way as far reaching but because it was almost as fiercely contested as that battle. The whole history of the GATT shows the difficulty of turning precept into practice. But the universal benefits of free trade are perhaps easier to demonstrate today than ever before. The alternative to going forward is distinctly unattractive for Europe, for North America and for Japan.

That is why I believe that we will move to a more open trading system, but only if we all move. There can be no opting out. We dare not be complacent. We must work for it and hope. We must lose no chance of proclaiming that if these hopes should not be fulfilled, the world will deny itself the widening prosperity that beckons in the 1990s.

Notes

1. This is the average for 1980–87: see *OECD National Accounts*.
2. See, for example, George N. Hatsopoulos and Harvey Brooks, *The Cost of Capital in the United States and Japan* (Cambridge, MA: Kennedy School of Government, Harvard University, 1987).
3. For example, the 'earnings stripping' provision in the 1989 Reconciliation (Tax) Bill was designed to limit the tax deductibility of interest payments to foreign parent companies, and the draft regulations implementing the Exon–Floria Amendment to the Trade Act would give the Administration powers to block foreign acquisitions of US firms whose operations have a 'national security' aspect.
4. *The Financial Times*, 26 October 1989.
5. See Bill Emmott, *The Sun Also Sets: Why Japan will not be Number One* (New York: Simon & Schuster, 1989).

6 Trade Blocs and the Prospects for Japan's Relations with Eastern Europe

Abdul M. Turay

The economic transformation taking place among the Eastern European countries of Bulgaria, the Czech and Slovak Federated Republic (CSFR, formally Czechoslovakia), Hungary, Poland and Romania has enhanced the prospects for economic and trade relations between Japan and these countries. What is the potential value of such relationships? What will be the nature and scope of the relationships? Can economic and trade relations be the answer to some of the challenges facing Eastern Europe?

Uncertainties abound in analyzing these questions in present circumstances because the global market economy is itself undergoing dramatic structural transformations independent of the entry of former Communist-ruled nations into that economy. Specifically, the enactment of EC 92 and NAFTA will substantially alter the structure of the international economy. The EC is now largely devoid of internal barriers to the flow of goods and services, capital and labour, while NAFTA eliminates barriers to the free flow of goods and services. Thus, the nations of Eastern Europe are entering the international economy at a time when the international flows of trade and investment are being transformed by the elimination or reduction of trade barriers among nations in each of the two blocs, as well as by their own entry into the global economy.

Japan remains the largest economy that is not a member of either of these two trading blocs, and the evolution of trade and investment relations between Japan and the nations of Eastern Europe will inevitably both shape and be shaped by the emergence of trade blocs in Western Europe and North America. This chapter presents an assessment of the prospects for economic and trade relations between Japan, Bulgaria, the CSFR, Hungary, Poland and Romania (referred to hereafter as the Eastern European countries).

ECONOMIC AND TRADE RELATIONS: A PREVIEW OF SOME ISSUES

As with most nations of the world, Japan and the Eastern European countries are bound by a complex network of global economic, political and social interrelationships. These ties will determine the nature and scope of any future economic relations that might emerge between Japan and the nations of Eastern Europe. However, the network of relationships in which Japan finds itself embedded and into which the Eastern European countries are entering is undergoing a profound structural transformation as a result of the integration of the economies of Western Europe under EC 92, on the one hand, and the nations of North America (Canada, the USA, and Mexico) under NAFTA on the other. The objective of this section is to preview some of the issues that can influence these relations.

As economic and political transformation continues to gain momentum in Eastern Europe, there is renewed interest in regionalism. Therefore, the prospects for economic and trade relations between Japan and the Eastern Europeans become increasingly important. For Japan, there is concern about the effects on its trade and investment flows of the SEA and NAFTA between the USA, Canada, and Mexico. To the extent that EC 92 evolves into the much-feared 'Fortress Europe' and NAFTA evolves into a protectionist bloc in Japan's other major export market, Japan will be compelled not only to seek ways to preserve its market shares in Europe and North America, but also to seek new markets to offset any loss of market share in Europe and North America. The nations of Eastern Europe, as new entrants into the global economy, could provide an alternative for Japanese exports and for Japanese investments, especially investments in production facilities to supply the European markets. On the other hand, the Eastern European countries are concerned about developments in bilateral payments and trade as a result of the collapse of the Council of Mutual Economic Assistance (CMEA) of which they were members. These issues will influence substantially the prospects for economic and trade relations between Japan and the Eastern European countries.

The Single European Act: EC 92

The SEA has been discussed in other chapters. However, this section will present an overview of the possible impact of EC 92 on the nations of Eastern Europe, recent developments in relations between the EC and Eastern European countries and the ways in which the new links forged between the EC and the nations of Eastern Europe may affect the potential for Japanese and Eastern European relations.

The SEA was enacted in 1986 and became effective in 1987. The Act calls for the elimination of all barriers to the flow of goods and services, capital, and labour among EC members by 1992; the deadline was later postponed to 1993. In anticipation of EC 92 and in recognition of the dramatic reforms taking place in Eastern Europe, the EC signed a series of bilateral trade and economic agreements with Hungary and Poland in 1988 and 1989. The agreements provided for reciprocal MFN status for both countries (Hungary and Poland), providing those two with non-discrimina-tory tariff reductions and favourable access to the markets of the EC member states. Generally, if a group of countries contract to extend MFN status to each other, they are also undertaking the extension of the same commercial advantage to a third party.

In 1990, the trade accord between the EC and two Eastern European countries, Hungary and Poland, was modified. The modification was based on similar status granted to both countries by the Group of 24 industrialized countries under the programme entitled 'Poland–Hungary Aid for Restruc-turing of Economies' (PHARE). Under this programme, the EC agreed to shorten the time frame for the elimination of all quotas placed on imports from both Hungary and Poland. This modification may result in favourable access to markets in the EC for the two former CMEA nations.

In further support of the political and economic reforms in Eastern Europe, the EC in 1991 signed an association agreement with Poland, Hungary and the CSFR. This agreement went into effect in 1992 on an interim basis. The agreement calls for a free trade zone that will cover a wide range of products for a period of ten years. The agreements cover such issues as: (1) political dialogue; (2) economic, financial and cultural co-operation; (3) the free movement of goods, services, people and capital among the three economies; (4) the gradual application of EC laws to Hungarian and Polish goods; and (5) the right of establishment. The agreements also contain provisions dealing with 'Special Protocols' that cover sensitive products such as textiles, steel, agriculture and fisheries. Finally, all three agreements call for all parties to work towards the harmonization of laws dealing with customs policy, banking and financial services, intellectual property, worker and consumer protection, environ-mental laws and standards.

The three Visegrad countries – Poland, Hungary and the CSFR – have all indicated their willingness to enter into membership talks with the EC by 1996. However, the three Visegrad countries may need a sustained period of adaptation and growth before being considered for membership. The reasons are obvious when we examine Table 6.1. However, to gain admission into the EC, economic reforms must continue. As Table 6.1 shows, all three Visegrad countries are moving towards a complete reform of their economies. For example, the pace at which privatization laws are implemented and the progress towards privatization may well be one of the major determinants for admission into the EC. In the CSFR privatization laws were passed in 1990–91. In Hungary the agency responsible for carrying out privatization was established in 1990, and in Poland the plans for massive privatization were unveiled in 1991. The actual process of privatization has gone very well. In the CSFR, a substantial number of enterprises have been privatized through auctions and large-scale joint ventures. In 1991 the Hungarian Government privatized 2120 small and 245 medium and large firms. All retail and wholesale trade has been privatized in Poland. This includes nearly 800 small and 20 large industries.

In addition to the privatization laws and the process of privatization, reforms in other areas may also play an important role in any future negotiation for admission into the EC for the three Visegrad countries. Some of these changes may involve price liberalization, wage controls, import liberalization, exchange rate and interest rate liberalization, banking, money and capital market reforms as well as budget reforms, to name just a few. All three economies of the Visegrad countries have made substantial progress in these areas, as shown in Table 6.1. When these reforms are completed, they will enable these countries to compete effectively in the EC as well as in Japan.

As for the other Eastern European countries, the EC in 1992 approved the mandate to negotiate a bilateral association agreement with the Bulgaria and Romania. The agreement between the EC and the Visegrad countries may act as a model, even though the provisions are not expected to be as far reaching as those found in the agreement with the Visegrad countries. The reasons are that Bulgaria and Romania have not been as progressive as Poland, Hungary and the CSFR in implementing market reforms, and neither are they as highly developed economically as the Visegrad countries. In addition, the EC feels that since the prerequisites for democratization and sustained economic growth have not yet been achieved in Bulgaria and Romania, it would then take a long period of transition in both countries before membership in the EC would be considered. Even though membership in the EC for Bulgaria and Romania is a long way off, negotiations over trade dealing with sensitive products such as textiles, agriculture and steel continue to progress.

In light of the SEA, negotiations between the EC and the nations of Eastern Europe present Japan with a new set of opportunities that may help

Table 6.1   The status of economic reform in the CSFR, Hungary and Poland

Policy issues	CSFR	Hungary	Poland
Privatization laws	Restitution and Privatization Laws passed, 1990–91	Legal framework established, 1989; privatization agency established, 1990	Passed, July 1990; plan for privatization unveiled, June 1991
Privatization	Large share of small enterprises privatized through auctions and restitution; some large-scale joint-ventures concluded; comprehensive large-scale privatization beginning 1992	2120 small and 245 medium and large firms privatized by the end of 1991	All retail and wholesale trade privatized; nearly 800 small and 20 large industrial firms privatized or commercialized
Price liberalization (per cent of prices that are free)	95 per cent, the majority since January 1991	90 per cent of consumer and 93 per cent of producer prices by end of 1991	100 per cent of agricultural, 88 per cent of industrial producer, 93 per cent of consumer prices
Wage controls	Wage limits in large enterprises enforced by penalty tax	Tax-based wage policy, lifted in in early 1992	Tax-based wage policy with partial indexation in state-owned sector
Import liberalization	All imports liberalized except oil, gas, arms and drugs	90 per cent of imports free of control	All imports liberalized; licences required for arms and radioactive materials

(Table 6.1 continued)

Policy issues	CSFR	Hungary	Poland
Exchange rate	Unified in December 1990	Unified rate pegged to a basket	Unified official rate pegged to a basket; legal parallel market with no significant differential in rates
Interest rate liberalization	Flexible rates with maximum ceilings on bank lending rates	Deposits and lending rates freed for the enterprise sector since 1987; deposit rate ceilings for households lifted in 1991	Banks are permitted to set interest rates, but central bank informally influences some spreads
Money and capital markets	Stock market planned for late 1992; money markets being developed	Stock market established in 1990; active money market	Stock market established in April 1991; money market established in 1990
Tax reform	VAT and modernization of income tax system beginning January 1993	VAT and personal income tax introduced in 1988; enterprise profit tax introduced in 1989	Personal income tax introduced in January 1992; VAT introduced by 1993
Budget reform	Subsidies reduced and streamlined in 1990	Social Security separated from budget in 1989; local and central government finances separated in 1991	Most extra budgetary funds incorporated into state budget; local budgets devolved to local authorities
Unemployment benefits	Established in 1991; 65 per cent of previous wages in first 6 months and 55 per cent in remaining 3 months	70 per cent of previous wages for first 6 months and 60 per cent for next 6 months	36 per cent of the average wage in the economy in the previous quarter, payable for 12 months

offset the risk of lost market shares in Europe which otherwise might result from EC 92. To the extent that the implementation of the PHARE programme results in preferential access to the EC market for goods produced in Hungary and Poland, Japanese investors should be attracted to these two nations as production sites for goods destined for the EC. The creation of the single market in the EC should result in substantial growth in the economies of the member nations, making the European market even more lucrative. However, it will also make goods produced in the nations of the EC more competitive throughout the twelve member nations than they were prior to integration. The obvious strategy by which Japanese firms could maintain their competitiveness in the European market and hedge against the possibility of protectionist barriers to goods produced outside the EC would be to invest in production facilities in Europe. However, the cost of land and labour is cheaper in Poland and Hungary than in the EC. A Morgan Stanley International study found that average hourly labour costs in West Germany were $22.49, compared to $15.34 in France, $15.27 in the USA, $13.41 in Great Britain and $13.23 in Japan, while in Hungary they were $1.38 and in Poland about $1.00.[1] Even at Western-owned plants that are employing the most highly skilled Eastern European workers, wages are less than half what they would be if the plant were in an EC nation, and Western managers are finding that most Eastern European workers are as well-educated and trainable as their Western counterparts.[2] Thus, to the extent that the PHARE programme results in Hungarian and Polish goods being given preferential access to the EC market, investment in these two nations could develop into an attractive alternative to direct investment in the EC. In this sense, the creation of the single European market should enhance the prospects for trade and investment relations between Japan and the Eastern European countries, especially Poland and Hungary.

NAFTA

The second issue that may provide Japan an opportunity for expanded trade relations with the Eastern European countries is the signing of NAFTA by the USA, Canada and Mexico. NAFTA is a preferential trade agreement between Canada, Mexico and the USA. Prior to the agreement, the three countries were already major trading partners. As Table 6.2 shows, trade flows between Canada and Mexico are substantially smaller relative to those between each of these two countries and the USA. Thus, the potential economic effects of NAFTA on countries outside the region have been a major concern to policy makers in Japan. They have expressed concern about the potential loss of market shares, especially in the USA and Canada. For Japan, the anticipated loss of market shares will provide an opportunity

Table 6.2   Export trade between Canada, Mexico and the USA,
1990 (US$ billions)

Origin	Destination				
	Canada	*Mexico*	*USA*	*Others*	*Total*
Canada	–	0.5	95.3	35.4	131.2
Mexico	0.5	–	21.9	7.5	29.9
USA	82.9	28.3	–	282.0	393.2

Source: IMF Directions of Trade Statistics, Yearbook 1991.

for the exploration of trade relations with other countries, such as those of Eastern Europe.

Furthermore, since NAFTA is expected to expand the current pattern of trade among the three member countries, it is important for a country such as Japan to look to other markets as an outlet for its exports. The current pattern of trade among the three NAFTA member countries is clearly structured around the concept of comparative advantage. For example, consumer goods and fuels account for 30 per cent of US imports from Canada and Mexico, while they comprise only 15 per cent and 10 per cent, respectively, of Canadian and Mexican imports from the USA. In contrast, approximately three-quarters of Canadian and Mexican imports from the USA are in the form of industrial supplies, machinery and equipment, while similar items account for 60 per cent of total US imports from both Canada and Mexico. In addition, manufactured goods represent 80 per cent of the US and Canadian exports to Mexico and only 36 per cent of Mexico's total exports to the USA and Canada, while oil and minerals account for 57 per cent of the Mexican exports to the USA and Canada.

Therefore, since trade within NAFTA will continue to be based on comparative advantage and can have significant effects on non-member countries such as Japan, it is essential for Japan to explore trade relations with other countries such as Bulgaria, the CSFR, Hungary, Poland and Romania in order to maintain its competitive edge over members of NAFTA, especially the USA.

The Collapse of the Council of Mutual Economic Assistance

The third factor shaping the evolution of the Eastern European countries' trade and investment relations with Japan is the collapse of the CMEA, of which all five Eastern European countries were members. The CMEA was established in 1949 as a counterpoint to the US Marshall Plan for the reconstruction of Europe after the Second World War. The CMEA in some sense was a very narrow common market. Membership consisted of mostly former Soviet satellite nations, including the former Eastern European nations. The CMEA was built on a centralized, administrative and state-directed system of economic management. One major objective of the CMEA was to eliminate all forms of market impulses and rationales among member nations.

However, as a result of the dramatic changes that took place in the former Soviet Union and Eastern Europe in the late 1980s and early 1990s, the CMEA collapsed. The collapse of the CMEA may also be attributed to three other factors: (1) the switch by member countries from domestic prices set by the government to world market prices; (2) the settlement of international transactions in hard currencies; and (3) the shortage of foreign exchange due to the inability CMEA member nations to export.

The collapse of the CMEA has now cleared the way for a complete dissolution of all trade agreements among Eastern European countries.[3] However, the possibility exists that the CMEA may be reorganized into a Preferential Trade Area (PTA), in which lower trade barriers exist among member nations than between member nations and non-member nations. A PTA is often referred to as the lowest form of economic integration.

It is too early to measure the impact of the dissolution of the CMEA on the East European countries. However, one thing is clear: these countries will have to find new outlets for their exports in order to raise the necessary foreign exchange to finance economic growth. Prior to the dissolution of the CMEA, most of the member nations' trade was with other members of the CMEA. In the aftermath, each member nation is faced with both the substantial loss of exports to markets in the former CMEA member nations, and the lack of competitiveness of their goods in the markets of non-CMEA members. Thus, their exports have dropped precipitously, resulting in a substantial depletion of foreign exchange reserves. As we saw earlier, the shortage of foreign exchange was one of the factors responsible for the collapse of the CMEA. Thus the possibility of bilateral trade agreements with Japan is attractive to the former CMEA members as a possible alternative outlet for goods and services from Eastern Europe.

RELATIONS WITH JAPAN: THE ECONOMIC CHALLENGES IN EAST EUROPE

Much has been written about the political and economic reforms among the East European countries of Bulgaria, the CSFR, Hungary, Poland and

Romania. There are exhaustive analyses on bilateral trade agreements between these countries and the EC as well as between them and the USA. In this section, we plan to examine some key issues related to the prospects of trade relations between Japan and the countries of Eastern Europe.

Bulgaria

In the 1980s, the economic growth rate in Bulgaria fell to 2 per cent annually. By 1990, Bulgaria's foreign debt had skyrocketed to over $10 billion, and 40 per cent of its hard currency earned from exports was used to service its debt. In 1990, the inflation rate in Bulgaria was 100 per cent, while the unemployment rate was 2 per cent. The GNP was estimated at $47.3 billion, which represents a per capitum income of $5300. By 1989, the government started restructuring the economy with a partial decentralization of production decisions and foreign trade. Such restructuring efforts should have some positive impact on trade relations with Japan. However, the extent of this impact will depend upon the extent to which the Bulgarian government extends liberalization of the economy.

Revitalization of the Bulgarian industrial sector is vital to establishing trade relations with Japan. However, the growth rate in Bulgaria's industrial production in 1990 was estimated at −10.7 per cent. Its major industries are food processing, machinery and metal buildings, electronics and chemicals. Agriculture still accounts for 15 per cent of the GNP, and agricultural products such as oilseeds, vegetables, fruits and tobacco account for a large part of Bulgaria's exports. In fact, Bulgaria is the world's fourth-largest tobacco exporter. The foreign trade data in Table 6.3 clearly show substantial trade activities between Bulgaria and the industrial countries (including Japan).

Before the collapse of the CMEA, 82.5 per cent of Bulgaria's exports went to fellow members of the CMEA. The developed market economies received only 6.8 per cent of Bulgaria's exports and developing countries another 10.7 per cent. As for imports, 80.5 per cent of Bulgaria's imports are from the CMEA, with another 15.1 per cent coming from the developed market economies and 4.4 per cent from the developing countries. With the collapse of the CMEA, Bulgaria's pattern of trade will be drastically altered as exports to former CMEA member nations plunge and the government looks to the developed market economies as an alternative outlet for Bulgarian exports. This will open a window of opportunity for an expanded trade relationship with Japan. The remaining question is how to make Bulgarian goods competitive in the Japanese market (as well as other markets such as the EC and North America).

Prior to the collapse of the CMEA, machinery and equipment accounted

Table 6.3 Bulgarian imports and exports, 1984–90 (US$ billion)

	Exports							Imports						
	1984	1985	1986	1987	1988	1989	1990	1984	1985	1986	1987	1988	1989	1990
USA	28.2	35.5	55.4	42.9	28.6	59.9	47.9	48.3	114.4	106.2	97.2	140.0	199.1	92.7
EC	405.2	433.7	504.4	576.3	520.0	542.6	716.4	1078.6	1393.0	1608.6	1858.2	1825.3	1803.2	1610.9
Japan	6.2	20.5	16.4	22.8	44.9	40.7	31.5	91.7	137.2	178.0	130.4	176.2	180.0	59.7
Czechoslovakia	242.9	269.7	333.5	371.3	361.5	286.2	152.5	263.8	289.8	36.4	454.6	448.2	370.7	189.0
Hungary	104.4	111.9	118.5	113.3	116.3	69.6	60.4	137.3	134.4	158.6	153.6	138.5	77.3	31.7
Poland	227.1	202.7	190.6	189.6	219.3	165.9	131.5	310.9	257.2	250.7	274.3	313.1	289.6	309.6
Romania	174.4	262.8	230.2	246.3	237.6	231.3	212.7	192.4	209.0	242.5	287.5	260.8	205.8	123.1

Source: IMF Direction of Trade Statistics: Yearbook 1991.

for 60.5 per cent of Bulgaria's total exports. However, most of these sales were to other CMEA nations and this market has collapsed along with CMEA as an institution. Expanding trade relations with Japan will undoubtedly result in a change in the composition of Bulgaria's exports. Bulgarian machinery is not competitive in world markets and it will be difficult to restore machinery's share of exports. However, demand for other Bulgarian commodities may increase. For example, agricultural products account for 14.7 per cent of total exports, manufactured consumer goods account for 10.6 per cent of the total exports, and fuels, minerals, raw materials and metals comprise 8.5 per cent of exports. Exports of these commodities are likely to increase, both in absolute terms and certainly as a share of total exports. Much of this increase may come as a direct result of preferential tariff reductions if both Japan and the Eastern European countries sign a trade agreement.

Since the implementation of political and economic reforms in Bulgaria, prices and interest rates have been liberalized. The economy has been opened to international trade, with private sector activities increasing rapidly. However, most political and economic reforms are associated with high domestic costs and *sectoral dislocations*. High domestic prices and widespread unemployment have plagued the economy since reforms were instituted.

What emerges from the brief analysis of the Bulgarian economy is that the transformation to a well-functioning market economy will be a prolonged and painful process. A strong international trade policy in the form of enhanced trade and economic relations with Japan can aid in the transformation of the Bulgarian economy to a market economy.

The Czech and Slovak Federal Republic

The CSFR is one of the most highly industrialized countries in Eastern Europe. The industrial sector accounts for well over 50 per cent of the nation's GNP. On the other hand, agriculture and forestry account for 7 per cent of the GNP, even though 95 per cent of the agricultural land is in collective or state farms. The CSFR's economic growth rate has been sluggish, averaging less than 2 per cent from 1982 to 1989. However, GNP per capitum remains the highest in Eastern Europe. Inflation and unemployment rates in 1990 were 9 per cent and 0.8 per cent respectively.

Prior to the current economic and political transformation taking place in Eastern Europe, the centrally planned economy of the CSFR was linked by trade to other former CMEA members. As Table 6.4 shows, trade with CMEA members was second only to the trade with the EC. Machinery and

Table 6.4 CSFR's imports and exports, 1984–90
(US$ millions)

	Exports							Imports						
	1984	*1985*	*1986*	*1987*	*1988*	*1989*	*1990*	*1984*	*1985*	*1986*	*1987*	*1988*	*1989*	*1990*
USA	79.4	109.9	80.7	90.8	91.2	261.6	91.3	49.6	44.9	54.0	37.8	57.4	54.0	76.2
EC	2557.9	2597.4	3047.9	3548.7	3537.8	1224.8	3733.0	2503.8	2518.7	3216.1	3859.5	3855.8	3675.6	4264.5
Japan	47.6	42.1	49.2	66.9	89.5	574.0	88.7	74.0	59.7	89.8	102.2	82.4	73.9	63.7
Hungary	428.1	413.2	520.9	641.2	630.1	89.2	492.4	474.7	507.0	570.7	600.9	623.7	683.8	453.8
Poland	612.3	688.7	885.9	1096.6	1195.7	3625.2	746.0	616.7	700.8	913.5	1144.6	1196.4	1227.9	1691.6
Romania	149.1	179.1	216.3	240.2	229.0	93.9	140.3	174.6	184.1	222.7	234.9	260.7	236.5	96.5

Source: IMF Direction of Trade Statistics Yearbook, 1991.

equipment accounted for 42.7 per cent of total exports in 1989, and the same items accounted for 38.6 per cent of total imports in the same year.

When we examine the foreign sector of the CSFR's economy from the view point of other former CMEA members, it faces stiff competition in the future because all of its former CMEA partners are concentrating on expanding their market share and export volume. With respect to the trade and economic relations with Japan, the CSFR's industrial growth will play a major role in any bilateral relationship with Japan because the growth in industrial production in 1990 was 3.3 per cent for such commodities as iron and steel, machinery and equipment, cement, sheet glass and chemicals. Furthermore, because of its highly developed industrial base, industrial labour force, infrastructure to support further industrial expansion and its proximity to Germany and Austria, the CSFR will become an attractive site for Japanese investment.

Hungary

The industrial sector of the Hungarian economy accounts for 40 per cent of the GNP and 30 per cent of the employment in the country. In contrast the agricultural sector accounts for 15 per cent of the GNP and 19 per cent of the national employment. Prior to the current political and economic reforms, 40 per cent of it foreign trade was with the former members of CMEA and about 30 per cent with the EC (see Table 6.5). Hungary exports mostly capital goods, food, consumer goods and fuels, and imports capital goods, fuels, manufactured goods and agricultural products.

Between 1989 and 1990, the economy experienced a sluggish growth rate, reflecting the inability of a Soviet-style economy to stimulate growth. The GNP declined by 1 per cent in 1989 and by almost 6 per cent in 1990. The external debt has almost doubled during the same period. In 1990, unemployment and inflation were 1.7 and 30 per cent respectively.

As with most of the Eastern European countries, Hungary continues to experiment with decentralization and market-oriented enterprise. Consequently, Hungary will be in a better position than other Eastern European countries as it pursues trade relations with Japan. There seems to be every likelihood that Hungary will be a beneficiary if an economic and trade relationship is established with Japan.

Romania

The industrial sector of Romania employs one-third of the labour force and generates about half of the GNP. The agricultural sector accounts for 15 per

Table 6.5 Hungary's imports and exports, 1984–90

| | Exports | | | | | | | Imports | | | | | | |
	1984	1985	1986	1987	1988	1989	1990	1984	1985	1986	1987	1988	1989	1990
USA	228	197	214	287	294	319	337	199	245	194	251	210	222	228
EC	1408	1368	1586	1896	2239	2390	3090	1629	1776	2159	2395	2356	2534	2662
Japan	34	29	48	70	100	111	111	87	139	142	151	135	140	181
CSFR	444	483	540	481	533	489	396	407	408	497	531	473	452	402
Poland	366	327	388	328	323	304	159	358	386	453	390	380	290	206

Source: IMF Direction of Trade Statistics Yearbook, 1991.

cent of GNP and 28 per cent of the work force in the economy. Both the industrial and agricultural sectors will play an important role in any trade and economic relationship with Japan. However, industries in Romania are faced with ageing capital plants and persistent shortages of energy, which will severely diminish their ability to compete in the Japanese market. The agricultural sector has been burdened with mismanagement and shortages of inputs. Real growth rate in Romania in 1990 was –10.8 per cent. However, the GNP was $69.9 billion and per capitum income was $3000. The 50 per cent inflation rate during the year was caused by the expansionary monetary policy of the government.

As with the case of all the other former CMEA countries of Eastern Europe, Romania's foreign trade was mainly with members of the CMEA. In 1990, 27 per cent of total exports went to the former Soviet Union, and 23 per cent to other Eastern European countries. On the other hand, 60 per cent of Romania's total imports came from former Communist countries. The composition of exports included machinery and equipment, fuel and minerals, and manufactured consumer goods. Imports consisted mostly of fuels, minerals and metals, machinery and equipment, manufactured consumer goods, and agricultural and forestry products (see Table 6.6).

For Romania and other Eastern European countries, continued progress towards price liberalization is essential because it raises the level of efficiency in the product, labour and capital markets in Romania and other East European countries. Price liberalization usually means removal of price controls. This may force prices upwards or cause inflationary pressures. However, to enhance the prospect for trade relations with Japan, price liberalization in Romania and Eastern Europe should be accompanied by appropriate macroeconomic policies to prevent inflationary pressures that may affect the prospect for trade relations with Japan. Before the political and economic reforms in Romania, prices did not play an allocative role, but were used to control income distribution. In the Romanian economy there is generally a gap between production costs and sales price which tends to distort the allocation of resources.

JAPAN AND EASTERN EUROPE: A GENERAL FRAMEWORK FOR BILATERAL TRADE

The major challenge confronting Japan as it seeks to establish trade relations with the Eastern European nations may lie in tailoring the nature and scope of its bilateral trade relations with each of the Eastern European nations to the unique characteristics, strengths and weaknesses of each

Table 6.6   Romania's imports and exports, 1984–90
(US$ millions)

	Exports							Imports						
	1984	*1985*	*1986*	*1987*	*1988*	*1989*	*1990*	*1984*	*1985*	*1986*	*1987*	*1988*	*1989*	*1990*
USA	703	647	544	627	627	612	351	270	265	252	240	233	183	428
EC	793	2705	2293	2992	3060	2838	1894	878	885	821	564	529	511	1838
Japan	82	62	73	154	165	185	96	72	92	105	92	57	48	79
CSFR	231	291	323	340	413	351	194	197	287	315	342	358	414	294
Hungary	204	267	279	329	336	303	158	180	240	268	338	324	294	228
Poland	379	398	445	473	467	340	85	431	475	464	436	426	362	405

Source: IMF Direction of Trade Statistics Yearbook 1991.

nation's economy. This means that successful trade relationships with the nations of Eastern Europe will depend on resolving a number of trade issues such as MFN status for the Eastern European countries. As mentioned in the previous section, the USA granted MFN status to some Eastern European countries. The reciprocity in trade that the MFN principle provides represents a new approach to international trade policy for Eastern Europe. Therefore, we will examine the general framework for bilateral trade relations between Japan and the Eastern Europe countries. It is plausible to argue that the trade relations should be based on the following provisions: (1) the MFN clause; (2) the balance of trade clause; (3) the safeguard clause; (4) a Joint Committee; and (5) an investment provision.

A bilateral trade relationship between Japan and the Eastern European countries should be based on MFN treatment. The MFN principle discourages discrimination on tariff policies and provides access to certain markets for some countries. What form should the MFN status take? The 'unconditional' form of MFN status is the most commonly used in bilateral trade relations today. Unconditional MFN tariff reduction requires reciprocal concessions to be extended to all parties without any requests or expectations of compensation. In contrast, a conditional MFN is characteristic of a situation in which, for example, Country A grants tariff reductions to Country B in exchange for reciprocal tariff reductions. MFN is, in principle, a non-discriminatory tariff reduction that may help stimulate international trade activities between Japan and Eastern European countries. Traditionally, the impact on trade flow resulting from the MFN can be classified into trade creation and trade diversion. Trade creation may result if exports of the beneficiaries of MFN status expand as a result of MFN tariff reduction. On the other hand, if domestic consumers substitute lower priced imports from beneficiaries for domestically produced goods and imports from non-beneficiaries of the MFN, this will result in trade diversion.

The desire for MFN tariff cuts by the Eastern European countries is just one manifestation of the economic transformation sweeping the region, along with their desire to expand their international trade activities. In the past, their international trade was limited to some extent to members of the CMEA. When trade was expanded to countries outside the CMEA, it was intended to satisfy the demand for goods and services required to meet the target goals of their economic plan. Today, however, international trade is expected to play a vital role in the economic growth and development of these countries. Trade policies such as the MFN tariff cuts will provide an incentive for the efficient use of exports to earn foreign exchange to finance growth and development.

How important are MFN tariff reductions? A form of MFN tariff reduction for exports from East European countries would generate trade creation incentives for Eastern Europe producers. Since Japan generally excludes certain imports from tariff reductions under the Generalized System of Preferences (GSP), it is likely that under a general MFN plan a broader range of products originating from Eastern Europe will be purchased by Japan. GSP is a form of preferential tariff treatment on imports of manufactured and semi-manufactured products from developing countries. In contrast, economic and trade relations between Japan and Eastern Europe may mean full benefits of an MFN tariff reduction for Eastern European countries.

More importantly, the Eastern European countries collectively stand to benefit more from MFN tariff reductions than does Japan. This conclusion is based on the structure of the MFN programmes and the benefits associated with such programmes. For example, MFN tariff cuts are usually permanent when compared to GSP programmes. Furthermore, MFN tariff reductions typically provide more favourable access to world markets for unlimited trade volume.

In addition to the MFN clause, there are other provisions that may be considered in the establishment of economic and trade relations between Japan and the East European countries, as listed on p. 131.

In a balance of trade provision, both parties agree to foster a harmonious expansion of reciprocal trade. In addition, they work towards preventing a long-term and serious imbalance in trade between the two parties. If a trade imbalance does occur, the problem can be examined by a Joint Committee established by the parties involved. This will be the case with Japan and the Eastern European countries. The current foreign trade strategy of the Eastern European countries is to maintain the capacity to finance imports and economic development. However, if trade with Japan suffers from an imbalance (or a trade deficit), then a Joint Committee will be in a position to recommend measures to correct the trade deficit.

Another provision is the safeguard or escape clause. This is a provision which states that concessions in a trade agreement could be withdrawn if a trade agreement produces an unforeseen injury to the domestic industry of a trading partner. This clause is consistent with the GATT rules in the sense that a country injured by such a withdrawal can retaliate by imposing restrictions on trade if a mutual agreement cannot be reached. A safeguard or escape clause has been referred to as the tool of 'new protectionism'. For example, in the USA, an injured industry may petition for and receive relief from the International Trade Commission. In the case of a Japanese–Eastern Europe economic and trade relationship, an injured industry may petition for relief to the Joint Committee established in accordance with the agreement.

A Joint Committee will be established in accordance with the agreement which established economic and trade relations between Japan and the Eastern Europeans. The role of the Joint Committee will be as follows:

- to monitor the agreement and its various functions
- to deal with questions of the accord such as issues that might hinder the flow of trade
- to examine new opportunities for trade
- to make policy recommendations on trade and financial issues, such as trade imbalances

Finally, the trade and economic accord between Japan and the Eastern European countries should consist of an investment provision. Basically this clause calls for all parties to agree on a framework to promote and encourage greater and mutually beneficial investment. There are several such investment agreements that a Japanese–Eastern European economic and trade agreement can use as a model, such as the 1986 Sino–UK Investment Agreement which requires the UK and China to 'promote and encourage greater and mutually beneficial investment'. Some of the general provisions of the Sino–UK Investment Agreement include the following points.

1. All parties to the agreement shall provide investors from member countries with the same investment climate they create for investors who are not party to the said agreement.

2. Signatories will allow others to transfer freely to their respective countries their investments and returns. More specifically, up to 20 per cent per year of all profits, interest, dividends, royalties or fees can be transferred under the Sino–UK Agreement. Finally, the exchange rate to be used will be the official exchange rate of the country receiving the investment.

3. All parties to the agreement should make use of consultation through diplomatic channels if a dispute arises from the interpretation of the agreement and related law. The dispute may be submitted to international arbitration if it has not been settled within six months of the date on which it arose.

4. Compensation must be made if any of the parties decides to expropriate or nationalize the investment of another party. If there is disagreement on the terms and amount of compensation, the case may be submitted to a court of law or to an international arbitration tribunal for settlement.

ECONOMIC COSTS AND BENEFITS OF TRADE RELATIONS BETWEEN JAPAN AND THE EASTERN EUROPEANS

What are the possible economic benefits and costs of economic and trade relations between Japan and Eastern European countries? Traditionally, international trade theory addresses two types of gains and losses in economic and trade relations. They fall into two major categories: the static and dynamic effects.

Static effects of trade relations between Japan and the Eastern European countries will be in the form of reallocation of resources. The dynamic effects will be associated with the productive capacity of firms in both Japan and Eastern Europe. More specifically, the static affects from trade relations will depend on the relative size of the gains from trade creation.[4] Since the economic and trade relationship between Japan and Eastern Europe will involve tariff reductions on imports from individual Eastern European countries, this would make some imports relatively cheaper than domestically produced goods in Japan. Thus trade creation will occur for the Eastern European countries if Japan replaces goods produced domestically with imports from Eastern Europe. In contrast, trade diversion will arise if Japan uses low-cost imports to replace more expensive products from Eastern Europe.

On the supply side, economic and trade relations will force the Eastern European countries to reallocate resources from costly producers for the home market to producing exports for Japan. On the demand side, consumers in both Japan and the East European countries will increase demand for goods and services as a result of the lower prices and greater variety.

The possibility of losses may also exist if economic and trade relations cause consumers in both Japan and Eastern Europe to buy from less efficient producers. This is what we refer to as trade diversion. When such diversion of trade occurs it may affect the East European countries because a large share of their trade will be involved with Japan. Another impact of the trade diversion is a deterioration of the terms of trade with Japan for most of the Eastern Europe countries. Terms of trade represent the behaviour of export relative to import prices. This deterioration in the terms of trade in the long run will affect the export and growth performance of the Eastern European countries.

Another static gain for the Eastern European countries is in the form of the so-called rents from preferential market access as a result of the MFN status extended to them by Japan.[5] For example, with the granting of MFN status, the Eastern European counties can export to Japan at the current international market price minus the external tariffs or mark-up cost from

NTBs. However, countries not receiving MFN tariff status from Japan may sell their products in the Japanese market at the current international market price plus the external tariff or mark-up cost. The counterpart of this rent from preferential market access on the part Japan is the trade diversion and a loss of tariff revenue.

Moreover, both Japan and the East European countries may experience some transitional adjustment costs as these economies shift from one equilibrium position in the economy to another. Consider that a substantial short-run cost will be a transitional welfare loss in the form of temporary unemployment and idle capacity.

Finally, the projected net gains for the Eastern European countries resulting from an economic and trade relationship with Japan may be affected as a result of national preference for industries.[6] In other words, nationalism will play a vital role in the decision as to which industries should be shut down as resources are reallocated to more efficient industries. Under these circumstances, policy makers in Eastern Europe will be well advised to reduce excessive costs of inefficiency by closing inefficient plants.

Let us now turn to some of the dynamic effects of economic and trade relations between Japan and Eastern Europe. One such dynamic effect would be a sustainable increase in the rate of growth of income in Eastern Europe. Dynamic gains may also be realized by the Eastern European countries through increased consumption made possible by unrestricted access to the Japanese market.

Dynamic effects may also arise from economies of scale being realized by firms in Eastern Europe. Access to the Japanese market provides an opportunity for firms in Eastern Europe to expand production. Therefore gains from economies of scale will be a result of the declining costs of production while production is increasing among firms in Eastern Europe. Finally, economic and trade relations with Japan are likely to improve the investment climate in Eastern Europe. As a result of the expanding market opportunities and the rising profitability among firms, the dynamic gains will come as investments are attracted to these countries.

THE POLITICS OF JAPAN'S INTERNATIONAL ECONOMIC POLICY AND THE RULES ON IMPORTS FROM EASTERN EUROPE

Since the Second World War, Japan has successfully achieved its two major economic goals: (1) rapid economic growth, and (2) international competitiveness. However, it is important to point out that, for Japan, both economic goals are related. Japan's trade policy for most of the post-Second

World War period has been governed by two specific domestic goals: namely, to attain a higher standard of living for Japanese people, and to become an economic power force among industrialized nations.

During the period 1950–70, the Japanese trade policy can be best described as straightforward, with a strong and successful export promotion policy counterbalanced by a strong restrictive import policy to protect domestic industries. Policy makers in Japan believed very strongly that their government could promote global competition by investing in physical and human capital as well as by protecting domestic industries. The protective nature of this economic strategy encouraged the domestic flow of resources to those industries that are now the backbone of the Japan's international economic policy. The success of this policy has greatly depended on quantitative restrictions (QRs), quotas, import tariffs and import licensing used by the Japanese Government over the years. For both the government and domestic producers in Japan, the use of import quotas has meant that they knew the quantity of an item that was being imported and the effect that such a quantity could have on the competing domestic industries in Japan. Import tariffs have been less predictable because they depend on elasticities of supply and demand, which are generally not known by the government issuing the import licences.[7] They are issued to a limited number of importers which gives them the right to import a stated quantity of an item.

Finally, let us examine Japanese international monetary regimes and exchange rates. Foreign trade analysts have frequently ignored the implications of international monetary regimes on international trade relations. For example, a critical element in Japan–Eastern European economic and trade relations will be capital flows. Such non-trade transactions are very critical to the balance of payments of both parties, and particularly to the overall international economic strength of the Eastern European countries. Moreover, overvalued or undervalued exchange rates among the parties may influence policy makers to subsidize the international trade competitiveness of the country in question. Therefore, international monetary relations and exchange rate factors in Japan and among the Eastern European countries represent a major element in their economic and trade relations.

What, then, are Japan's international monetary and exchange rate policies, and how do these policies affect economic and trade relations with Eastern Europe? The appreciation of the Japanese yen typically has a very modest impact on Japanese imports. Traditional international monetary theory states that when a country's currency appreciates, it should have a significant impact on its imports. In the case of Japan, the answer may be found in her trade policy (discussed in this section). Japan's trade policy discourages imports even when the yen appreciates in value. Thus the

Japanese business cycle is as much a determinant of the volume of imports as the Japanese exchange rate policy.

What is the significance of Japan's international economic policies on trade relations with Eastern Europe? First, it is important to note that an appreciation of the Japanese yen may significantly shrink Japan's competitive edge over most of the Eastern European countries. However, this is not likely to happen because of Japan's trade policies. When the yen does appreciate, Japanese exporters have been known to reduce export prices, preferring lower profit margins to loss of market share. In the wake of lower yen costs for imports, Japanese importers frequently raise their prices. There are certain products in which Japan controls substantial proportions of the market (such as 35mm cameras and videotape recorders). Therefore, price increases for these items may not translate into a resurgence of domestic production among competitors in Eastern Europe.

We have discussed the possible benefits for East European countries from trade relations with Japan. However, there are three major factors which are likely to affect long-term productive relationships. First of all, individual countries will want to realize economic benefits. The distribution of benefits must be controlled and apportioned because of the economic disparities which exist among the Eastern European countries. Second, each country will have to modify its domestic policies in order to accommodate a number of policies in the agreement with Japan. Third, adjustments may have to be made by the individual countries in areas such as transportation and communications. Finally, exchange rates and balance of payment policies must be negotiated for a successful agreement: for example, an inefficient transportation system may have a similar effect to a customs duty because it will cause trade and exchange to be more costly. In many of the Eastern European countries, transportation and exchange systems are still geared towards export markets of the collapsed CMEA. Improvements are essential for effective economic and trade relations with Japan. Similarly, if the exchange rate of a single country is out of line (such as an overvalued currency), this could become a barrier to economic exchange.

There are two ways to achieve the distribution of benefits among Eastern European countries from the trade and economic relations with Japan. One is through the establishment of an investment provision in the agreement, and another is to develop a programme to compensate the countries that would be left with less than a fair share of the long-term benefits from the trade relations.

All of the problems associated with Japanese–Eastern European trade relations cannot be solved by efficient distribution of benefits, the modification of domestic policies, or the adjustment of various sectors. The goal should be to make sure that neither the Eastern European countries nor Japan are worse off after an economic and trade agreement is signed. However, in the case where a country is experiencing a deterioration in its balance of payments with Japan or has an increase in the average price level (inflation), then each country may have to formulate policies to deal with the problems it faces. Therefore, the survival and success of an economic and trade relationship between Japan and the Eastern European countries will greatly depend on the three policies discussed and the specific policies outlined as precautions.

SUMMARY AND CONCLUSION

The economic and political transformation taking place among the Eastern European countries of Bulgaria, the CSFR, Hungary, Poland and Romania have increased the prospects for economic and trade relations between them and Japan. However, any form of Japan–East European trade relationship may be influenced by the complex network of economic, political and social interrelationships around the world. This is evidenced by the SEA or the so-called EC 92, NAFTA between the USA, Canada and Mexico, and the collapse of the CMEA of which the East European countries were members.

In 1988 and 1989, for example, the EC signed a series of bilateral trade and economic agreements with Hungary and Poland. The agreements provide Hungary and Poland with MFN status. With MFN status, both Eastern European countries are given the opportunity to expand their market size. The NAFTA, on the other hand, is expected to expand the current trade pattern between its three members.

Finally, the collapse of the CMEA may also have an impact on a Japanese–Eastern European relations. It provides an opportunity for Bulgaria, the CSFR, Hungary, Poland and Romania to find new outlets for their exports. Japanese–East European relationships may provide such an opportunity.

A bilateral trade agreement between Japan and the East European countries should be based on (1) MFN status for the Eastern European countries; (2) a balance of trade clause; (3) a safeguard clause; (4) a Joint Committee; and (5) an investment provision. The MFN status for the East European countries is important because of the ongoing efforts to transform these economies from non-market to market economies. Furthermore, having a MFN status would generate trade creation incentives for producers (or exporters) from Eastern Europe. On the other hand, a balance of trade clause will enable both parties to work towards preventing a long-term and serious imbalance in trade. The safeguard or escape clause would protect industries that are affected by the agreement. If the effect includes the loss of market share, the affected firm can petition (and receive relief from) the Joint Committee.

The economic costs and benefits of a Japanese–East European trade agreement may fall within the traditional static and dynamic effects of a trade agreement. Within the static effects, there will be some reallocation of resources, while the dynamic effects will take place in the areas of enhanced productive capacity of firms in both Japan and the East European countries. Furthermore, the possibilities of a trade diversion exists if consumers in both Japan and Eastern Europe make purchases from less efficient producers. One impact of the trade diversion will be a deterioration in the terms of trade. Trade creation can occur for Eastern European countries if Japanese consumers substitute imports from Eastern Europe for domestically produced goods.

Japanese international economic policies will be a significant factor in the trade relations with Eastern Europe. An appreciation of the Japanese yen at any time should shrink Japan's competitive edge. However, current Japanese trade policy seems to protect their market share during periods in which the yen appreciates in value.

Finally, there are three precautions for successful trade relations between Japan and the Eastern European countries. They are: (1) the benefits from trade and economic relations with Japan; (2) modifications of domestic policies by the East European countries; and (3) structural adjustments. Thus, the potential for economic and trade relations between Japan and the Eastern European countries is becoming increasingly important as world events continue to unfold.

Notes

1. Richard W. Stevenson, 'East Europe's Low Wages Luring Manufacturers from West Europe', *New York Times*, 11 May 1993, p. C2.
2. Ibid, p. C2.
3. A meeting in Moscow on March 1991 failed to dissolve the organization formally, leaving the possibility for a reorganization of the CMEA into a more traditional economic integration organization.
4. For more discussion on the international theory on trade creation and trade diversion see Jacob Viner, *The Customs Union Issues* (New York: Carnegie

Endowment for International Peace, 1950); J.M. Meade, *The Theory of Customs Unions* (Amsterdam: North-Holland, 1955); and R.G. Lipsey, 'The Theory of Customs: Trade Diversion and Welfare', *Economica*, 24 (1957) pp. 40–6.

5. See Paul Wonnacott and R. Wonnacott, 'Is Unilateral Tariff Reduction Preferable to a Customs Union? The Curious Case of the Missing Foreign Tariffs', *American Economic Review*, 71 (1981) pp. 704–14.

6. For a detailed discussion on this issue, see C.A. Cooper and B.F. Massell, 'Towards a General Theory of Customs Unions for Developing Countries', *Journal of Political Economy*, 73 (1965) pp. 461–76.

7. The responsiveness of demand for imports to changes in the price, as a result of tariff reduction.

7 Trade Blocs and the Prospects for Japan's Relations with Russia

Gordon B. Smith

Upon coming to power in 1985, Mikhail Gorbachev undertook an active policy designed to forge a new relationship between the Soviet Union and Japan. Despite the break-up of the Soviet Union, the Russian President, Boris Yeltsin, seems committed to continuing that momentum. However, whether these efforts will succeed remains unclear, given the uncertainty surrounding the future of the Commonwealth of Independent States (CIS), the stability of the Russian economy, the volatility of political conflicts between Yeltsin and conservative elements dominating the Russian Parliament, and the ability of the Russian state to fulfil any commitments it might undertake in bilateral negotiations.

In January 1986 the Soviet Foreign Minister, Eduard Shevardnadze, visited Japan, the first such diplomatic visit to Japan in more than ten years. Unlike previous diplomatic encounters, Shevardnadze did not refuse to discuss controversial issues such as human rights or the long-standing Northern Territories dispute over the four Kurile islands that have been occupied by the Soviet Union since the end of the Second World War but which are claimed by Japan. Shortly after Shevardnadze's visit to Tokyo, a 250-member Japanese trade mission went to the USSR at the invitation of its Premier, Nikolai Ryzhkov. Ryzhkov had already stated his intention to pursue an aggressive trade promotion campaign with Japanese business leaders. He noted that it was necessary 'to eliminate in our exports the emphasis on raw materials and to increase the share of manufacturing'.[1]

On 24 April 1986 the Soviet Government unveiled what it called 'The Pacific Document' that set forth Soviet interests in the region, including the call for an all-Asian forum to establish a nuclear-free zone in the Asia–Pacific region. The document declared:

The Soviet Union is deeply convinced that the establishment of broad cooperation on the basis of equality and mutual advantage among all countries of the Asian and Pacific region, regardless of differences in their social systems, is in the fundamental interest of the states in this part of the world and will facilitate a restructuring of international relations on an equal, democratic basis. Our country is prepared to take a very active part in this regional peaceful cooperation and to use for this purpose the economic, scientific, and technical potential at its disposal.

During Foreign Minister Shintaro Abe's return visit to Moscow in May 1986, he was told by Gorbachev that 'we have made a principled political decision to utilize all possibilities for developing and improving relations with Japan in all areas, regardless of relations with other countries'.[2] During Abe's Moscow visit several agreements were reached relating to trade, taxes, cultural exchanges, reactivation of the Japan–Soviet Scientific and Technological Cooperation Committee and visits by Japanese citizens to ancestral grave sites in the Northern Territories.

Perhaps the most ambitious statement of Gorbachev's intent to improve Soviet relations in Asia, and with Japan in particular, came during his visit to Vladivostok on 27–8 July 1987. He proclaimed that 'the Soviet Union is also an Asian and a Pacific country'.[3] He went on to observe:

About relations with Japan, here too signs of change for the better are being noticed. It would be good if this turn does take place. The objective position of our two countries in the world is such that it requires extensive cooperation on a healthy, realistic basis and in an atmosphere of tranquility unburdened by problems. A start was made this year. There was an exchange of visits by Ministers for Foreign Affairs. On the agenda is an exchange of visits at the highest level.[4]

In the same month, Gorbachev appointed a new ambassador to Japan, Nikolai Solovyev. Solovyev is a professional diplomat fluent in Japanese. In contrast to his predecessor, Dmitri S. Polianski, Solovyev impressed the Japanese by his sensitivity to their culture and traditions.

Both sides worked feverishly to bring about the first ever visit of a Soviet General Secretary to Japan. Following his decisive election victory, Nakasone reportedly dispatched Ichiro Suetsuge to Moscow in June 1986.[5] Another source indicates that Michael Deaver, the former Reagan staff assistant, served as the intermediary, drawing on his connections to former Soviet Ambassador to Washington, Anatoly Dobrynin.[6] Arrangements for Gorbachev's visit hit a snag in October 1986 after the US–Soviet summit in Reykjavik. Numerous attempts by the Japanese to extract a commitment from the Soviets on a date for the visit proved fruitless. Some sources indicate that the Japanese Foreign Ministry officials were dragging their feet.[7] The Reagan Administration was also concerned about the prospect of a Gorbachev–Nakasone summit. In early December a senior Soviet official, attending a 'private-level' meeting in Tokyo, conveyed to Nakasone that the visit could not be scheduled without prior agreement on the agenda.[8] The Soviets wanted Japan to conclude agreements on long-term economic co-operation and on 'bilateral friendship', but the Japanese held to their position that no such accords could be reached until a peace treaty was signed.

A period of renewed Japanese–Soviet hostilities followed. In May 1987 two officials of Toshiba Machine Company were arrested for selling strategic equipment to the USSR in violation of COCOM restrictions. A few days later V.V. Aksyutin, the third secretary in the Soviet embassy in Tokyo, was accused of theft of classified documents and advised to leave the country. A *Pravda* commentary on the treatment of Aksyutin accused the Japanese of mounting an anti-Soviet campaign.[9] The article also complained that the Japanese Ministry of Foreign Affairs was imposing unreasonable visa restrictions on Soviet trade officials in Japan.

In August 1987 a Soviet Foreign Ministry spokesman announced that a diplomatic representation had been issued to the Japanese Ambassador regarding 'the continuing hostile propaganda campaign being waged in Japan against the USSR'.[10] The announcement also indicated that two Japanese diplomats in the USSR, and one Japanese businessman, had engaged in intelligence-gathering activities and were being expelled from the country.

In November 1987 Noboru Takeshita succeeded Nakasone as Prime Minister. The change of leadership of the Liberal Democratic Party (LDP) did not, however, promise any substantive changes in the Japanese position towards the USSR. A commentary in *Pravda,* concerning the leadership transition in Japan, accused the Nakasone Government of 'attempting to blow the Toshiba affair out of proportion and [mounting] slander campaigns designed to intimidate the Japanese with fabrications about the Soviet military threat'.[11] The commentator observed that Takeshita's statements soon after taking office indicated that Takeshita would probably follow Nakasone's general approach to the USSR.

The new Japanese Prime Minister had been in office approximately eight months when the Recruit scandal came to light. The remainder of his tenure in office was largely consumed with domestic political problems, making it difficult for him to undertake major foreign initiatives, even if he had desired to do so.

Reaffirming his commitment to a restructured Asia policy, Gorbachev renewed his call for an Asian security conference in a major address in Krasnoyarsk on 18 September 1988.[12] While acknowledging several points of disagreement with Japanese policy, the tone of Gorbachev's remarks were much more conciliatory than any since the breakdown of discussions on a summit meeting. Gorbachev called on the USA and other nuclear powers to refrain from additional deployments in Asia. He also issued various proposals for reducing naval deployments and ensuring the safety of sea lanes in the region.

In December 1988 Shevardnadze again travelled to Tokyo, where he engaged in discussions with Takeshita and the Foreign Minister, Sosuke Uno. Both sides agreed to convene regular negotiations aimed at concluding a peace treaty. The first session of these talks was held in Tokyo in March 1989. I.A. Rogachev, the Deputy Foreign Minister representing the Soviet side, took an uncompromising stand on the Northern Territories, and the session concluded without having achieved any progress.

Frustrations surfaced again in May 1989 when Uno met Gorbachev in Moscow. Gorbachev noted, 'It is obvious that the dynamics of Japanese–Soviet relations are lagging noticeably behind what has been taking place, especially recently, in the Soviet Union's relations with other major states.'[13] He went on to criticize the USA and Japan for carrying out a military build-up in the Pacific, and expressed disappointment at the lack of Japanese response to his initiatives made in Vladivostok and Krasnoyarsk.

A potential breakthrough came on 28 September 1989 when it was announced that Japan and the Soviet Union had reached an agreement in principle that Gorbachev would visit Japan some time in 1991. The date of the proposed visit was sufficiently distant to enable the sides to manoeuvre on a number of outstanding issues dividing them. The summit finally occurred on 16–19 April 1991, beginning with great expectations but ending in disappointment on both sides. Three additional rounds of unscheduled talks on the disputed Northern Territories ended without any solution. Negotiations over the status of the islands had become complicated by a jurisdictional dispute between Gorbachev and Yeltsin. The latter had been arguing for several months that Gorbachev and the government of the USSR had no jurisdiction to negotiate the status of the islands without the approval of the government of the Russian Federation.

Prior to the summit, rumours circulated that the Japanese were willing to expend up to $28 billion in aid, conditional upon the return of the disputed territories. With the failure of both sides to resolve this issue, Gorbachev came away from the summit largely empty-handed. In stark contrast to the chilly atmosphere of the Soviet–Japanese summit, Gorbachev was warmly received in South Korea. The South Koreans pledged $800 million in credits and greatly expanded cultural, educational, trade and diplomatic ties.

Gorbachev returned to Moscow without the bold diplomatic and economic victory he had hoped to obtain from his trip. The unravelling domestic situation, compounded by Yeltsin's rise in popularity and legitimacy as Russian President, forced Gorbachev to concentrate on domestic matters. The August coup attempt in Moscow, and the eventual dismantling of the Soviet Union as a sovereign entity, left Yeltsin to revive any initiatives with Japan.

Clearly, the Soviet leadership was according Japan, and its neighbours in the Asia–Pacific region, much higher priority than in the past. Whether their ambitious plans for Japanese–Soviet rapprochement can be resuscitated as guidelines for Japanese–Russian rapprochement is the subject of this chapter. It is argued here that the outlook for trade expansion between Russia and Japan is at best limited. Furthermore, we will argue that the primary impediments to a rapid expansion of trade are economic rather than political in nature. Consequently, the resolution of various outstanding bilateral political issues that Boris Yeltsin inherited from Mikhail Gorbachev, such as the Northern Territories dispute, will not necessarily result in the rapid expansion of Russian and Japanese commercial cooperation. Finally, we will argue that the primary political influence affecting Japanese trade activity with Russia is American pressures on Japanese export control policy.

THE POLITICAL FACTORS

Two major political issues divide the Russian Republic and Japan, and their resolution will undoubtedly have considerable bearing upon the future course of their bilateral relations. The two issues relate to the Northern Territories and the security threat that Russia still poses to Japan. We will discuss each issue in turn.

Northern Territories

The seizure by the USSR of four islands just off Hokkaido at the end of the Second World War remains a major stumbling block to the normalization of relations between Japan and the Russian Republic. Unlike his predecessors, Gorbachev took a somewhat more flexible position as to the territorial dispute. During his Tokyo visit in 1986, Shevardnadze reportedly discussed the problem with Abe for more than three hours.[14] As a result of those discussions, they agreed to resume long-suspended negotiations on a peace treaty, including discussions of the Northern Territories dispute.

At the Moscow Shevardnadze–Abe meeting in May 1986, Shevardnadze announced that the Soviet Union would allow Japanese citizens to visit the graves of their ancestors on the islands.[15] Initially, the Soviets only allowed non-visa visits to two of the four islands. In August 1986, 56 Japanese visited their ancestors' graves on these two islands.[16] However, on 1 April 1992, people from all four of the islands came to Hokkaido, and in May 1992 people from Hokkaido visited all four islands without visas for the first time.[17]

Although these are positive signs, successful resolution of the dispute has proved difficult because, in the past decade, the Soviet armed forces have built sophisticated intelligence-gathering facilities and other military installations on the two northernmost islands. These islands guard the entrance to the Sea of Okhotsk, where the largest submarine force in the Soviet Navy was deployed.

For the last years of Gorbachev's tenure rumours circulated that the Soviet leadership might be willing to exchange the two southern islands for closer economic ties with Japan.[18] Others indicated that the price for a return of some or all of the islands would be the severing of Japan's security ties to the USA.[19] Still other proposals called for a return of two of the islands and joint development of the remaining two islands.[20] Reports circulated in August of 1989 that the USSR had sent a secret message to the Japanese Government proposing the return of the four islands in exchange for large-scale investments in the Soviet economy.[21] A month later the Japanese press reported that Japanese officials in Paris had been approached with a proposal which would grant Japan 'tenant rights' to the islands, as well as to Sakhalin Island, and create a special economic zone near Vladivostok for joint development.[22] However, these reports were vigorously denied by Soviet Foreign Ministry officials.

For the Japanese, the return of all four islands is an issue of national pride. Should the Yeltsin leadership prove willing to negotiate over the status of the islands, it is likely to present the Japanese with a real political crisis. Are the islands negotiable? Should Japan have to agree to a quid pro quo to ensure the return of islands which were properly their territory in the first place? If the answer to the latter question is yes, then what price is politically acceptable to the majority of the Japanese public? Heretofore, the Japanese benefited politically from the Northern Territories stalemate in that they could raise it as an excuse for not proceeding faster towards economic cooperation and diplomatic normalization with the Soviet Union. Post-Second World War Japanese governments have been able to argue, with a high degree of credibility, that they were actively pursuing a return of the islands but that the Soviet Union was simply intransigent. Once the Soviet leadership indicated its willingness to be flexible on the Northern Territories issue, it forced the Japanese leadership to assess how important those islands really are in the larger panoply of Japanese national priorities.

Security Dilemmas

In the past two decades the Soviet Union has engaged in a massive military build-up in the Far East. Most notable have been the deployment of approximately one division of military forces on three of the disputed islands, deployment of three aircraft carriers in the Pacific fleet, and deployments of the Backfire bombers and SS-20 missiles in the Far East within easy striking range of Japan.

Although we have seen less dramatic turnabouts in the security dimension, some departures under Gorbachev are worthy of note. During Abe's visit to Moscow in May 1986 Gorbachev proposed that the issue of medium-range missiles be solved bilaterally.[23] In essence he was proposing that, in exchange for the Soviet Union destroying its missiles located in the eastern part of the USSR and aimed at Japan, the USA would destroy its corresponding nuclear weapons located in Japan and its coastal waters. Such proposals were not well received in either Japan or the USA. This issue was rendered moot when the Soviet Union signed the Intermediate Nuclear Forces (INF) agreement with the USA. This agreement called for the destruction of all intermediate-range nuclear missiles, including SS-20s based in Asia and aimed at Japan.

THE ECONOMIC FACTORS

Throughout the 1960s and 1970s, Japan embarked upon a course of economic cooperation with the USSR. From 1965 to 1982 Japanese–Soviet trade increased more than twelve-fold, from $408 million to more than $5.5 billion.[24] This rapid expansion of Japanese–Soviet trade resulted from a unique combination of political and economic factors. Since 1982, however, Japanese-Soviet trade has fallen by almost 20 per cent.[25] One of the most critical factors affecting the overall Japanese–Soviet trade relationship was the Soviet Union's ability to finance imports. The collapse in world oil prices severely reduced the Soviet Union's hard currency reserves by as much as 30–40 per cent in 1986.[26] Thus, the USSR was forced to cover its imports by export earnings in other commodities.

As we see in Table 7.1, total trade turnover between Japan and the USSR increased very rapidly over the period 1965–82, but also netted a large trade surplus in favour of the USSR. For example, in 1969, the year after the initiation of the first timber development project in the Far East region, Soviet exports exceeded imports by almost 84 million roubles. Similar surpluses in exports to Japan were also recorded in 1973 and 1974, and were directly linked to the rapid expansion of raw material exports. During the decade 1965–75 the USSR enjoyed a favourable trade balance with Japan of some 320 million roubles. Beginning in 1975, however, the USSR consistently ran a trade deficit with Japan, a deficit largely financed out of hard currency reserves from its oil and gas exports to Western Europe.

Table 7.1   Soviet exports to Japan and imports from Japan, 1965–87 (million roubles)

Year	Exports	Imports	Total	Balance
1965	166.5	159.6	326.1	+6.9
1966	214.8	201.8	416.6	+13.0
1967	317.7	352.1	669.8	–34.4
1968	149.1	166.5	315.6	–17.4
1969	321.3	237.4	558.7	+83.9
1970	341.1	377.4	718.5	–36.3
1971	377.4	356.2	733.6	+21.2
1972	381.7	433.9	815.6	–52.2
1973	622.0	372.4	994.4	+249.6
1974	905.7	777.5	1683.2	+128.2
1975	668.9	1253.5	1922.4	–584.6
1976	784.5	1372.1	2156.6	–587.6
1977	853.4	1444.4	2297.8	–591.0
1978	736.1	1583.7	2319.8	–847.6
1979	944.4	1653.5	2597.9	–709.1
1980	950.2	1772.6	2722.8	–822.4
1981	816.8	2212.7	3029.5	–1395.9
1982	756.6	2915.8	3672.4	–2159.2
1983	828.5	2175.5	3004.0	–1347.0
1984	840.0	2054.3	2894.3	–1214.3
1985	958.0	2287.1	3245.1	–1329.1
1986	979.0	2205.4	3184.4	–1226.4
1987	1411.2	1537.8	2949.0	–126.6
1988	1184.2	1950.9	3135.1	–766.7
1989	1343.0	2138.0	3481.0	–795.0

Source: Vneshniaia torgovlia SSSR (Foreign Trade of the USSR) (Moscow: Finansy i statistika, 1965–89).

As US–Soviet détente began to falter in the late 1970s, Japanese–Soviet trade continued to expand, albeit at a slower rate. The most noticeable result of the changed political climate was that no further joint projects were undertaken, despite repeated expressions of interest from the Soviet side. After this period of rapid trade expansion, Japanese trade with the USSR grew only by 4.8 per cent in 1980. The slowdown in trade that year can be attributed to Japanese support for the US-led embargo in reaction to the Soviet Union's invasion of Afghanistan. The growth rate in Japanese–Soviet trade recovered the following year, and by 1982 soared to a record 3.6 billion roubles.

In the period 1983–87, however, Japanese–Soviet trade contracted by almost 20 per cent. The cause of this decline is clearly attributable to a precipitous decline in Soviet imports of Japanese manufactures and high technology. From 1982 to 1984 Japan fell from being the second leading trading partner of the USSR (behind West Germany) to sixth (behind Germany, Finland, Italy, France and Britain). Although there was a slight rebound reported in 1985, total trade turnover for that year recovered only to the 1981 level and declined further for the remainder of the decade.[27] Soviet–Japanese total trade turnover for the first quarter of 1988 was again on the rise, increasing by approximately 50 per cent over the same period in 1987.[28]

By mid-1991, Soviet outstanding debts to Japanese firms approached $500 million, prompting Japanese banks to suspend credits to the USSR. Under increasing pressure from Japanese firms seeking repayment of their Soviet debts, MITI announced in late July 1991 that it would underwrite $200 million of a $350 million bridging loan provided by Japanese commercial banks to give the Soviet Union some breathing space.

The underlying causes of the trade downturn in 1983–87 appear to be more economic than political; they lie in the structural nature of the Japanese and Soviet economies, in particular in the changing nature of Soviet exports to Japan, as we see below. The transformation of the USSR into the CIS will do little if anything to alter the structure of trade opportunities between Japan and the CIS or any of its constituent republics, including the Russian Republic.

Soviet Exports to Japan

Until recently, Soviet exports to Japan were dominated by raw materials. Indeed, in 1985 more than 80 per cent of all exports to Japan came in this form.[29] The leading export items were timber and forestry products (round timber, rough-sawed lumber and pulpwood), coal and oil products (see

Table 7.2). Together timber and forestry products accounted for almost one-half of all Soviet exports to Japan in 1986. Energy products (primarily oil and coal) accounted for another 25 per cent of all Soviet exports. The commodity composition of Soviet exports to Japan remained remarkably stable over the period 1975–87. There has been a tendency for de-concentration of exports items, especially in 1987, yet the top ten export commodities still accounted for more than 77 per cent of the total.

Since 1975 Japanese economic growth has slowed, resulting in less demand for raw materials. The sectors most affected by the slower rate of economic growth – energy, steel and construction – are the same sectors which absorbed the vast majority of imports from the Soviet Union.

On closer scrutiny, even the issue of proximity of USSR and Japan does not argue forcefully in favour of long-term trade expansion. The South Yakutian coal fields are located more than 2600 km from Nakhodka, from where the coal is shipped another 1700 km to Yokohama.[30] Irkutsk, in Eastern Siberia, is located closer to the Urals than to the Pacific, while the major new oil and gas fields being developed in North-west Siberia are more than 3000 km closer to Western Europe than to Japan.

The commodity composition of Soviet exports to Japan began to alter in 1986, and especially in 1987. For the first time, exports of processed items were growing at a faster pace than exports of raw materials, indicating a reorientation of Soviet trading behaviour. Processed items accounted for 31.9 per cent of all exports in 1987, while raw materials fell to only 22.9 per cent of all exports.[31] In 1987 processed items rose by 65.2 per cent, foodstuffs by 32.8 per cent and mineral fuels by 20 per cent, while raw materials (including forestry products) declined by 12.5 per cent over the previous year's figures.[32]

Within the raw materials category, non-ferrous metal ingots commanded the largest share with 22.9 per cent.[33] This trend reflected both the desire of Soviet trade officials to export more finished and semi-finished goods and the greater demand in Japan for metal products. Forestry products, raw cotton, scrap metal and steel exports all declined.

Particularly noteworthy were the large amounts of gold and other precious metals exported to Japan in 1986 and 1987.[34] In 1986 gold accounted for 19.6 per cent of total exports, and in 1987 gold exports constituted 18.3 per cent of total exports.[35] Gold is a special commodity and is normally purchased outside usual trade contacts. If gold is removed from the overall trade figures, we see that Soviet exports to Japan in 1987 grew by 21.3 per cent. In 1988 gold became the single largest export item to Japan. During the first four months of the year gold exports trebled from 4204 to 12 711 kg, while platinum exports jumped five-fold to 7270 kg.[36] This led to a 58

Table 7.2 Soviet exports to Japan, 1975–87

RANK	1975	%	1985	%	1986	%	1987	%
1	Round timber	27.6	Round timber	23.6	Round timber	24.7	Coal	17.5
2	Rough sawed	25.1	Rough sawed	20.2	Rough sawed	22.1	Round timber	17.5
3	Coal	12.3	Coal	16.7	Coal	17.2	Rough sawed	15.6
4	Cotton fibre	10.6	Oil and products	13.8	Oil and products	6.9	Oil and products	8.7
5	Oil and products	7.6	Scrap metal	3.8	Fish	6.6	Fish	6.3
6	Non-ferrous metals	3.1	Pulpwood	3.3	Scrap metal	4.2	Sea products	3.4
7	Potassium salt	2.1	Chemicals	2.9	Cotton fibre	3.8	Cotton fibre	2.8
8	Construction lumber	1.6	Cotton fibre	2.8	Pulpwood	2.5	Cast iron	2.1
9	Minerals, clay	1.3	Fish	2.3	Chemicals	1.7	Pulpwood	1.8
10	Scrap metal	1.0	Potash fertilizer	2.0	Scrap wood	1.4	Chemicals	1.8
TOTALS		92.3		91.4		91.1		77.5

Source: Vneshniaia torgovlia SSSR (Moscow: Finansy i statistika, 1975–87).

per cent jump in the value of Soviet exports to Japan, which in turn enabled the Soviets to finance a 28 per cent rise in imports during the same period. Japanese traders eventually began receiving gold and platinum shipments directly from the Soviet Union, in addition to buying Soviet ingots on international markets such as those in London and Zurich.

The changing pattern of Soviet exports to Japan cannot be fully appreciated by relying solely on aggregate level data, but must be analyzed on a sector-by-sector basis. Below we discuss some of the particular features of the major Soviet export sectors.

Forestry Products

In terms of volume, the USSR was the second leading supplier of timber products to Japan; only Canada provided more. Most Soviet timber exports consisted of round and rough-sawed logs from the Far Eastern region. Construction grade lumber and plywood constituted a relatively small portion of Soviet exports to Japan due to a lack of the necessary processing equipment. During the 1960s and 1970s timber exports grew rapidly, by as much as 12 per cent per annum, peaking in 1977 at 8.9 million cubic metres.[37] Between 1977 and 1989, however, timber exports declined by more than one-third. In the early 1980s reports began to appear in the Soviet press of lumber shortages in the Ukraine, indicating that the opportunity costs of exports of lumber were rising.[38] The Soviets also faced greater competition from the USA, Canada, Australia and New Zealand for the Japanese market for forestry products. In 1985 the US Administration targeted forestry products as one of four sectors in which they intended to urge the Japanese to expand imports to redress the growing US–Japanese trade imbalance.

With the decomposition of the Soviet Union into its constituent republics, the future development of what is now the Russian Republic's Far Eastern timber reserves depends to a very considerable degree on the Japanese market. The break-even point in shipping lumber to the west is Krasnoyarsk in Central Siberia.[39] If the Japanese market does not recover to 1977 levels, there will be little incentive for Russia to develop the Far Eastern reserves. The irony is that much of the early planning for the BAM project (a rail line commenting the late Baikol reign with the Paljin Coast), as well as the construction of port facilities at Wrangel Bay, Vostochny and Sovietskaia Gavn', were predicated upon the assumption of expanding exports to Japan of timber and forestry products. Alarmed by the decline in timber trade, both sides engaged in intensive government-to-government discussions in 1983 and 1984 to stabilize commercial relations. In August 1985 the Japan Chip Trading Company reached an agreement to double (to 11.2 million cubic metres) pulp purchases over a 10-year period, beginning in 1986.[40] In exchange, the Soviets would buy some Japanese processing equipment. A second agreement was reached in 1985 for the supply of $500 million worth of wood chips between 1985 and 1995.[41] In addition, in late 1986 the USSR and Japan agreed to a fourth forest development programme in Siberia and the Far East. The eight-year project called for the export of 12 million cubic feet of logs and lumber, while the Japanese side would provide the necessary equipment and supplies.[42]

Coal
Soviet exports of coal to Japan peaked in 1976, declined by 50 per cent from 1977 to 1981, and beginning in 1981 eventually recovered to 85 per cent of the 1976 level.[43] The bulk of Soviet coal exported to Japan came from the South Yakutia region, which has been in operation since 1940. In 1974 the USSR and Japan signed a joint agreement for the development of coking coal reserves in South Yakutia. Under the terms of the agreement the Japan Export-Import Bank (EXIM Bank) provided $450 million in credits, and the Soviet Union was to supply six Japanese steel firms with a total of 104.4 million tons of coal over a 20-year period.[44] The Nakhodka terminal was expanded to handle up to 6.2 million tons of coal per year. The development of the South Yakutian reserves has been hampered, however, by the discovery of a layer of rock approximately 350 metres thick on top of the coal deposit. Japanese hydraulic equipment had to be imported to drill through the rock. However, operating at extremely cold temperatures, the equipment frequently broke down. It is estimated that the drilling equipment was operating only 60 per cent of the time.[45] Due to these difficulties, the first deliveries of South Yakutian coal only began reaching Japan in 1983, four years behind schedule.

At the same time Japanese demand for coal has diminished substantially since the mid-1970s, when the agreement was signed. As a result of rapidly rising energy costs, Japan scrapped almost one-half of its aluminium production during the 1970s.[46] Similarly, investments in the steel industry declined throughout the decade as the Japanese sought to develop their less material-intensive industries (motor vehicles, electronics and ceramics).[47] Massive efforts were also undertaken to conserve energy in Japan. In 1980 7.7 per cent of all Japanese outlay on plant and equipment was earmarked for energy-saving investment; another 1.7 per cent was directed towards fuel conversion.[48] Nuclear energy is also being rapidly developed and now accounts for 22.9 per cent of all electricity generated.[49] Foreign competition is also affecting Japanese purchases of Soviet coal. The USA and Australia are aggressively attempting to expand coal exports in order to lessen their severe trade imbalances with Japan. In 1986 an agreement was reached for the Soviets to supply 3.7 million tons of coal, well below the 6.5 million tons projected at the time of the original agreement.[50] Specialists with Keidanren indicate that Japan might be interested in substantially increasing its imports of Siberian coal or natural gas by the mid-1990s, but not before then.[51]

Oil

Japanese purchases of Soviet oil showed more or less steady increases from 1977 to 1985, declined in 1986, and began to rise again in 1987.[52] The Japanese are now able to purchase oil on the spot market or on short-term contracts at competitive prices and thus do not need to negotiate long-term contracts, which have been preferred by the Soviets. Since the lifting of the US Congressional ban on the foreign sale of north slope Alaskan oil, the Japanese have also been under some pressure from the USA to increase their oil purchases as a means of addressing the trade imbalance between Japan and the USA.

The centrepiece of Japanese–Soviet energy cooperation was the joint venture in off-shore drilling near Sakhalin, begun in 1977. So far, that project has tapped a few small gas wells, but no major oil fields. The Sakhalin project is indicative of the caution with which Japanese corporations view large compensation-trade deals. The project was estimated to cost in excess of $4.55 billion. The Soviet side was asking Japan to put up 50 per cent of this investment cost in return for guaranteed shipments of three million tons of gas and oil annually for 20 years beginning in 1991. However, Japan has already entered into contracts for ample gas and oil supplies through to the end of the 1990s from Indonesia, Abu Dhabi, Malaysia, Australia, Canada and elsewhere, and there are no plans for additional liquified natural gas imports.[53] A compromise position was apparently worked out in November 1987 whereby the Soviet Union would purchase all Sakhalin-produced natural gas, while the Japanese would purchase only crude oil. Since Japanese companies will not be purchasing natural gas, they will not provide credits for the construction of the proposed gas liquification facility.

Other Commodities

Japanese steel production is dependent upon manganese ore imports, but requirements are met primarily by non-Soviet sources. Similarly, Japanese industries obtain palladium, platinum, gold, silver, rhodium, vanadium and other rare metals primarily from South Africa, Canada and other countries in Asia. With the destabilization of South African production of rare metals, however, the Japanese began expressing some interest in expanding purchases from the USSR.[54] The share of these precious metals began rising in 1986, and by 1989 represented the single largest Soviet export to Japan. Of the nations outside the Eastern bloc, Japan was the leading importer of Soviet asbestos. Imports from the USSR accounted for as much as one-quarter of all Japanese asbestos purchases, and these purchases seriously eroded the Canadian share of supplies to Japan.[55] Cotton exports to Japan from the Soviet Union rose from 7 per cent of all imports in 1965–69 to 16 per cent in 1976. However, more than 36 per cent of all cotton imported into Japan comes from the USA.[56]

Thus, in its principal export sectors, the CIS and the Russian Republic particularly are confronting rising development costs, greater foreign competition for the Japanese market and declining demand within Japan for energy resources and other raw materials.

JOINT VENTURES: PROSPECTS AND PROBLEMS

Given the difficulties of covering the cost of Soviet imports of Japanese technology and equipment with exports to Japan, the Soviets turned to joint ventures as a way to attract Western capital and technology. Since the enactment of the Law on Joint Ventures in January 1987, only a few of the more than 100 ventures negotiated with Western companies have involved Japanese firms. However, approximately 50 more Japanese joint ventures were under discussion as of 1991.[57] After the Toshiba affair, the Japanese appeared to favour joining consortia involving several partners, including at least one American company. Japanese trading companies say that US participation is essential because of American 'technical pre-eminence'. However, a more likely reason is that they apparently believed that with American partners they would run less risk of being accused of breaching COCOM regulations.[58]

One of the most promising joint ventures involving substantial Japanese participation concerned the construction of a $6 billion petrochemical complex at Tengis, near the Caspian Sea. Partners to the project included Occidental Petroleum, Montedison, Ente Nazionale Idrocarburi and the Marubeni Corporation. A second joint venture, potentially even bigger, involved Mitsubishi, Mitsui, Chiyoda and two American partners, Combustion Engineering Inc. and McDermott International, in the construction of a petrochemical complex at Surgut in Western Siberia. At least four large Japanese trading companies, including Mitsubishi, Mitsui, Nissho Iwai and Tokyo Maruichi Shoji, presented proposals to the Ministry of Foreign Trade for other joint ventures dealing with forestry, food processing and machine-tool manufacturing.[59]

Initially, Japanese companies were reportedly hesitant to pursue joint ventures when they were only permitted a 49 per cent share. Moreover, there was an expectation (if not a requirement) that the manager of the enterprise be a Soviet, and there were relatively stringent restrictions on the repatriation of profits in hard currency. Nevertheless, after the Soviet Government amended the law to enable foreign partners to hold majority interest, the number of Japanese companies interested in joint ventures did not increase substantially. The actual reasons for Japanese coolness towards joint ventures in the USSR or its constituent republics lie elsewhere.

The Soviets were reluctant to grant foreign joint venture companies access to the Soviet market. Like other Western firms, Japanese companies encountered difficulties in repatriating profits. A particularly difficult stumbling point in recent joint venture negotiations was that the Japanese partners were refusing to enter into contractual arrangements unless profit margins could be determined in advance.[60] The Soviet side refused to accede to such a demand.

Thus, a three-tiered system of Japanese–Soviet commercial relations emerged at the end of the 1980s, and we can expect a similar pattern to prevail between Japan and the newly sovereign republics of the CIS, including Russia. Under the aegis of bilateral, long-term development projects, the two nations continued to develop forestry, coal and other natural resources of Siberia and the Far East. One might expect trade under similar agreements to continue between Japan and Russia basically as compensation agreements, exchanging raw materials for equipment.

A second category of trade is bilateral trade not under the aegis of one of the joint development programmes. This category of activities will continue with greater attention on the part of the Russian Federation to ensure that such trade remains in approximate balance. Increasingly, Russian purchases of Japanese goods and equipment will be financed by the sale of gold and other precious minerals, as well as by the export of processed goods.

Finally, the Russians are banking on the proliferation of joint ventures with Western firms to eliminate the necessity of having to purchase large quantities of Western technology or to borrow investment capital from Western banks. Whether such plans materialize, however, depends to a great extent on how flexible the Yeltsin leadership proves to be in addressing the qualms of Western firms regarding strictures on joint venture development. The relative posture of Japanese firms in joint ventures also remains in doubt. It is instructive to note that neither of the two Japanese joint ventures currently operating in Russia is located in Eastern Siberia or the

Russian Far East. The majority of the industrial infrastructure in the CIS remains west of the Urals. Thus, the geographic factors in the critical machine building, chemical and electronics sectors are disadvantageous to the Japanese. Based on this analysis of economic factors, we do not foresee a major increase in Japanese–CIS trade or Japanese–Russian trade, regardless of the outcome of the political and security issues noted above.

Following the lead of other international banks, the Bank of Tokyo announced in May 1992 that it will open a branch in Moscow, the first Japanese bank in the CIS.[61] This will facilitate financial dealings for Japanese companies in the CIS, but it does not necessarily signal a major expansion of trade between the two countries.

TRADE BLOCS AND JAPANESE–RUSSIAN RELATIONS

Japanese–Russian relations in the aftermath of the break-up of the Soviet Union cannot be viewed in a vacuum. The prospects for Japanese–Russian political and economic relations depend to a considerable degree on a number of other powers, or constellations of powers, and their relations with both the Russian Federation and the CIS generally, as well as its other constituent republics and Japan. Rather than assess these multiple relationships in terms of bilateral interactions, we have opted to explore them in terms of triangular relations. We will begin with what is obviously the most important, the USA–Japan–Russia triangle.

USA–Japan–Russia

The USA represents a significant constraint on Japanese policy towards the CIS generally and the Russian Federation specifically, in the political/security and the economic area. The past decade has witnessed a growing commitment in both Tokyo and Washington to strengthening their security alliance in North-east Asia. Japan has deployed more destroyers than Britain has in its entire fleet.[62] The Japanese have more P-3 anti-submarine aircraft than does the US Seventh Fleet. In 1986 Japan abandoned its self-imposed 1 per cent of GNP limit on defence spending. In January 1987 the Japanese Government agreed to participate in Strategic Defense Initiative research programmes. Although it was fraught with difficulties, Japanese–American cooperation in the development of the FSX aircraft symbolized the community of interest both powers feel concerning their mutual security arrangements. And recently the Japanese Diet passed legislation that would allow Japanese Self Defence Forces personnel to participate in international peacekeeping operations, although only in roles that would not allow them to become involved in combat. The subsequent participation of Japanese personnel in the UN-sponsored operation in Cambodia represents the first time since the end of the Second World War that Japanese military personnel have been allowed to serve beyond the borders of Japan.

Despite its increasing commitment to defence, Japan remains deeply reliant upon the USA for its defence *vis-à-vis* Russia. The neutralization of Japan as a quid pro quo for the return of the Northern Territories would be unacceptable, not only to the USA but to the majority of the Japanese themselves. Nevertheless, it is apparent that the Soviet leadership and their successors in the Russian Federation and the other CIS republics would like to decouple their relations with Japan from their policies toward the USA. The most dramatic statement of this posture was Gorbachev's proposal for destruction of Soviet SS-20s targeted on Japan in exchange for Japanese commitment to a nuclear-free strategy. Gorbachev's remarks to Shintaro Abe during the foreign ministers' meeting in Moscow in May 1986, calling for improving relations with Japan 'regardless of relations with other countries', revealed a similar intention. However, overly aggressive or blatant attempts to drive a wedge between Japan and the USA are likely to raise suspicions and ultimately harden Japanese attitudes toward the CIS generally and the Russian Federation specifically.

Japanese–Soviet commercial relations are also complicated by the ever-present superpower rivalry. First, US Government officials have long harboured suspicions that Japanese businesses would sell strategic technologies to the East in violation of COCOM and US regulations governing the licensing of strategic technologies.[63] The disclosure that Toshiba Machine Company illegally exported four machine tools to the USSR in 1982 and 1983, which were used to grind submarine propellers to specifications the Soviets could not have achieved otherwise, aroused considerable anger in the US Congress. On 1 July 1987 the Senate voted to ban Toshiba and the Norwegian company Konigsberg Vaapenfabrikk from selling products in the USA for at least two years, and possibly as many as five years.

The Toshiba case was used by the USA to coerce the Japanese into greater financial support for COCOM and more cooperation with American experts on export control and enforcement. New export control legislation, which significantly increased criminal penalties for export control violations, was prepared and approved by the Japanese Cabinet on 31 July 1987. As we noted above, Japanese firms have been reluctant to enter into joint ventures in the USSR without co-participation by American firms. This reluctance may well reflect Japanese sensitivity to American pressures on export controls in the wake of the Toshiba case. This sentiment is likely to persist among the Japanese business community with respect to its dealings in the CIS, and especially in the Russian Federation.

We also noted above that during the 1980s the US–Japanese trade imbalance generated considerable pressures on Japan to purchase raw materials such as coal, timber, oil and foodstuffs from the USA rather than from the USSR. The American market is vital to Japan's continued economic prosperity, certainly to a much greater degree than is the market of the CIS or of any of its constituent republics. Thus, Japan is and will remain for the foreseeable future much more likely to be influenced by American political and economic leverage than by prospects for political and economic cooperation with the CIS or any of its member states.

China–Japan–Russia

China has also emerged as a significant factor in the development of Soviet–Japanese relations. Since the signing of the Sino–Japanese Treaty of Peace and Friendship in 1978, Japanese investments in China have flourished to the point that China is now Japan's second largest trading partner. Sino–Japanese trade rose from $8.9 billion in 1983 to $19.6 billion in 1989, while during the same period Japan's share of Soviet trade fell from second to fifth place among Western industrial powers.[64]

From the Japanese perspective, China had more to offer economically than did the USSR. China is an important source of raw materials such as coal, iron, timber, cotton and foodstuffs; in short, China can supply much of the same commodities that Japan purchased from the Soviet Union. In addition, however, the more flexible approach that the Chinese have demonstrated towards foreign investment and the greater access they provide to their own domestic market made China a more attractive target for Japanese companies than the USSR.

For its part, the Gorbachev Administration pursued a policy of normalization of relations with China. While such a process inevitably proved difficult, the withdrawal of Soviet forces from Afghanistan and the demobilization of several units in Mongolia demonstrated a degree of flexibility never before seen in the Soviet leadership. A rapprochement between the USSR and China would not have posed a serious threat to Japanese interests, and Sino–Russian rapprochement poses even less of a threat. The converse is not true, however: to a considerable degree, Japanese economic relations with Russia and China are a zero-sum game.

Europe–Japan–CIS

As European integration proceeds under the banner of EC 92, Japanese companies have devoted a great deal of attention to establishing a foothold on the continent. Japanese direct investment in Europe rose by 79.7 per cent in 1986, 89.6 per cent in 1987, and 24.6 per cent in the first half of 1988.[65] As of January 1989, the Japanese had built 411 manufacturing plants in Europe, almost one-quarter of them in Britain.[66] Collectively, Europe represents a market larger than that of the USA, and in the past decade Japanese companies have begun to penetrate the European market successfully. Japanese companies have made a conscious decision to establish manufacturing facilities in Europe in order to secure their position in the European market and in an attempt to minimize the threat of trade frictions. The dramatic increase in Japanese investment in Europe, however, diverted resources and attention from the USSR and now from Russia and the other member states of the CIS.

The European economies also competed with Japanese firms for the most lucrative deals in the USSR. Since 1982, Japan's share of machinery and equipment sales to the USSR fell consistently. In 1982 Japan ranked second among the advanced Western economies as a source of equipment and technology sold to the Soviet Union. By 1985, they had fallen to sixth, behind Germany, Finland, Italy, France and Britain.[67] As we noted earlier, geographical factors as well as established trading patterns appear to favour European firms competing for equipment sales to enterprises in the CIS which are attempting to modernize their production facilities.

Asia–Japan–Russia

Japan represents a critical factor in the Russian Federation's attempts to improve its relations elsewhere in Asia. Easing relations with Japan will be essential if Russia wishes to gain entrance to the Asia Development Bank and the Pacific Economic Cooperation Conference (PECC). The Soviet Union sent a delegation in 'observer' status to the past several meetings of the PECC. The delegation was headed by the Academician Yevgeni Primakov, Director of the Institute of World Economy and International Relations.

The Japanese were reportedly alarmed by the attempts of the USSR to penetrate various Asian multilateral organizations, such as PECC, and they used their considerable political and economic influence to exclude the USSR where possible. In November 1989 the Asia Pacific Economic Conference convened in Canberra. The Soviet Union, together with Taiwan and China, were not invited to participate, despite the participation of most other major actors in the region, including the USA and Canada. The Soviet Union, together with China, was invited to attend the 1991 ASEAN meetings for the first time as observers. However, progress towards full membership in PECC, ASEAN and the Asia Pacific Economic Conference was halted by the August 1991 coup and subsequent collapse of the Soviet Union.

Japan's interest in the rest of Asia is also motivated by clear economic self-interest. Beginning in 1988, Japanese investment in Asia rose faster than in any other region of the world, with the exception of North America. In the first six months of 1988, Japanese direct investment in ASEAN countries rose by 52.2 per cent, and investment in the Asian NICs rose by 32.4 per cent.[68] Whereas 1986 and 1987 saw a rapid increase in Japanese investment in plant and equipment in Europe, in 1988 Japanese financial institutions began investing heavily in Asia. According to one report, Japanese financial institutions are turning their attention away from the USA and Europe and concentrating their expansion in Asia because profits are easier to earn there, due to lessened competition.[69] The Japanese are targeting their investments primarily through large-scale loans, joint ventures, new branch networks and establishing strategic stakes in key industries. As in the case of Europe, Japanese investment in Asia has absorbed capital that might otherwise have been directed to the member states of the CIS.

A recent study conducted by GATT concluded that Japan and the rest of Asia represent a potential market even larger than that of North America.[70] The Japanese are aware that the ASEAN nations and the NICs of Asia offer the most rapidly expanding market in the world and one in which the Japanese would enjoy a strong comparative advantage. No doubt Japan wishes to guard its newly acquired dominant position as the Asian superpower. For this reason, it has not encouraged Soviet diplomatic or economic involvement in the region.

The combined thrust of these triangular relations points to only a modest potential for Japanese–CIS trade expansion. While the Japanese praised the reform efforts of Gorbachev, the cautiousness of their actual policies towards the USSR and now towards the CIS speaks even more loudly. Japanese hesitancy towards committing themselves in the USSR goes far beyond the territorial dispute or the absence of a peace treaty. The underlying dynamics motivating Japanese foreign economic behaviour today appear to be determined by a strong desire to secure and expand market share in those economies upon which Japan most depends: North America, Europe and the newly emerging economies of Asia.

Notes

1. Cited in Roy Kim, 'Gorbachev's Challenge to Japan', *Atlantic Community Quarterly*, 25 (Autumn 1987) p. 357.
2. Ibid, p. 355.
3. *Pravda*, 29 July 1986, p. 1.
4. Ibid.
5. Cited in Kim, 'Gorbachev's Challenge', p. 359.
6. Ibid.
7. Ibid, p. 361.
8. Cited in *Far Eastern Economic Review*, 10 December 1986, p. 28.
9. *Pravda*, 7 June 1987, p. 5.
10. *Pravda*, 21 August 1987, p. 4.
11. *Pravda*, 13 November 1987, p. 5.
12. *Pravda*, 18 September 1988, pp. 1–3.
13. *Pravda*, 6 May 1989, p. 1.
14. Cited in Kim, 'Gorbachev's Challenge', p. 354.
15. Cited in Peter Berton, 'Soviet-Japanese Relations: Perceptions, Goals, Interactions', *Asian Survey*, 26 (December 1986) p. 1280.
16. Ibid.
17. *Asahi Shimbun*, 12 May 1992.
18. See *Far Eastern Economic Review*, 18 December 1986, pp. 28–9.
19. Fuji Kamiya, 'The Northern Territories: 130 Years of Japanese Talks with Czarist Russia and the Soviet Union', in Donald S. Zagoria (ed.), *Soviet Policy in East Asia* (New Haven, CT: Yale University Press, 1982) p. 150.
20. Cited in *Japan Times*, 28 December 1985, p. 1.
21. *Izvestiia*, 10 August 1989, p. 4.
22. *Izvestiia*, 29 September 1989, p. 5.
23. Cited in Kim, 'Gorbachev's Challenge', p. 355.
24. Calculated from SOTOBO data published in *Monthly Bulletin on Trade with the USSR and East Europe*, January 1965–April 1985.
25. Ibid and *Vneshniaia torgovliia SSSR* (Foreign Trade of the USSR) (Moscow: Finansy i statistiki, 1981–85).
26. Cited in Charles Smith, 'Courting the Bear Market', *Far Eastern Economic Review*, 23 June 1988, p. 80.
27. Cited in ibid.
28. *Vneshniaia torgovlia* (1987).
29. Ibid.
30. For an extensive discussion of proximity and Japanese–Soviet trade, see Leslie Dienes, 'Soviet–Japanese Economic Relations: Have They Begun to Fade?', *Soviet Geography*, September 1985.
31. These figures cited in Yasuo Kaji, 'Japan–Soviet Trade Sharply Down in Exports, but Up in Imports on Japan's Part', *The Japan Economic Review*, 15 July 1988, p. 10. Note that these figures do not agree with the Soviet figures presented in Table 7.2.
32. Ibid.
33. Ibid.
34. Gold exports are not reported by Soviet authorities and thus are not included in the data in Table 7.2.
35. Kaji, 'Japan–Soviet Trade', p. 10.
36. Smith, 'Courting the Bear Market', p. 80.

37. *Vneshniaia torgovliia.*
38. Cited in Peter Blandon, *Soviet Forest Industries* (Boulder, CO: Westview Press, 1983).
39. Ibid.
40. *Japan Times*, 14 March 1986, p. 9.
41. Cited in Michael J. Bradshaw, 'Soviet Asian–Pacific Trade and the Regional Development of the Soviet Far East', *Soviet Geography*, 24 (April 1988) p. 383.
42. *The Japan Economic Review*, 15 March 1988, p. 12.
43. *Vneshniaia torgovliiia.*
44. From consultations with Yukihiro Kato, General Manager, External Relations Department, South Yakutian Coal Development Cooperation Co Ltd, Tokyo (6 March, 1986).
45. Ibid.
46. M.M. Kostecki, *Soviet Impact on Commodity Markets* (London: Macmillan, 1984) p. 119.
47. *Japan 1984: An International Comparison* (Tokyo: Keizai Koho Centre, 1984) p. 21.
48. Cited in Dienes, 'Soviet–Japanese Economic Relations'.
49. *Japan Times*, 27 October 1984, p. 2.
50. Bradshaw, 'Soviet Asian–Pacific Trade', p. 383.
51. Sophie Quinn-Judge, 'Siberian Spring', *Far Eastern Economic Review*, 10 September 1987, p. 95.
52. *Vneshniaia torgovliia.*
53. Cited in Teruji Suzuki, 'Japanese–Soviet Trade: Past Trends and Future Prospects', *Coexistence*, 25 (1988) p. 296.
54. From consultations with officials at Keidanren and SOTOBO (30 June 1985 and 4 March 1986).
55. Kostecki, *Soviet Impact*, p. 180.
56. Ibid, p. 228.
57. Cited in Donald S. Zagoria, 'Soviet Policy in East Asia: A New Beginning', *Foreign Affairs*, 68, 1, p. 127.
58. *Far Eastern Economic Review*, 23 June 1988, p. 80.
59. Ibid, 11 September 1986, p. 117.
60. Ibid.
61. *Asahi Shimbun*, 13 May 1992.
62. For a discussion of Japanese military capabilities, see Myles L.C. Robertson, *Soviet Policy Towards Japan* (Cambridge: Cambridge University Press, 1988) pp. 104–8.
63. For example, see remarks of US Commerce Secretary Malcolm Baldrige, *Christian Science Monitor*, 17 July 1987, p. 3.
64. Cited in Berton, 'Soviet–Japanese Relations', p. 1273. On Sino–Japanese trade, see Tomozo Morino, 'China–Japan Trade and Investment Relations', in F.J. Macchiarola and R.B. Oxnam (eds), *The China Challenge: American Policies in East Asia* (New York: The Academy of Political Science, 1991).
65. Cited in *Far Eastern Economic Review*, 8 June 1989, p. 60.
66. *Far Eastern Economic Review*, 18 May 1989, p. 68.
67. *Japan Times*, 5 March 1986, p. 7.
68. *Japan Times*, 5 March 1986, p. 7.
69. *Far Eastern Economic Review* 1 June 1989, p. 54.
70. Cited in *Far Eastern Economic Review*, 15 June 1989, p. 53.

8 Prospects for an Asian Trade Bloc: Japan, the Association of South-east Asian Nations and the Asian Newly Industrializing Economies

Shigeko Fukai

The spectacular economic growth of Japan, the Asian newly industrializing economies (NIEs) and some members of ASEAN has been achieved through the expansion of trade, investment and other economic ties in the Asia–Pacific region. This expansion has taken place without a formal regional institutional framework comparable to that of either the EC or the OECD. Recently, however, there has been much speculation about these fast-growing countries – South Korea, Taiwan, Hong Kong, Singapore, Thailand, Malaysia, Indonesia and the Philippines – forming a regional bloc centred on Japan in response to the EC and North American economic integration.[1]

This chapter seeks to explore the implications for the Asian economies of the changing world economic power configurations and of the apparent erosion of the commitment of major powers to the liberal international economic order. How do Japan, the Asian NIEs and ASEAN members react to the integration of the EC and the creation of the free trade zone in North America? Do they wish to establish a bloc of their own to ensure continued economic growth in case the European and North American markets should be further closed to their exports? Which countries would join such a bloc?

The prospects for an Asian trade bloc depend on (1) how protectionist Europe and North America become, and (2) whether a shared perception of regional interests emerges. An influential view among Asians is that economic integration of the EC and the melding of the US, Canadian and Mexican economies could foster more self-sufficient, inward-looking economic groups that favour intraregional trade and investment.[2] It was this

164

fear, observers agree, that inspired Australian Prime Minister Robert Hawke's 1989 initiative to hold a government-level conference to promote Pacific economic cooperation. Hawke originally excluded the USA and Canada from the conference he envisioned, but both were invited at the insistence of Japan and ASEAN. That same fear made his initiative materialize quickly into the Asia–Pacific Economic Cooperation Council.[3]

Whether regional interests coalesce into an Asian trade bloc hinges on how individual nations view the costs and benefits of such a bloc, including in particular their international economic standing and domestic social welfare. Important variables here are the values and goals of the ruling elites of the Asian nations. Their perceptions in turn will be built on the economic reality of the region. What change, then, has occurred in the economic reality, particularly in the trade and investment relations between Japan, the Asian NIEs and other ASEAN countries, and what has been Japan's role therein?

JAPANESE BUSINESS ACTIVITIES AND ASIAN ECONOMIC INTEGRATION

We can recognize a clear change in the nature of interdependence within the Asia–Pacific region before and after the Plaza Accord of September 1985. Until the mid-1980s, Japan's trade with other Asian countries had been characterized by a vertical relationship in which Japan imported raw materials and fuel from them and exported manufactured goods to them. As the industrial sectors grew in those countries, so did Japan's exports of parts, intermediate goods and capital equipment. Their finished products were exported mostly to the USA. This pattern created chronic trade surpluses and trade friction between those countries and the USA, on the one hand, and chronic trade deficits between them and Japan, on the other.

The yen's appreciation since 1985 has changed this pattern by inducing structural changes in the Japanese economy. The yen's sharp rise against the dollar has reduced the international competitiveness of many products made in Japan but has also transformed Japan into the largest source of exportable capital in the world. Japan's nominal wealth increased by about 50 per cent between September 1985 and late 1986. Japanese investments in the USA and Europe soared. A logical response to these circumstances was for Japanese manufacturers to relocate their production bases to their Asian neighbours, where labour and land costs are lower. At the same time, in response to US pressure to reduce their exports to American markets, many Japanese manufacturers increased their efforts to cultivate domestic demand.

Let us look at how changes in Japanese business strategy and consumer behaviour have influenced the evolution of a multi-layered horizontal division of labour among the Asian nations. First, FDI is aimed at cutting production costs by establishing subsidiaries where labour and other factor costs are low, and to supply parts and intermediate goods from Japan. Second, different production processes of specific goods have been allocated to different locations according to the levels of available technology and value-added considerations.[4] In the emerging pattern Japanese firms use ASEAN as the production base for low-technology exports and labour-intensive production processes, and they use the NIEs as sites for investment in higher value-added manufacturing and services such as retail trade, property transactions, financial services and the leisure industry.[5]

To take advantage of the high yen, Japanese retailers and wholesale distributors have adopted what they call 'developed imports': importing products they developed or designed from subcontracted Asian manufacturers. These developed imports are mostly garments and processed foods, furniture, bicycles and consumer electronics.[6] The so-called original equipment manufacturing (OEM), which refers to the overseas production of manufactured goods under the importer's brand name, has also increased. Parallel to these developments, Japanese consumers have begun to appreciate lower-priced imports as well as high-value-added brand name products. Still another development is the notable increase in catalogue orders by Japanese consumers of foreign brand goods.[7]

The result has been a substantial expansion of Japan's imports of manufactured goods from its Asian neighbours. The share of manufactured goods in Japan's total imports from Asian countries almost doubled, from 25.7 per cent in the third quarter of 1985 to nearly 50 per cent in the third quarter of 1988.[8] Relocating Japanese plants has increased East and South-east Asian countries' imports of capital and capital goods from Japan. These plants assemble Japanese parts and export their products to Japan and the USA. Haruhiro Fukui observed that 'Japan's neighbors thus looked more and more like offshore extensions of the constantly aggrandizing Japanese economy. The Greater East Asia Co-prosperity Sphere of World War II vintage had come out of mothballs.'[9] *The Economist* describes the change in the following terms: 'The economies of East and South-East Asia are becoming horizontally integrated, with the trade benefits of exporting more manufactures and components being offset by imports of capital and of capital goods from Japan.'[10]

In sum, under the influence of Japanese companies' strategies on trade and direct investment, the East and South-east Asian economies are being horizontally integrated into a regional system dominated by Japan.[11]

The horizontal integration has been deepened by changes in the exchange rates of the NIEs' currencies which realigned the comparative advantages of the Asian countries and stimulated intraregional investment and trade flows. In the process, too, Japan has played a significant role. In 1986 alone, Japan's direct investment in Asian NIEs increased by 113 per cent, in Hong Kong by 282 per cent and in Korea by 225 per cent.[12] That same year witnessed sharp increases in Asian NIEs' trade surpluses with the USA, resulting in pressure from the USA to revalue their currencies against the dollar. The economic expansion tightened labour markets in these countries. In Korea, for example, increased labour disputes pushed wages up substantially.

In 1987, Japan's direct investment in the NIEs slowed down and began to shift to ASEAN countries, causing a dramatic reversal of the previous trend. Whereas in 1986, direct investment in the 'ASEAN Four' decreased by 7 per cent from the previous year, in 1987 it sharply increased, by 86 per cent.[13] Thailand in particular was so flooded by Japanese investment that it stopped accepting new applications because the country's infrastructure could not accommodate any more investment. Japanese firms then began to shift their attention to Malaysia and the Philippines. Meanwhile, the Asian NIEs began shifting production sites to ASEAN to counteract the appreciation of their own currencies and wage increases in their own labour markets.[14]

Three trends have emerged as a consequence: (1) conspicuous increases in capital goods and other imports by the six fastest-growing Asian economies (Hong Kong, Malaysia, Singapore, South Korea, Taiwan and Thailand); (2) a shift in their exports from cheap consumer goods to high-technology and industrial products; and (3) a rapid rise in intraregional trade. Those six economies imported $57 billion and exported $47 billion in capital goods in 1987.[15]

These development have had two important effects on Asian economies. One is the acceleration of industrialization through the transfer of capital, technology, management skills and markets from Japan. The transfer of markets is a particularly important factor for the recent Japanese investment. The rapid industrialization, however, has often taken place (except perhaps in Taiwan, where small and medium-sized industries have strong roots) without leading to the growth of a technology-intensive component sector.[16] The other impact has been a reduction in Asian countries' dependence on US markets for their exports and an increased dependence on Japanese markets. Overall, these changes improved the standards of living and the distribution of income in those countries, which in turn expanded domestic demand for the goods and services within these Asian countries.[17]

In many countries, however, increased urban–rural income disparities and competitiveness gaps between indigenous and foreign capital intensified social tension. The weakness of intermediate capital goods industries concerns those wishing to establish a viable local industrial base.[18] Fraught with these and other problems, economic integration in East and South-east Asia has been a consequence of economic events rather than of a grand political scheme. Saburo Okita observes three consecutive waves of growth in the region, starting in Japan in the 1960s, spreading to the Asian NIEs in the 1970s and on to the ASEAN countries in the 1980s.[19] The pattern fits well a V-formation of 'flying geese', first postulated by Kaname Akamatsu in the mid-1930s to characterize the pattern of Japanese development.[20] As Japan upgrades its industrial structure and moves into more advanced stages, it transfers its labour-intensive industries to the geese following it (the Asian NIEs), who subsequently transfer industries to ASEAN countries. Following Japan, Taiwan and Hong Kong began to shift their plants to Thailand to become the latter's second and third largest sources of investment, surpassing the USA and closely followed by Singapore and South Korea.[21] The geese that take off later catch up in a shorter time by benefiting from the forerunners' experience, so the V-formation gradually results in horizontal integration.[22] Whether or not this last prediction proves right, the formulation itself captures the central feature of economic restructuring in the Asian subregion that occurred through FDI decisions made by Japanese businesses. In other words, it was a restructuring that was not masterminded by the Japanese Government.

JAPANESE GOVERNMENT POLICY AND THE ASIAN ECONOMIC ORDER

Nevertheless, analysts note the critical role that Japan's aid has played in the restructuring of the Asian economic order. With some $13.7 billion appropriated for the fiscal year 1988–89, Japan was the largest donor of Official Development Assistance (ODA). Japan is the largest aid donor to every country in Asia except Cambodia, South Korea and Vietnam.[23] That aid is used to build basic infrastructure, such as roads and dams for power generation; to nurture basic industries; and to provide capital for the recipient government to finance activities in the private sector to help the national economy 'graduate' from the developing stage to maturity.[24] Many Asian critics point out, however, that Japanese companies exploit their cheap labour and cheap land to assemble parts and components brought from Japan, then export those products. The Japanese Government simply tries to create a favourable investment environment. Recipients complain that the Japanese are increasingly reluctant to transfer high technology and to localize entire production operations.[25] Some Western observers find in the Japanese Government's statements and actions evidence that Japan's goal is to integrate the Asian economies into the Japanese economy or to expand the sphere of influence of 'Japan, Inc.'[26]

Whatever their motives, the various Japanese actors have clearly encouraged interregional trade and interdependence. The key factors in this process have been Japan's direct investment, its official economic assistance, and its increased role as the regional import 'absorber'. We have seen over time how these factors have indirectly contributed to the rapid rise in Asian NIEs' investment in ASEAN countries, which has become another key factor in regional integration,[27] hence the following observation: 'From South Korea to Thailand, across the vibrant sweep of Pacific Asia, the hum of economic activity has become almost deafening. And for the most part, the tune these countries are playing has been composed in Japan.'[28]

During the eras of *Pax Britannica* and *Pax Americana*, the hegemons' currencies served as the means of international exchange, and the hegemons enjoyed the advantages of seigniorage. Naoki Tanaka argues that, in a similar fashion today, three factors are encouraging the formation of a yen bloc, where the yen acts as a common unit of value in the rapidly emerging East Asian economic community. First, an increase in manufactured exports to Japan promotes a shift away from dollar towards yen settlements. Second, growing exports of Japanese capital goods are 'the very pith' of production networks of regional industrial specialization and are 'an irreplaceable asset for countless East Asian entrepreneurs'. Third, Japan has both low interest rates and an abundant supply of cash to finance the expansion of these networks. Tanaka predicts that the credit institutions of other countries will also try to increase their business opportunities through yen loans.[29] Krause also points out that determinants of key-currency status are foreign traders and investors. If they earn and must make payment in yen, the yen will become the unit of account and the transaction currency. They will then choose the yen as reserve currency. He believes the yen may well replace the dollar as the world's key currency.[30]

An article in *The Economist* predicted that Asian integration would start with a currency alignment instead of a free trade bloc. The yen now plays a bigger role in international trade and capital markets and in Asian countries' foreign reserves. Several Asian countries – notably Thailand, South Korea and Taiwan – have already edged towards managing the value of their currencies against the yen. The next likely step is greater harmonization of monetary policies.[31]

Does this mean that an economic bloc is now in the making? The Japanese Ambassador to Thailand, Hisahiko Okazaki, says no for the following reason: 'Things are going well without any artificial mechanisms for discussion and coordination among the countries. Why do we need an economic bloc? Why do we need to talk about it? Such talks will simply give an excuse for some Europeans to promote protectionism.'[32]

Miles Kahler raises conceptual issues against the establishment of a Pacific economic organization. Among these are the heterogeneity of political and economic norms among the regimes in the region, the potential risk of undermining the non-discriminatory norms of the post-Second World War global economic organizations, and the ineffectiveness of adjusting policy differences between governments by mere 'consultation', which would be the highest authority member governments would confer on a prospective regional organization.[33] These observations suggest that a closed Asian bloc will be on the Asian agenda only in desperate reaction to protectionism in Europe and America. Policy makers and observers agree that an economic bloc would become an official policy issue among governments only if Asians are cut off from their markets in Europe and America.[34] Okazaki's statement reflects his concern about ASEAN's sensitivity to a Japanese initiative and the EC's exploitation of any move to create a *formal* Asian trade bloc as a means to justify their own bloc formation. Kahler also focuses on the problems in establishing a *formal* organization in the Asia–Pacific region rather than in its East and South-east Asian subregions. Neither observation denies *de facto* formation of an *informal* economic bloc in the subregion.

Let us now examine the nature of the economic order taking shape, particularly in the East and South-east regions of Asia, in the aftermath of the decline of US hegemony in Asia.

JAPAN AND THE THEORY OF HEGEMONIC STABILITY

The rapid growth of production in, and international trade between, Japan, the Asian NIEs and ASEAN have given rise to debate on the decline of American hegemony and the future of the liberal international economic order 'after hegemony'. From the above overview, Japan's central role is clear in this process of reshaping the economic structure and making the subregion of Asia 'a powerhouse of the world economy'.[35] Is it then appropriate to characterize Japan's role in terms of hegemony in the region?

The theory of hegemonic stability holds that maintaining an open and liberal world economy requires the existence of a hegemonic power. It assumes that the hegemonic power is both able and willing to establish and maintain the norms and rules of a liberal economic order, and that its decline greatly weakens such an order.[36] The hegemon must be committed to the values of liberalism and, to be so committed, its societal disposition and domestic distribution of power must be such that it favours a liberal international order.[37] In other words, the hegemon builds international regimes that reflect its own domestic regime. Such hegemony has existed only twice. The first was the era of *Pax Britannica*, which lasted from the end of the Napoleonic Wars to the outbreak of the First World War. During that era, British economic success, general acceptance of liberal ideals and recognition of the benefits of trade among the major European powers led to negotiated tariff reductions and ushered in an age of free trade.[38] After the Second World War, the USA assumed a world leadership role, and under its initiative GATT and the IMF were established. Under the *Pax Americana*, open international markets and global economic interdependence significantly expanded.[39]

The hegemon uses its influence to create international regimes, which consist of 'principles, norms, rules and decision-making procedures around which actor expectations converge in a given issue-area'.[40] Its influence derives mainly from economic power: its control of financial capital, markets, certain valued technologies and natural resources overseas. It must have enough funds to serve as a single lender of last resort in the system, and a large enough domestic market to serve as a market of last resort for the goods of other nations.[41]

In his 1987 book, Robert Gilpin rejected the possibility of Japan's replacing the USA as a global hegemon. Although he is concerned with global rather than regional hegemony, Gilpin's argument raises relevant questions for us to ponder:[42]

The Japanese have been equally [as have been the Europeans] poor candidates to assume economic leadership. The nature of their economy has made it difficult if not impossible for them to carry out hegemonic responsibilities. Their trade structure – the importation of raw materials and the exportation of manufactured goods – has made it unlikely that they would provide a large market for the exports of the industrializing countries as Britain and America have done. Unless Japan is able to shift significantly away from its economic strategy of moderating domestic demand in favour of export-led growth, it can hardly displace the United States as the world's 'engine of economic growth.' ... Japan could not really exercise a global leadership role without military power ... [A]s an influential report on Japan ... put it, the Japanese people and Japan's domestic systems ... are not yet adequately prepared for the tasks of international leadership.

My view is that Japan's actual performance, particularly in the years since Gilpin's book was published, casts doubt upon this argument. First, Japan has substantially increased its imports of manufactured exports from the Asian NIEs and ASEAN countries, while significantly increasing its consumption of local goods and services in these countries through both tourism and business operations. Growing consumer preference for lower-priced foreign imports and corresponding changes in the policies of import distributors and retailers in Japan point to a greater import penetration of the Japanese market of 100 million affluent consumers.[43]

Second, given an ever deeper, more complex economic interdependence, physical and direct control over raw materials is no longer an indispensable condition for exercising effective hegemonic power. Interdependence has created a new 'resource' for an economic superpower: the ability to cripple another country's economy by withdrawing or simply withholding capital, technology, or markets.

Third, the relative weight of military power as a source of international influence or leadership has declined. The dramatic increase in the destructive capacity of nuclear arms that precludes their utility as either a diplomatic or a military weapon, the increased interdependence among nations, and the end of the Cold War with the disintegration of the Soviet Union have increased the relative effectiveness of non-military deterrence. The momentous changes in Eastern Europe will also have far-reaching implications for a global as well as regional equation of power and security.

Perhaps the most relevant of Gilpin's arguments is the last one. Japan may indeed lack the desire or willingness to be a hegemonic leader. Kenneth Pyle's chapter in this volume explores this question in more depth. The reason for Japan's reluctance to assume the role of hegemon is not Japan's domestic systems, as Gilpin suggests, but rather the Japanese reluctance to insist, as self-righteous Americans do, that their values and goals be shared by other peoples. This reluctance has characterized Japanese foreign policy behaviour since the Second World War.[44] But cannot Japan provide the public goods required of the hegemon without becoming self-righteous in the process? This questions broaches a more fundamental reason for Japanese unwillingness to assume hegemonic responsibility: their failure to discover or invent a sufficiently inspiring ideal or vision of a future world order to motivate them to aspire to a leadership position, and, as a consequence, their inability to define the nature of the public goods vital to the alternative, post-*Pax Americana* world order. The Japanese have yet to forge a consensus even among themselves on an alternative to their singular post-Second World War goal of maximum economic growth. With material affluence attained, the Japanese now search for alternative values to give meaning to their newly acquired wealth and altered lifestyle.

Nevertheless, I believe that Japan has become a new regional hegemon as defined by Antonio Gramsci. Gramsci's concept of hegemony is not the same as Gilpin's, but it better suits the conditions created by the profound changes underway in the structure of the global system, changes that demand redefinitions of many concepts including the concept of hegemony. These changes give special relevance and poignancy to Gramsci's conception of hegemony, which was developed as a tool first for understanding and then changing the state–society relationship.[45] Gramsci defined hegemony as a relationship, not of domination imposed by force, but of consent generated by political and ideological (or intellectual and moral) leadership.[46] It is, in short, the organization of consent. A hegemonic class gains the consent of other classes and social forces by creating and maintaining alliances through political and ideological struggle.[47] Gramsci explained bourgeois rule in a stable capitalist society in terms of beliefs and values common to both the elite and the masses. The consensus formation involves changes in the belief system through persuasion of the masses to accept their own subordination by the bourgeois class. This acceptance is achieved through the bourgeoisie's subtle control over the mass media, schools, trade unions and other social institutions.[48] When the majority of society takes for granted the present structure of the social system and does not question its legitimacy, it presents a formidable barrier to the penetration of revolutionary consciousness. Yet, as Gramsci saw it, capitalism was an increasingly decadent system, failing to solve underlying problems of political, economic and social inequality.[49] For the working class to change the situation, it must gain hegemony by organizing not only its own class but also other classes and social forces. It must become the national representative of broad interests.[50] To cement diverse classes, the working class must develop an ideology that incorporates compromises and has a broader appeal beyond its own class.[51]

Extending Gramsci's concept, Robert W. Cox distinguishes between a hegemonic and a non-hegemonic world order. A hegemonic structure is characterized by an ideological consensus which legitimates the leading role of a dominant power in the world order. A non-hegemonic world order is composed of rival powers, none of which 'has been able to establish the legitimacy of its dominance'.[52] Cox proposes a redefinition of hegemony as a state of fit between three factors: a power configuration, a widely accepted ideology and institutions to administer the order of the world. Equating stability with this reformulated concept of hegemony, he points out that the dominance by a powerful state may be a necessary but not a sufficient condition for stability of the world order. On the other hand, he notes, the strong may dominate without resorting to force if they can make the weak accept the prevailing power relations as legitimate by characterizing the mission of the strong as hegemonic, rather than as merely dominant and dictatorial, and marked by a willingness to make concessions to secure the acquiescence of the weak in their leadership. Institutions in this context may serve as the anchor for such a hegemonic strategy by facilitating both the representations of diverse interests and the universalization of policy.[53]

Robert Keohane uses Gramsci's concept to explain the willingness of a hegemon's partners to accept hegemonic leadership. Hegemony, he writes, 'rests on the subjective awareness by elites in secondary states that they are benefiting, as well as on the willingness of the hegemon itself to sacrifice tangible short-term benefits for intangible long-term gains'.[54]

Two key factors are relevant to the present discussion about the birth and growth of a new hegemonic economic order in East and South-east Asia: (1) the emergence of a regional leader and of participants' willingness to defer to the emergent leadership, resulting in a consensus for building a new regional order; and (2) the leader's willingness to take a long-range view of its own interests as a criterion for action and to sacrifice short-term benefits for long-term goals, a condition that would require relative autonomy of its ruling elite from interest group pressures. To be a hegemon, the dominant power must have a sense of leadership and be willing to use its wealth for producing public goods. In other words, it must be willing to bear the costs of creating and maintaining a new order, and it must be able to create a vision of a future order by which to mobilize the followers.

Japan's performance on these two conditions can be measured by two types of activities. First there are Japan's political and organizational efforts aimed at the formation of an international and a domestic consensus on a regional integration regime. These efforts amount to 'a set of principles, norms, rules, and decision-making procedures governing actor behavior in an issue-area'.[55] Second, there are Japan's efforts to build networks of economic interests through a coordinated use of economic aid, technical cooperation and private sector FDI.

CONSENSUS-BUILDING EFFORTS IN THE ASIA–PACIFIC REGION

To determine the willingness and desire of the Japanese elite to create and lead a regional economic order, let us examine the activities of Japanese politicians, bureaucrats, businessmen, academics, the media and others to create a regional and domestic consensus in support of a regional economic order guided by Japanese leadership. In Japan, the idea of regional cooperation in Asia and the Asia–Pacific area is rooted in pre-war Pan-Asianism. In 1960, the first proposal for Pacific economic cooperation after the Second World War was criticized for its close ideological resemblance to the pre-war concept of the Greater East Asia Co-prosperity Sphere. Morinosuke Kajima, a businessman and Diet member of the ruling LDP, suggested creating an Asia development fund modelled after the Marshall Plan in order to give grants rather than credits to help Asian countries develop their economies. He reasoned that the historical trend was moving towards Asian integration.[56]

The founders and the driving force in the current movement in Japan to promote Asia–Pacific economic cooperation (referred to as either the Pacific Community Concept or the Pacific Basin Movement) are two economists, Kiyoshi Kojima and Saburo Okita. Okita traces his interest to the pre-war experience with the Showa Institute and Prime Minister Fumimaro Konoe's idea of an 'East Asian Cooperative Union' announced in 1938.[57] Okita and Kojima formed an official study group in 1961. Supported by four major business groups, Okita established in 1963 the Japan Economic Research Centre (JERC), which has been one of the most influential academic promoters of the Pacific Community Concept.[58] To counterbalance the formation of the EEC, Kojima proposed in 1965 a Pacific Free Trade Area (PAFTA) with the USA, Canada, Japan, Australia and New Zealand as full members, and East Asian developing countries as associate members.[59]

The then Foreign Minister, Takeo Miki, endorsed the PAFTA plan and, in a 1967 speech, called on the Pacific developed countries jointly to assist Asian developing economies.[60] Miki traveled to several Asia–Pacific nations to probe regional interest in the concept and found that Japan's Asian neighbours were still wary of a resurgence of Japanese economic power. They suspected that the economic gains from PAFTA would heavily favour the developed countries, especially Japan.[61] The idea proved unacceptable to the USA as well because its global stature and commercial interests were incompatible with its membership in discriminatory regional trading arrangements. The less populous developed countries – Australia, Canada and New Zealand – feared Japanese economic domination. They saw that any potential economic gains heavily favoured Japan. Inside Japan itself were sceptics who found in the proposal shadows of the discredited concept of a Greater East Asia Co-prosperity Sphere.[62] With the formation of ASEAN, the Japanese Government terminated its sponsorship of Ministerial Confer-

ences on Economic Development in South-east Asia. Thus, government
initiatives foundered on issues of leadership and fears of Japanese economic
domination. The stalemate, however, ultimately resulted from the gap between the proposed concept and the Asian reality.

Meanwhile, inspired by a JERC report, another important non-govern-
mental transnational forum, the Pacific Basin Economic Council (PBEC),
was established in April 1967 under the leadership of Japanese and Australian businessmen who shared concerns about the EC developing into a
discriminatory bloc.[63] Composed initially of businessmen from the five
developed Pacific Rim countries (the USA, Canada, Japan, Australia and
New Zealand), its membership has since expanded to include representatives from developing countries in the region such as Indonesia, Malaysia,
the Philippines and Chile. PBEC promotes private sector cooperation through
its annual general meetings.[64]

Another important transnational forum for academics to discuss the concept of Pacific Rim cooperation, the annual Pacific Trade and Development
(PAFTAD) conference, is organized under JERC auspices on the initiative
of Okita and Kojima. Its first meeting in January 1968 was funded by the
Japanese Foreign Ministry. PAFTAD has since met annually in participants' countries and has become an important consensus-forming forum for
economists from both developed and developing countries of the Asia–
Pacific area. As Kojima puts it, the forum has created a 'Pacific Economist
Community'.[65]

Government-level participation in the discussion of the Pacific Community Concept resumed in the late 1970s, inspired mainly by fear of protectionism in Western Europe and growing US pressure on Japan to increase
its share of the defence burden in the Western Pacific.[66] In 1977 the Prime
Minister, Takeo Fukuda, visited ASEAN countries and announced in Ma-
nila the 'Fukuda Doctrine', or 'heart to heart' diplomacy. In his electoral
campaign of 1978, the Prime Minister, Masayoshi Ohira, offered a 'Pacific
Rim Community' idea to compete with Fukuda's ASEAN policies. Ohira's
plan aroused interest in the US Senate.[67] In 1979 a US Congressional
Research Service report on Pacific cooperation, prepared by Hugh Patrick
and Peter Drysdale, proposed the creation of an intergovernmental Organization of Pacific Trade and Development (OPTAD). Kojima endorsed the
OPTAD concept as more realistic than his earlier proposal for an EC type
of free trade area.[68]

In September 1980, at the joint request of Australian Prime Minister
Malcolm Fraser and Ohira,[69] the PECC was convened at Australian National University in Canberra. The conference was attended by unofficial
tripartite delegations composed of a government official, a business leader

and an academic or professional from eleven Pacific Rim countries, including the five developed countries, the five ASEAN countries and the Republic of Korea. The conference studied the Pacific Basin Cooperation Concept (PBCC) proposed by the Ohira Study Group in May 1980. Essentially a political document, it was, as some critics observed, vague in its goals; it was overly cautious in defining the nature of the commitments required of the participating governments; and it left many issues of organizational structure open-ended.[70] A typical ASEAN view was that the PBCC would merely freeze 'the present international division of labour and the entrenchment of the current political and military divisions of the developed North'.[71] The suggestion for the use of the yen as a regional currency was seen as evidence of the hidden Japanese scheme to turn their economic strength into political influence and to secure control of markets, natural resources and strategic waterways in the region.[72]

The Canberra conference abandoned as premature the idea of a formal governmental organization modelled on the EC. The delegates reached a consensus on the need to focus on creating a sense of community among the participants rather than on the specific shape, functions and composition of the Pacific Community. They proposed establishing a Pacific Cooperation Committee (PCC) as a private, informal body of 25 members that would study such matters as trade, FDI, energy, marine resources, communications and educational exchange. The membership includes government appointees who participate in deliberations in an unofficial capacity.[73]

Some analysts have characterized the development from the publication of the Ohira group document to the Canberra seminar as a 'diffusion phenomenon': 'a move away from strict EEC-type institutional organization to a more loosely structured consultative body; from institutional integration to functional cooperation; from a preoccupation with trade to the inclusion of a wider range of areas for cooperation, including the socio-cultural field'.[74]

The second PECC met in 1982 in Bangkok, and the third convened in Bali, Indonesia, in 1983. In 1984, the USA established a National Committee on Pacific Economic Cooperation, signalling the growing US interest in the Pacific Community idea. The fourth PECC, held in Seoul, was attended by some 140 participants, including twelve ministry-level officials from twelve countries. For the fifth PECC, held in Vancouver, both China and Taiwan were present as full members, and the Soviet Union sent observers. These developments indicate the evolution of PECC into a forum superseding the East–West ideological divide. The sixth PECC, which met in May 1988 in Osaka, Japan, was attended by more than 700 academics, government officials and businessmen. The Soviet delegation applied for full membership. The conference endorsed Japan's proposal to establish a $1 million fund to enable continued participation from developing countries.[75]

The PECC series has explored and publicized the benefits of regional cooperation between its members.[76] It has widened communication channels and provided a mechanism of consultation on economic policy issues. It has also contributed to the clarification of the central goal of Pacific economic cooperation. As Peter Drysdale observes, the goal is 'the development of common or mutually consistent approaches' to trade, foreign investment, aid, structural adjustment and commercial policy rather than such matters as macroeconomic coordination of monetary and fiscal policy, or the management of the exchange rates and the international monetary system.[77] The meetings have created a climate favourable to building institutions that reduce uncertainty in international economic exchanges and provide a framework within which members coordinate their approaches to various issues.[78]

Analysts argue that to make the PECC more effective in promoting regional cooperation, Japan must share leadership with the USA. In other words, Japan should be prepared to shoulder more of the costs of developing and maintaining the PECC apparatus.[79] So far, however, in fear of rekindling their Asian neighbours' suspicion of Japanese intentions and without domestic consensus on the matter, the Japanese have maintained a low profile in the PECC process, while eagerly organizing or hosting a variety of Asia–Pacific-related regional conferences in Japan.[80]

It was on the initiative of the Australian Prime Minister, Robert Hawke, that the first formal governmental-level APEC Conference was convened in Canberra in November 1989. It was attended by 23 leading ministers of state from twelve countries (the six ASEAN countries, Australia, Canada, Japan, South Korea, New Zealand and the USA). The *Summary Statement* of the conference encouraged future participation by China, Hong Kong and Taiwan.[81] As we have seen, the various organizations formed since 1960 promoted the idea of Pacific cooperation, but the creation of an official Cabinet-level body was a major leap forward.

The overview of developments presented above indicates several key features of the patterns of cooperation emerging in the Asia–Pacific region. First, Japan and Australia have played central roles in developing the Pacific Community Concept and have demonstrated their willingness to form a regime or institution for ensuring cooperation. Second, the deep-rooted ASEAN concern and wariness about being dominated by larger countries, especially Japan, still persists. Third, the gradual change in the perception and attitudes of ASEAN's elites towards the creation of an exploratory mechanism is becoming increasingly evident.

An important new motivation for promoting a Pacific economic cooperation scheme is the shared fear of trade blocs forming in Europe and North
America. The more fundamental motivation behind the movement lies in
the deepening economic interdependence within the region that has created
both problems to be dealt with and potentials for benefits to be shared by
forming regional regimes. Let us now turn to the Japanese Government's
efforts to help build a cohesive regional economic network that will minimize the problems created by economic interdependence while maximizing
benefits gained by cooperation.

COHESIVE REGIONAL ECONOMIC NETWORK FORMATION

The Japanese Government, especially MITI, has been keen to use its aid to
assist in restructuring and upgrading the Japanese economy by relocating
industrial production facilities in what it sees as the most efficient way. An
immediate goal is to facilitate the establishment of lower cost component-
making and export bases for Japan's manufacturing industries in East and
South-east Asia in order to maintain its edge over its competitors in the
region.[82] The government has also been eager to aid the economic development of the Asian nations, again in the manner and direction that it believes
will increase complementarity with the Japanese economy, reduce the region's dependence on American markets and increase intraregional trade
and investment.

For these purposes, MITI developed a New Asian Industries Development Plan to channel Japan's direct investment flow into the NIEs and
ASEAN countries by coordinating the flows of aid, trade and private capital
to those nations. Its guiding rule still is 'to intervene in order to strengthen
the market forces, not to combat them', a rule that seems to be shared by the
targeted countries of the Asian subregion. As Chalmers Johnson observes:
'Interventionism, in the sense of regulatory interference, is limited in Asian–
Pacific developing countries because they lack the mistrust of markets and
private entrepreneurship that motivates large-scale doctoring in other Asian
countries and in African and South American countries.'[83]

In these efforts, the Japanese Government is systematically focusing on
the fast-growing subregion that encompasses the Asian NIEs and ASEAN.[84]
Japanese aid policy is shifting from symbolic large-scale infrastructure
building and the creation of export orders for contractors and equipment-
makers in Japan to the development of specific industries in the recipient
countries that will increase complementarity with the Japanese economy
and among themselves. The establishment of the ASEAN–Japan Develop-

ment Fund under Japan's $20 billion recycling plan is designed to expedite the implementation of these policies.[85] While the Japanese private sector today often professes its distaste for MITI's interventionist posture, Japanese aid policy has clearly been facilitating the integration of the Asian economies into a regional horizontal division of labour centred on Japanese business activities. Given these developments, Japanese policy makers seem to be increasingly convinced that Japan's long-term national interest lies in the creation of a new economic order in East and South-east Asia that would benefit the entire region.

Although Peter Drysdale wrote in December 1988, 'Japan seems destined to lead from behind',[86] Fukui observed that Prime Minister Takeshita demonstrated his willingness to assume the role of an Asian leader during his official overseas trips. Fukui attributes Takeshita's unexpectedly (or unlikely, given his personality) activist diplomatic posture to Japan's economic position in the world.[87]

> Takeshita's assumption of the role of an Asian leader at the Toronto summit meeting was one response to the political implications of Japan's evolving economic relationships with its Asian neighbors. A MITI plan to set up a formal advisory council to look into the feasibility, and the desirability, of a Pacific Basin regional bloc was another. Interestingly, Japan's neighbors did not strongly react to those Japanese moves one way or another in 1988.

Numerous reports and proposals on regional economic cooperation have been produced in Japan in the last few years by a growing number of study groups and committees, often associated with one ministry or another. This proliferation reflects the enthusiasm for promoting regional cooperation under Japanese leadership. Also, a shift in the tone of debate is clearly towards a more activist leadership role for Japan. For example, an Economic Planning Agency's (EPA's) advisory council set up in August 1988 and headed by Shoichi Akazawa has called for the establishment of an international organization to coordinate macroeconomic policies among the nations of the region. The report, issued in June 1989, defines the goal of the proposed organization as that of becoming 'the driving force of the free-trade system' in the Asia–Pacific region, and eventually 'to make the region an full-fledged economic dynamo with loose multilateral ties'.[88] The Foundation for Advanced Information and Research (FAIR) of the Ministry of Finance has organized a Committee for Asia–Pacific Economic Research. Its subcommittees produced a variety of recommendations. Here, again, an activist leadership role is anticipated for Japan.[89]

At a three-day symposium entitled 'The Present and Future of the Pacific Basin Economy', held in Tokyo in July 1989, a panel urged that Japan should play a leading role in linking the economies of the Pacific Basin region and promoting harmonious development among them.[90] Naoki Tanaka called for efforts to set up a network of global manufacturing operations that would make Japan a supplier of technology-intensive capital goods and facilitate the transfer of manufacturing jobs from Japan to other parts of East Asia. The symposium was attended by 47 scholars and experts from fourteen nations in the region, the EC and six international organizations, as well as some 300 observers.

It seems not only that the East and South-east Asian economies are developing an increasingly cohesive structure among themselves but that common interests are perceived among government officials, politicians, businessmen and scholars and experts in the region, in no small part because of the Japanese private sector and informal government initiatives and the series of international conferences reviewed earlier. The implications of this development go beyond the market-oriented Asian economies. As Steffan B. Linder prophetically noted in this 1986 book, *The Pacific Century*, the demonstration effect of 'spectacular economic success in the Pacific Basin' is undermining the legitimacy of Communist regimes, not at the grass roots but at the level of ruling elite. In so doing it is eroding the dominance of the military-industrial complex that was entrenched in the Cold War structure and psychology and that has determined the post-Second World War allocation of resources worldwide.[91]

JAPAN'S ROLE IN ASIA: REGIONAL HEGEMONY?

The developments reviewed seem to confirm Japan's hegemony in the region in terms of the Gramscian theory of hegemonic stability. The criterion here is not whether the Japanese elite and public are determined to assume leadership. Many analysts believe the Japanese would shun a leading world role because of wartime memories, still strong suspicions among Asian countries, and the lack of a strong, appropriate philosophy.[92] True, they may not want to exercise an assertive, let alone commanding, theatrical type of leadership, but that is mainly a matter of presentation or style. What counts is substance. We must examine whether Japan's actions led to the formation of consensus and legitimation of its dominant role in reshaping the structure of the regional economy. Restructuring the economy under Japan's influence is, like it or not, a fact of life:[93]

Japan provides 65 per cent of all the funds (both government aid and private investment) that flow into the rest of Pacific Asia; Japan is the largest aid donor to every country in Asia except Pakistan, and the source of 64 per cent of the aid to the developing countries of Southeast Asia; Japan's total trade with Asia is now the largest of any nation, and its imports from Pacific Asia have almost doubled in the past two years.

These developments seem to support another influential view that international regimes would emerge as devices for facilitating decentralized cooperation among egoistic states as American hegemony erodes.[94] This argument, however, must be examined by asking whether such devices (fully institutionalized or not), are operated by co-equals rather than controlled from behind by a dominant power, what they can decide and implement, and what impacts they make in changing the economic landscape of the region.

The crucial questions are these: are the Japanese able and willing to sacrifice short-term economic gains for their enlightened long-term view of national interest, which would include the creation of a new regional economic order to benefit all of its members? Can they articulate goals that legitimize an economic cooperation forum, if not a bloc, under their leadership? Is it possible to guide the flow of investment, aid and trade so as to develop networks of interests as the basis for establishing an economic bloc that will satisfy the self-interests of both Japan and its associates?

One question has been omitted: are the Japanese willing to make sacrifices to support the free trade system? An alternative vision of regional economic order that benefits its members may not be the free trade system. The critical question – ideological, ethical and practical – is how Japan will, and whether it should, use its resources to improve the welfare of the entire region. Here the test for legitimate leadership – a condition for hegemony – is no longer simply the maintenance of the liberal international economic system. It is, I think, the willingness and ability to tackle problems of uneven development in such a way as to broaden the basis of economic growth by fostering autonomous and viable indigenous entrepreneurship.

Asia's share of world GDP increased from 16 per cent in 1965 to 24 per cent in 1985. However, its share of world population was 59 per cent in 1985.[95] This disparity between income and population shares suggests a growing income gap between the rich and the poor countries in Asia and the still strong growth potential in the region. The growing gap between the rich and the poor is intensifying tensions both among and within nations, particularly the poorer ones in Asia. The Asian NIEs' economic growth has been achieved by their adopting market-oriented export promotion strategies, but the international environment has since changed. The success of Japan and the NIEs may not be easily repeated in other Asian countries. One lesson seems clear from the experiences of the Asian NIEs and ASEAN economic development: localization of industrial activity is necessary for sustained economic growth as it directly affects the incentives and motivation for both management and labour.

The agenda had changed for the hegemon. To establish legitimacy for its leadership, the hegemon must solve the potentially explosive problem of growing inequality. Paradoxically, the hegemon's task (and long-range interest) will lie in the advancement of a more egalitarian development. The answer to our questions of hegemony and the possibility of forming an economic bloc will depend on whether Japan exercises creative leadership in the region and how European and North American economic cooperation evolves.

Notes

1. See, for example: Richard Rosecrance and Jennifer Taw, 'Japan and the Theory of International Leadership', *World Politics*, XLII (January 1990) pp. 184–209; Lawrence B. Krause, 'Change in the International System: The Pacific Basin', *Annals of the American Academy of Political and Social Science*, 505 (September 1989) pp. 105–16; Peter Drysdale and Ross Garnaut, *A Pacific Free Trade Area?* Pacific Economic Papers, No. 171 (Canberra: Australian National University, 1989); *The Economist: A Survey of the Yen Bloc*, 15 July 1989; Daniel Sneider, 'Japan in Asia' (five-part series), *Christian Science Monitor*, 6, 13, 15, 17 and 27 November 1989; Peter L. Berger, 'Asian Capitalism and the Future: Trouble Ahead for Asian Predominance?' *Speaking of Japan*, 9 (February 1989) p. 9. See also Masao Fujioka, 'Toward Globalism: Japan's Role in Asian Development', *Speaking of Japan*, 9 (February 1989) pp. 15–20.
2. Ibid.
3. Daniel Sneider, 'Pacific Rim Nations Strengthen Economic Ties', *Christian Science Monitor*, 6 November 1989, p. 10.
4. Bank of Tokyo, *Tokyo Financial Review*, 14 (April 1989) p. 5.
5. *The Economist*, 15 July 1989, p. 10. For example, Hitachi makes semiconductors in Malaysia which are used as components of videocassette recorders sold in Singapore. Many firms producing consumer electronics shifted production from NIEs to ASEAN as the former's labour costs and currencies (except the Hong Kong dollar) started rising roughly three years ago. *Far Eastern Economic Review*, 15 June 1989, p. 58.
6. EPA, *Economic Survey of Japan, 1987–88* (Tokyo: Japanese Government, 1989) p. 76.

7. Ibid, pp. 77, 92.
8. *Tokyo Financial Review*, April 1989, p. 2; *The Economist*, 15 July 1989, p. 10. An increasing number of Japanese makers now import from their overseas manufacturing subsidiaries such products as consumer electronics (television sets, walkmen, stereo-cassette players, and so on), foods (confectionery and soft drinks) and motorcycles. Some of their subsidiaries in Asian countries export low-cost components to Japan for use in high-tech products and to other Japanese-owned factories in the region for products aimed at local markets. These include parts for general machinery and electronics equipment, small motors and car windows. The improved manufacturing technology and redundant capacity in the Asian NIEs and ASEAN (that is, lower costs), explain the rapid increase in imports of intermediates: EPA, *Economic Survey of Japan*, pp. 74–9.
9. Haruhiro Fukui, 'Japan in 1988: At the End of an Era', *Asian Survey*, January 1989, p. 7. For FDI in the Asian NIEs, see Steffan Haggard and Tun-jen Cheng, 'State and Capital in the East Asian NIEs', in Frederic C. Deyo (ed.), *The Political Economy of the New Asian Industrialism* (Ithaca, NY: Cornell University Press, 1987) pp. 84–135.
10. *The Economist: Survey*, 15 July 1989, p. 9.
11. Ibid.
12. Thomas A. Layman, 'Financing Growth and Development in Asia', in Robert Scalapino, Seizaburo Sato, Jusuf Wanandi and Sung-joo Han, (eds), *Pacific–Asian Economic Policies and Regional Interdependence* (Berkeley: Institute of East Asian Studies, 1988), pp. 203–307; *Tokyo Financial Review* (*TFR*), April 1989, p. 2.
13. *TFR*, April 1989, p. 3.
14. Ibid.
15. GATT report cited in *Wall Street Journal*, 9 November 1989. Japanese direct investment in the Asian region tends to concentrate in manufacturing industries: 34 per cent in 1987. The share of electric, ferrous and non-ferrous metal, and chemical industries increased after the yen's appreciation. The share of exports from Asian countries in Japan in total sales rose from 10.8 per cent in 1983 to 15.8 per cent in 1986.
    Horizontal division of labour between Japan and the Asian NIEs is most developed in steel, precision machinery, general machinery and motor vehicle parts and, since 1987, increasingly in electrical machinery. The general pattern has been for Japan to import low-cost items made by Japanese subsidiaries abroad and to process them into high-value-added products. Usually, core parts of products made by the Asian NIEs are supplied by parent companies in Japan, while peripherals for products manufactured in Japan are imported from the Asian NIEs: *Economic Survey of Japan*, p. 90.
16. The industrial structure of most advanced countries is marked by a broad base of basic industries, less broad but still large capital-intensive intermediate technology sectors, and a smaller high-technology sector on the top. Japan's direct investment in its Asian neighbours, particularly after 1985, has created instantaneous industrialization that focuses on high-technology assembly operations but that has neither a broad base nor a strong intermediate sector. Herein lie the difficulties in localizing production processes. According to Shohei Manabe, who has been in charge of plant exports to developing

countries in Asia and the Middle East, assembly plants are far cheaper to
build than basic industries; hence plants are often built by the Japanese
companies without long-range planning. Author's interview with Shohei
Manabe, 22 November 1989, Cambridge, Massachusetts.

17. Harry T. Oshima, *Economic Growth in Monsoon Asia: A Comparative Survey* (Tokyo: University of Tokyo Press, 1987) pp. 69, 311.
18. Takamitsu Sawa, 'Asia taiheiyo-jidai' (The Asia Pacific Era), *Asahi Shimbun*, 30 November 1988; Yuji Suzuki, 'Tonan ajia no "minshuka" to sono inpakuto' ('Democratization' of Southeast Asia and its Impact), *Sekai*, December 1988, pp. 92–8; To Tsuan En, 'NIEs jidai no higashi ajia keizaiken' (East Asian economic bloc in the NIEs era), *Sekai*, December 1988, pp. 123–32; Jun Nishikawa, 'Kaihatsu enjo to jiritsu: ODA wo kangaeru' (Development aid and self-reliance: Reconsider ODA), *Sekai*, October 1989, pp. 31–43.
19. Saburo Okita, 'Asian–Pacific Prospects and Problems for the Further Development of the Asian–Pacific Cooperative Framework', paper presented at First International Symposium, 'In Search of a New Order in East Asia', Santa Barbara, CA, 1–3 February 1980.
20. Kaname Akamatsu, 'A Historical Pattern of Economic Growth in Developing Countries', *The Developing Economies* (Tokyo: Institute of Asian Economic Affairs, 1962) p. 11.
21. *Economic Survey of Japan*, p. 90.
22. Okita, 'Asian–Pacific Prospects', p. 2.
23. *Nikkei*, 6 October 1989.
24. Nobuo Maruyama, cited in Sneider, 'Japan in Asia', 13 November 1989.
25. T. Sawa, *Asahi Shimbun*, 30 November 1988; Suzuki, 'Tonan ajia'.
26. Krause, 'Change in the International System', p. 114; Richard Cronin, cited by Sneider, 'Japan in Asia', 13 November 1989; *The Economist: Survey*, 15 July 1989, p. 10.
27. 'New Globalism: Japan and Economic Cooperation with the Asia-Pacific', *LOOK JAPAN*, 35 (September 1989) p. 12. See also MITI, *Tsusho hakusho 1989* (White Paper on International Trade) (Tokyo: Japanese Government, 1989).
28. Sneider, 'Japan in Asia', 13 November 1989.
29. Naoki Tanaka, 'The Dollar's Fin de Siècle, the Yen's Debut', *Japan Quarterly*, April–June 1989, p. 122.
30. Krause, 'Change in the International System', p. 115.
31. *The Economist*, 11 November 1989, p. 15.
32. Author's interview with Hisahiko Okazaki, Japanese Ambassador to Thailand, 14 October 1989, Cambridge, Massachusetts. A similar view was expressed by Toshio Watanabe, 'The Age of the Western Pacific: Interdependence Grows Among Asian NIEs and Japan', *Japan Update*, Autumn 1989, p. 22.
33. Kahler, 'Organizing', in Scalapino *et al.* (eds), *Economic Policies*, pp. 338–40.
34. Sneider, 'Japan in Asia', 13 November 1989; *The Economist: Survey*, 15 July 1989, p. 15.
35. *The Economist*, 11 November 1989, p. 15.
36. Robert Gilpin, *The Political Economy of International Relations* (Princeton, NJ: Princeton University Press, 1987), p. 72; Keohane, 'The Theory of

Hegemonic Stability', in Ole Holsti, R.M. Siverson and Alexander George (eds), *Change in the International System*, (Boulder, Co: Westview, 1980) p. 132.

37. John Gerald Ruggie, 'International Regimes, Transactions, and Change: Embedded Liberalism in the Postwar Economic Order', *International Organization*, 36 (1982) p. 382.
38. Gilpin, *The Political Economy*, p. 75.
39. Stephen D. Krasner, 'Structural Causes and Regime Consequences: Regimes as Intervening Variables', *International Organization*, 36 (1982) p. 185.
40. Ibid, p. 185.
41. Richard Rosecrance, *The Rise of the Trading State: Commerce and Conquest in the Modern World* (New York: Basic Books, 1986), p. 56.
42. Gilpin, *The Political Economy*, p. 376.
43. *Economic Survey of Japan*, p. 76.
44. Frank Langdon, *Japan's Foreign Policy* (Vancouver: University of British Columbia Press, 1973); Lawrence Olson, *Japan in Postwar Asia* (New York: Praeger, 1970).
45. Roger Simon, *Gramsci's Political Thought* (London: Lawrence & Wishart, 1982) p. 22.
46. Joseph V. Femia, *Gramsci's Political Thought: Hegemony, Consciousness, and the Revolutionary Process* (Oxford: Clarendon Press, 1981) p. 24. For the complexity and ambiguities of the concept, see Walter L. Adamson, *Hegemony and Revolution: A Study of Antonio Gramsci's Political and Cultural Theory* (Berkeley, CA: University of California Press, 1980) Chapter 6.
47. Femia, *Gramsci's Political Thought*, p. 21.
48. Ibid, pp. 228–9.
49. Ibid, p. 229; Robert Bocok, *Hegemony* (London: Tavistock Publications, 1986) p. 23.
50. Simon, *Gramsci's Political Thought*, p. 23.
51. Ibid, p. 25.
52. Robert Cox, 'Social Forces, States and World Orders: Beyond International Relations Theory', *Millennium*, 10 (Summer 1988) p. 153, n. 27.
53. Ibid, p. 229.
54. Robert O. Keohane, *After Hegemony: Cooperation and Discord in the World Political Economy*. (Princeton, NJ: Princeton University Press, 1984), p. 45. Also, see Krasner, 'Structural Causes'.
55. Krasner, 'Structural Causes'.
56. M. Hadi Soesastro, 'Institutional Aspects of Pacific Economic Cooperation', in M. Hadi Soesastro and Han Sang-joo (eds), *Pacific Economic Cooperation* (Jakarta: Centre for Strategic and International Studies, 1983), p. 16; James William Morley, 'The Genesis of the Pacific Basin Movement and Japan', in Roy Kim and Hilary Conroy (eds), *New Tides in the Pacific* (New York: Greenwood Press, 1987) pp. 11–34.
57. Saburo Okita, *In Search of a New Order*.
58. Ibid; Tessa Morris-Suzuki, 'Japan and the Pacific Basin Community', *The World Today*, December 1981; Asian Studies Centre, *The Pacific Community: Evolution of an Idea, Backgrounder*, 21 May 1987; David Arase, 'The Politics of Pacific Economic Cooperation', revised version of a paper first delivered at the 32nd International Conference of Orientalists in Japan, 3 May 1987.

59. Morley, 'The Genesis', p. 13.
60. Ibid; Miles Kahler, 'Organizing the Pacific', in Scalapino, *et al.* (eds), *Economic Policies*, pp. 330–3.
61. Soesastro, *Pacific Economic Cooperation*, p. 29.
62. Peter Drysdale, *International Economic Pluralism: Economic Policy in East Asia and the Pacific* (Sydney: Allen & Unwin, 1988) p. 208.
63. Morris-Suzuki, 'Japan and the Pacific Basin Community', p. 455.
64. Arase, 'The Politics of Pacific Economic Cooperation', p. 6; Han Seung Soo, 'The Place of Japan in Pacific Cooperation', paper prepared for the Second Korea–US Bilateral Forum, Kyungju, Korea, 6–9 August 1987, p. 2.
65. Kojima's written submission, Pacific Community Seminar in Canberra, 16 September 1980, cited in Soesastro, *Pacific Economic Cooperation*, p. 23.
66. Ibid, pp. 24–5; Drysdale, *International Economic Pluralism*, p. 215; Morris-Suzuki, 'Japan and the Pacific Basin', p. 459.
67. Bernard K. Gordon, 'Japan and the Pacific Basin Proposal', in Soesastro (ed.), *Pacific Economic Cooperation*, p. 246.
68. Soesastro, *Pacific Economic Cooperation*, pp. 30–7.
69. Ibid, p. 24.
70. Ibid, pp. 32–4; Hoon-mok Chung, 'Economic Integration in the Pacific Basin: A Historical Review', in Han Sung-joo (ed.), *Community Building in the Pacific Region: Issues and Opportunities* (Seoul: The Asiatic Research Centre, Korea University, 1981) p. 19; Gordon, 'Japan and the Pacific Basin Proposal', in Soesastro, *Pacific Economic Cooperation*, p. 245.
71. Speech by Tan Sri Ghazalia, Malaysian Minister of Home Affairs on 12 December 1979 at the Conference on Asian and Pacific Security, Pattaya, Thailand, cited by Gordon, 'Japan', p. 248.
72. Ibid.
73. Asian Studies Centre, *The Pacific Community*, p. 6; Gordon, 'Japan', p. 249.
74. Hoon-mok Chung, 'Economic Integration in the Pacific Basin: A Historical Review', in Han Sung-joo, *Community Building in the Pacific Region*, p. 19; cited in M. Hadi Soesastro, 'Prospects for the Pacific–Asian Regional Trade Structures', in Scalapino, *et al.* (eds), *Economic Policies*, p. 309.
75. *Asahi Shimbun*, 21 May 1988.
76. Arase, 'The Politics of Pacific Economic Cooperation', p. 32.
77. Drysdale, *International Economic Pluralism*, p. 220.
78. Ibid, p. 218–19.
79. Arase, 'The Politics of Pacific Economic Cooperation', pp. 29–30; Drysdale, *International Economic Pluralism*, p. 221.
80. Arase, 'The Politics of Pacific Economic Cooperation'.
81. Saburo Okita, 'Asian–Pacific Prospects and Problems for the Further Development of the Asian–Pacific Cooperative Framework', paper presented at First International Symposium, 'In Search of a New Order in East Asia', Santa Barbara, California, 1–3 February 1980, p. 16.
82. Urata, cited in *The Economist Survey*, 15 July 1989, p. 10.
83. Chalmers Johnson, *MITI and the Japanese Miracle* (Stanford, CA: Stanford University Press, 1982).
84. *Ibid.*
85. *The Economist: Survey* 15 July 1989, p. 16.
86. Peter Drysdale, *Japan as a Pacific and World Economic Power*, Pacific Economic Papers, No. 166 (December 1988) p. 18.
87. Fukai, 'Japan in 1988', p. 4.

88.   *Japan Times*, 13 June 1989.
89.   The recent history of FAIR reveals factors that interest Japanese policy makers in Asia–Pacific economic cooperation. Following a suggestion by Prime Minister Takeshita that it should study recent trends towards regional economic integration and protectionism in both North America and the EC, in September 1988 FAIR established the Committee for Asia–Pacific Economic Research. Commissioned by the Ministry of Finance's Customs and Tariff Bureau and in consultation with the Ministry of Foreign Affairs' Economic Affairs Bureau and other government agencies, including their research arms, the committee members were selected from academic and business circles and asked to make proposals for use in high-level consultations between policy makers. The committee is divided into seven research groups: the world's political-economic system; Pacific macroeconomic policy; international economic structure; Asian economic structure; opportunities for loans and investment and business strategies; international economic and tariff policies; and tariff policy and customs administration. See FAIR report, 'World's Political and Economic System Research Group' (Group 1), June 1989, Appendix, p. 1.
90.   *Asahi Evening News*, 28 July 1989.
91.   Steffan B. Linder, *The Pacific Century: Economic and Political Consequences of Asian–Pacific Dynamism* (Stanford, CA: Stanford University Press, 1986).
92.   *Christian Science Monitor*, 27 November 1989.
93.   *Christian Science Monitor*, 13 November 1989.
94.   Keohane, *After Hegemony*.
95.   Fujioka, 'Toward Globalism', p. 17.

9 A Japanese Perspective on the Pacific Rim in the 1990s[1]

Nobuo Matsunaga

At this time of revolutionary and historical change heralding the birth of a new world order, the common values which Australia and Japan share, as well as the common challenges which they will face in adjusting their mutual roles, will present these two countries with a golden opportunity to cement their constructive partnership in order to achieve their goals for growth and development in the twenty-first century. It is with such confidence that I hope to give you a glimpse of the Japanese perspective on the problems and issues facing the Asia–Pacific region.

Of all the many diverse countries in the region, Australia and Japan share a particularly strong and productive relationship. Japan's relationship with Australia for most of the past 30 years has been dominated by bilateral trade issues, with the two economies developing a complementarity that promotes mutual advantage. Since 1970, Japan has been Australia's major trading partner, with Australia emerging as Japan's third biggest supplier of imports. And yet one of the early certainties being confirmed for us in this post-Cold War, post-Gulf War world is that the narrowness of a primarily bilateral relationship will no longer meet the changing needs and realities of increasingly global circumstances, which require a more multilateral structure.

In addition to being two key members of the Western alliance in this region, it would also be fair to say that Australia and Japan are the key engines of growth in the region's northern and southern perimeters. Between them lies a region of developed and developing countries which is beginning to attract the more serious attention of the rest of the world. Defining this Asia–Pacific region will be a series of subregional economic partners founded on the indispensable principles of free trade, non-protectionism and democracy.

In 1989, Sosuke Uno, Japan's foreign minister at the time, characterized the Australia–Japan relationship as a 'constructive partnership', a concept which captured the forward-looking approach of the two countries based on

189

positive cooperation, mutual respect, cultural appreciation and recognition of their mutual roles and contributions within their respective bilateral and regional frameworks. As Australia's partner in this regard, Japan is the first to commend the Australian commitment and foresight in promoting Asia–Pacific cooperation. Australia took the lead in 1974 as the first country to establish formal relations with ASEAN, and it was Australia's foresight in advocating non-discriminatory trade liberalization throughout the Pacific Rim which led to the creation of the APEC forum in 1989.

In the May 1991 meeting of the Australia–Japan Ministerial Committee, the notion of a constructive partnership was further delineated to embrace four key elements: first, cooperation in the further development and diversification of the bilateral relationship; second, cooperation in maintaining and strengthening a free and open world economic system through international trade; third, security, with particular emphasis on cooperation in securing peace and prosperity in the Asia–Pacific region; and fourth, the resolution of international problems requiring cooperation, particularly in the area of the environment. In security and strategic areas, as well as in economic terms and in the realm of international diplomacy, both Australia and Japan remain leading actors in the region, and closer cooperation through a strengthened partnership should be a priority for both countries in the 1990s.

TOWARDS A FREE AND OPEN WORLD ECONOMIC SYSTEM

From one perspective, the Asia–Pacific region is an area of substantial political, social, cultural and linguistic diversity, all of which limits the development of a thoroughly defined sense of common identity. Having said this, one can just as forcefully argue that because of its economic dynamism and its relatively complex internal economic linkages, the region has the potential of becoming a truly open and interacting economic arena.

Yet despite the potential and productivity inherent in this region's diversity, it is also a reality that such differences can be destabilizing, especially if too much is attempted too quickly. This word of caution is intended in no way to discourage the progress towards regional multilateralism which holds great hope for the future; rather it is merely to advocate an incremental approach that utilizes a series of already established bilateral relations as the building blocks of the region's economic and political stability in the 1990s.

In its relations with Australia, the ASEAN states, the Republic of Korea, and other nations of the region, it is important that Japan cooperates for mutual benefit and fosters both bilateral and multilateral frameworks in its approach to political, economic and global issues relevant to regional stability and development. In addition to its bilateral ties, Japan's active participation in the ASEAN Post-Ministerial Conference with the Dialogue Partners (ASEAN–PMC), the ministerial meeting for APEC, the PECC and other multilateral fora for cooperation is also essential in strengthening the level of mutual trust between Japan and other nations of the Pacific Rim.

With the recently completed Uruguay Round as the most pressing challenge in the trade policy agendas of both Japan and Australia, the national interests of both countries have been advanced over the past few years through an initiative aimed at greater cooperation with regional economies in the APEC process. APEC was the original initiative of Australia, which saw in 1989 that continued economic growth in the Asia–Pacific region would be advanced by wider and more structured regional cooperation. Today the APEC region accounts for nearly 50 per cent of the global output of goods and services, and one-third of the world's trade.

The purpose of APEC is to secure open economic intercourse in the region, ranging from trade and services to technology transfers. The key word for the region is 'openness', and both Japan and Australia have much to do in achieving this goal. Like Australia, Japan firmly believes that any regional economic cooperation should forestall trade protectionism while remaining open to participation from the outside world. In addition, it is imperative that Japan keep to its present course of fiscal and monetary policy which is aimed at restructuring its economy and further opening its markets to foreign goods and services. For Australia, I believe this internal progress involves its continued economic restructuring and integration with the dynamic economies of the Asia–Pacific region.

SECURITY AND DIALOGUE IN THE ASIA–PACIFIC REGION

A crucial element in the security of the region is the presence of the USA, the importance of which has only been heightened in the aftermath of the Persian Gulf crisis and dissolution of the Soviet Union. American involvement and leadership are indispensable to efforts aimed at reducing tension and enhancing political stability in the region. In recognition of this, Australia has forged strong military ties with the USA, and this alliance, although not always easy, has been successful in promoting the stability of the Southern Pacific. Similarly, the US–Japan alliance is one of the most important bilateral relationships in the region, providing an essential basis for security assurances as well as a framework for foreign policy cooperation, which is essential for economic development and political stability. As we move into the changing international environment of this post-Cold-War world, these strategic alliances with the USA will have a purpose: that of safeguarding the peace and prosperity of the Asia–Pacific region as a whole.

It is also becoming increasingly important for both Japan and its fellow Asia–Pacific nations to maintain opportunities for close communication on a constant basis. In this regard, the ASEAN–PMC remains one of the most appropriate bases for addressing the regional peace and security issues and providing a forum for such necessary communication.

In the interests of ensuring long-term stability in North-east Asia, Japan intends to continue its policies regarding the Korean peninsula by maintaining contacts with the Republic of Korea, the USA and the People's Republic of China. However, the issue of nuclear proliferation remains a concern, together with a few other problems. Unless North Korea becomes more realistic, the prospects for a successful conclusion to talks do not seem bright.

The achievement of overall stability and development in South-east Asia hinges largely on the inclusion of Indochina in the framework of economic development in the Asia–Pacific region. Towards this goal, efforts must be focused on the reconstruction and development of Cambodia and Vietnam, a process which is already significantly underway. Japan confirmed its readiness to contribute more funds to the UN effort to maintain peace in Cambodia and contributed personnel to the peacekeeping effort.

The stability and development of the Asia–Pacific region also depend greatly on the promotion of active cooperation for economic and political reform and openness in China. Both Japan and Australia realize that an isolated and inward-looking China is contrary to their strategic and economic interests. Regional stability will be influenced also by China's key role in such issues as the Cambodian peace process and by its economic modernization reforms. Given China's 1.1 billion people, the direction and pace of reform in the next few years may have profound consequences for the stability and prosperity of the region.

Viewing these developments in their entirety, a conceptualization developed by the Japanese Foreign Ministry suggests that a multiplex mechanism for stability and security is becoming firmly entrenched in the Asia–Pacific region. This mechanism is composed of bilateral and multilateral frameworks of cooperation designed to enhance regional stability and security in a comprehensive manner. Thus, in the area of economic cooperation, such organizations as ASEAN, APEC, PECC and the ASEAN–PMC are already functioning as a stimulus to regional cooperation and policy coordination.

In the management of ongoing conflicts, frameworks of cooperation are emerging with respect to both Cambodia and the Korean peninsula. In the area of security there is a broad range of networks for cooperation, foremost of which is a set of alliance relations with the USA and growing cooperation among ASEAN members. Finally, there is the potential for the ASEAN–PMC to fill the need for a process of political dialogue on matters of mutual concern, such as the future of American and Japanese policy in the region.

TRANSNATIONAL ISSUES AND COMMON VALUES

The constructive partnership, which has been promoted enthusiastically by Australia and Japan, captures an important theme not only in the relationship of the two countries but also in relationships among all countries in the Asia–Pacific region. New priorities and new actors will emerge to play a greater role in global and regional economic and strategic affairs. Both Australia and Japan will be facing these new developments in a bilateral and multilateral set of frameworks.

As both countries meet these challenges individually and bilaterally, they will do so with common values rooted in the fundamental belief in freedom, democracy and the market economy. In view of the diversity and reality of the region, the approach should be a progressive one, taking into account the extent of the realistic feasibility. While this is not synonymous with acquiescing in the status quo, it does acknowledge that the common goal is to see freedom and democracy respected in the region. The way to achieve that goal, however, may vary and will require a policy which balances the universal application of certain principles with a country-to-country approach.

The international community is increasingly being challenged by transnational problems involving the global environment, refugees, illicit narcotics and terrorism. Through their partnership and participation in regional networks, Japan and Australia have an important role to play in contributing to the solution of these global difficulties. Japan has significantly increased its involvement in international environment issues and has begun exploring the possibilities for collaborative research with Australia in this area.

Recently, Japan hosted a major UN disarmament conference in Kyoto which addressed the entire range of post-Gulf-War multilateral disarmament and arms control options, and also hosted a meeting on drug abuse issues in the region. In addition, Japan has maintained its contribution to aid and humanitarian programs, and initiatives with Australia and other nations in the region have also been increased by Japan in an effort to promote a regional policy for development in these areas. Together with its guidelines for ODA, as announced in April 1991, which include the linkage of aid provision to a recipient nation's progress in democratic reforms and its level of arms spending, Japan will play an active role in the field of economic assistance towards developing countries.

In conclusion, as Japan and Australia's constructive partnership continues its progressive evolution, it should be the hope of both countries that these endeavours will contribute to a more open and free world and help to shape a new world order which draws heavily on the economic dynamism, stability and a spirit of regional cooperation exhibited by the nations of the Asia–Pacific area. As the rest of the world begins focusing its attention more seriously on the region, it is more important than ever that Australia and Japan embrace this historic opportunity to create a profoundly lasting legacy of peace and prosperity which will transcend the Asia–Pacific region and set the tone for the new world order of the twenty-first century.

Note

1.   This article is taken from the text of an address delivered on 12 April 1992, at the Eighteenth National Conference of the Australian Institute of International Affairs. This chapter previously appeared under the same title in the *Japan Review of International Affairs*, 6 (1992) in a special issue on 'Asia-Pacific Partnerships'. It is reprinted here with the permission of the author.

10 The Impact of Trade Blocs on the Future of Japan's Relations with China

T. David Mason

Since the inception of the Four Modernizations in the People's Republic of China and the signing of the Sino–Japanese Treaty of Peace and Friendship in 1978, Japan has emerged as China's leading foreign beneficiary in the pursuit of its economic development programme. During the 1980s, Japan was the largest single provider of the finance, industrial plant, and managerial and technical expertise required to achieve the technological modernization of the Chinese economy. Japan also served as China's major trading partner throughout most of this period, with total bilateral trade expanding from US$5.02 billion in 1978 to a peak of US$19.7 billion in 1989.[1] During the 1980s, Japan's share of China's annual trade was never less than 21.7 per cent and reached a peak of 26.7 per cent in 1985. The closest competitor throughout this period was Hong Kong, which provided 21.8 per cent of China's trade in 1985.[2]

It is against this backdrop that Japan was compelled to reassess its trade and investment relations with China as a result of the disturbing developmental trends in the Chinese economy that began appearing after 1986 and the political turmoil of 1989 which culminated in the massacre at Tiananmen Square. Soaring inflation in urban areas, chronic unemployment and underemployment in the countryside and in the cities, distortions in the economy created by the unstable coexistence of a state-controlled economy alongside a rapidly growing private sector, and the erosion of public faith in the ability or willingness of an ageing leadership to resolve its own internal conflicts and chart a consistent course for China's future coalesced to spawn the demonstrations in Tiananmen Square in the spring of 1989. The old guard's brutal repression of this challenge to its authority shocked the world and compelled China's major trading partners (including Japan) to reassess their official relations with China. The EC, the USA and Japan all imposed sanctions. However, in the case of the last two at least, the severity of the sanctions never approached the intensity of the verbal condemnations emanating from the official representatives of their respective governments.

By the end of 1991 Japan and the USA had quietly lifted most of the sanctions.

Although it appears that in the short term the events of 1989 are little more than a cyclical ripple in the burgeoning Sino–Japanese economic relationship, the dramatic transformation of the global system since 1989 compels us to consider whether the long-term prospects for Sino–Japanese economic ties are so inevitably positive. In this chapter, we explore the question of whether Japan's interest in China – as a trading partner and as a site for overseas investment – has been or is likely to be affected by these developments in China. This analysis of Sino–Japanese economic relations will then provide the context within which we can examine the broader question that is the subject of this book: will the emergence of trade blocs in Europe and North America impinge upon Sino–Japanese economic relations?

Both NAFTA and the creation of the single market in the EC created new opportunities and risks for Japan. The economic integration of these two regions into trade blocs will necessarily require a transformation in Japanese strategy for maintaining access to lucrative markets in North America and Europe. Will the creation of trade blocs induce Japan to shift some of its investment resources from China to the EC and North America in order to ensure continued access to these markets? Or will it induce a surge in Japanese investments in China, either as a consequence of reduced access to the North American and European markets or as a way to cut production costs of goods for export to Europe and North America?

The opportunity costs of doing business with China have been further altered by the dramatic events in the former Soviet Union and Eastern Europe. In 1989, the world witnessed the collapse of Communist Party rule in the nations of Eastern Europe and the transition to market economies and liberal democracy in Poland, Hungary and the CSFR. In 1991 the Soviet Union officially dissolved into its fifteen constituent republics. These new regimes in Eastern Europe and the CIS, heretofore isolated from the global economy, now exist as competitors with China for Japanese trade and investment. The fact that the former Communist states have skilled industrial labour forces and are next door to the largest single market in the world makes them especially attractive as low cost production sites for goods destined for the EC. While smaller in total population than China, these economies have at least the potential to develop more rapidly into lucrative markets for Japanese goods. Poland, the CSFR and Hungary already have substantially higher per capitum incomes than China. They contain proportionately much larger supplies of skilled labour, technical expertise and human capital compared to China. Likewise, their transportation, communication and energy supply infrastructures, though underdeveloped by EC standards, certainly provide a more supportive environment for industrial production than do all but a few of China's provinces. Wage rates are lower than in Western European nations, and the governments of several East European nations are considering or have adopted policies intended to attract foreign investment and gain preferential access to the EC market, even if full membership in the EC is as yet a remote possibility. If Japanese firms could find an effective economic 'gateway' from Eastern Europe into the EC market, they would be in a position to produce goods for the Western European market using highly skilled (compared to China) Eastern European labour at much lower cost than would be required to employ an equivalent work force of Western Europeans. The price of land and labour in Eastern Europe will be lower than the price of equivalent factors of production inside the EC itself, and the savings in transportation costs to EC markets will make production sites in Eastern Europe attractive alternatives to Asian sites.

Will these additional pressures and opportunities induce Japan to divert a portion of its investment capital, trade and economic interest away from China and towards these other regions? When these profound changes in the international environment of Japan's trade and investment policy are compounded by the economic uncertainties and political instability in China, will Japan's willingness to continue 'business as usual' as the primary partner of China's economic modernization programme begin to wane?

In theory, trade blocs would affect Sino–Japanese relations indirectly by altering the opportunity costs of investments in China: the emergence of trade blocs in North America and Western Europe creates pressures on Japan to increase investments in North America and Western Europe in order to preserve its competitive stance in those markets. EC 92 has created the largest and most lucrative single consumer market in the world, and even as a prospect it had already created pressures for Japan and other major industrial nations outside Europe to expand their production capacity within the Community in order to maintain or even expand their sales in the unified market. Likewise, NAFTA will make Canadian and Mexican goods more competitive in the US market and US goods more competitive in the Canadian and Mexican markets. For these reasons, Japanese firms will face increasing pressure to establish productions sites in Europe, the USA, Canada and Mexico in order to preserve their market share in each of the two newly integrated continental markets. As such, NAFTA and EC 92 raise the opportunity costs of investments in China at a time when the business climate there already appears uncertain and risky, owing to the unstable conditions in the economy, the persistence of political instability and uncertainty surrounding the imminent transition to a new generation of leadership. The opening of new markets and investments in Poland, Hungary, the CSFR and the member states of the former Soviet Union can only intensify these pressures. Hence, an environmental effect on Japanese investment flows to China which normally would be rather marginal may be magnified in the present circumstances.

THE EVOLUTION OF SINO–JAPANESE ECONOMIC RELATIONS IN THE 1980S

With the signing of the Sino–Japanese Treaty of Peace and Friendship in 1978 and the initiation of China's ambitious Four Modernizations programme, Sino–Japanese economic ties experienced a dramatic expansion in both the volume and the variety of exchanges throughout the decade of the 1980s. Both the Japanese Government, through a variety of Overseas Development Assistance packages, and the Japanese private sector, through a steady volume of credits, loans, joint ventures and other instruments, brought Japan to the point of being China's most important foreign partner in the modernization and internationalization of the Chinese economy.

There were political motivations for Japan to expand and strengthen its ties with China, and not the least of these was the perceived strategic advantages of having a China that was tied to and integrated with Japan and the West economically. By cultivating such ties, Japan and the USA could strengthen China and enhance its ability to play the role of mainland counterweight to Soviet expansionist ambitions in East Asia. With the demise of the Soviet Union, it remains to be seen how US and Japanese interests in China might evolve now that the strategic dimension which defined them throughout the 1970s and 1980s has all but disappeared.[3]

The growth in Sino–Japanese economic relations was fuelled by a fortuitous complementarity between the industrial sectors of the two nations: China emerged as a supplier of raw materials for Japan, and Japan served as a supplier of capital goods for China. In 1970–72 the Chinese Government explicitly identified finished steel, chemicals and petroleum products as their priorities for industrial development. In the aftermath of the 1973 oil crisis and the 'Nixon shocks', Japan was only too willing to serve as a supplier of the technology necessary for China to develop these industries.[4] The oil shocks of the 1970s engendered in Japan a heightened desire to diversify its energy supply sources and in China a desire to accelerate the exploitation of its coal and oil reserves for export as well as for its own industrial expansion.[5] Japan became a major supplier of extraction equipment, infrastructure development and technical expertise, as well as a proximate and lucrative export market for Chinese energy resources. Under the terms of the 1978 Long-Term Trade Agreement between Japan and the China, Japan agreed to purchase $10 billion worth of oil and coal from China between 1978 and 1985. In return, China was to balance the trade over this period through the purchase of plant and machinery from Japan.[6] Unfortunately, Chinese oil production did not expand as rapidly as anticipated and the agreement had to be extended until 1990.[7] Nonetheless, energy trade remains a central element of Sino–Japanese economic relations as indicated by the terms of their latest energy agreement, signed in December of 1990. This pact sets targets for Japanese purchases of Chinese crude oil at 8.8–8.9 million tons per year and coal at 3.7–4.5 million tons per year. In return, Japan is to provide $8 billion in technology and equipment (including construction equipment) to China.[8]

With such vital strategic and economic motivations, the Japanese Government took the lead in cultivating expanded economic intercourse with China, most visibly through the extension to China of Japanese Overseas Development Assistance. In the realm of government-to-government assistance, Japan has been China's primary beneficiary, providing 75.2 per cent of all the overseas development assistance China received in 1986. From 1982 to 1986 China was the recipient of a largest share of Japan's total overseas development assistance, and in 1987 it was the second largest recipient.

Since 1979, the Japanese Government has provided China with a series of low-interest loan packages for development projects. The first package ran from 1980 to 1984 and amounted to $1.5 billion. A second package of government loans worth $2.1 billion extended from 1984 to 1987, with an additional $670 million being extended in 1987. In addition, Japan provided some $4.4 billion in EXIM Bank credits between 1979 and 1984. These credits helped to finance a number of industrial projects as well as the development of coal and oil extraction projects.[9] Those projects were especially important to the Japanese Government in its effort to diversify its energy supply sources as a hedge against further instability and supply disruptions from the Middle East. In 1988, a $6.1 billion government loan package was announced to finance 42 specific economic development projects between 1990 and 1995. Included among these were a number of major infrastructure projects such as roads, dams, port facilities, communications networks and power plants in remote provinces such as Yunnan and Hainan Island.[10] This package was shelved in the aftermath of Tiananmen Square, and it was not until the G-7 meeting in Houston in July of 1990 that these loans were partially unfrozen.[11]

With the official encouragement of both governments and the financial backing of the Japanese Government, bilateral trade has grown steadily and dramatically since the normalization of relations in 1972 (see Table 10.1). From a total of $811 million in 1970, two-way trade grew to $5.08 billion by 1978. In the aftermath of the Long-Term Trade Agreement between the two nations in 1978, trade flows doubled again by 1981, reaching $10.4 billion for that year. Following a brief downturn in 1982–83, the growth in bilateral trade resumed for most of the decade, reaching nearly $19 billion in 1985 and levelling off at $19.7 billion in 1989.[12] Although there was a decline in Sino–Japanese trade flows in the aftermath of the Tiananmen Square massacre, the volume remained above $18 billion for 1990, and it is likely that the previous peak volume (reached in 1989) will be surpassed soon.[13]

Table 10.1   Japanese trade with China, 1972–90

Year	Exports to China	Imports from China	Total	Balance
1972	608.9	491.1	1 100.0	117.8
1973	1 039.5	974.0	2 013.5	65.6
1974	1 984.5	1 304.8	3 289.3	679.7
1975	2 258.6	1 531.1	3 789.7	727.5
1976	1 662.6	1 370.9	3 033.5	291.7
1977	1 938.6	1 546.9	3 485.5	391.7
1978	3 048.7	2 030.3	5 079.0	1 018.4
1979	3 698.7	2 954.8	6 653.5	743.9
1980	5 078.3	4 323.4	9 401.7	754.9
1981	5 097.2	5 291.8	10 389.0	−194.6
1982	3 510.8	5 352.4	8 863.2	−1 841.6
1983	4 912.3	5 087.4	9 999.7	−175.1
1984	7 216.7	5 957.6	13 174.3	1 259.1
1985	12 477.4	6 482.7	18 960.1	5 994.7
1986	9 856.2	5 652.4	15 508.6	4 203.8
1987	8 249.8	7 401.4	15 651.2	848.4
1988	9 476.0	9 858.8	19 334.8	−382.8
1989	8 515.9	11 145.8	19 661.7	−2 629.9
1990	6 129.6	12 053.5	18 183.1	5 923.9

Source: Tomozo Morino, 'China–Japan Trade and Investment Relations', in F.J. Macchiarola and R.B. Oxnam (eds), *The China Challenge: American Policies in East Asia* (New York: The Academy of Political Science, 1991) p. 88.

Despite the growth in bilateral trade, this relationship has not been without its problems. China has frequently complained about both the persistence of its trade deficit with Japan and the structure of the trade relationship, especially the preponderance of commodities in China's exports to Japan in contrast with Japan's high proportion of industrial goods and manufactured consumer goods in its mix of exports to China. In response to these complaints, the Japanese Government has taken steps to increase the share of manufactured goods in Japan's imports from China. Between 1985 and 1988, the share of manufactured goods in Japan's total imports rose from 31 per cent to 48.1 per cent (the result of yen appreciation and international pressures on Japan to reduce trade barriers). Other Asian nations besides China have been among the prime beneficiaries of this growth in manufactured imports. However, the share of manufactures in China's exports to Japan rose by 74 per cent during the period.[14]

The Japanese private sector has followed the lead of the Japanese Government in expanding its investment relations with China. Shortly after the signing of the Sino–Japanese Treaty of Peace and Friendship, a consortium of Japanese commercial banks extended an $8 billion package of short-term and medium-term credits to China. In 1985, an additional $2 billion package of in medium-term credits was extended by a similar consortium.[15]

Throughout this period Japanese firms have served as China's most important source of imported industrial plants and technology. Japanese firms won 59 per cent of the total plant and technology contracts for the first half of the 1970s, and in the second half provided plant and technology for the construction of such key industrial complexes as the Baoshan Iron and Steel complex in Shanghai, the Daqing Petrochemical Complex in Heilongjiang province, the Qilu Petrochemical Complex in Shangdong province, and the Yangzi Petrochemical Complex in Jiangsu province.[16] From 1978 to 1988, Japanese businesses provided China with approximately 42.3 per cent of its imports of 'turnkey' plants and high technology. Japanese firms accounted for $11.6 billion of the $27.6 billion in such contracts that China signed with foreign suppliers between 1978 and 1988.[17] Japanese firms have been especially active in China's development of production capacity in steel, petrochemicals and consumer electrical appliances. Japanese firms have been the major suppliers of the equipment and managerial expertise needed for China to retool large portions of its existing industrial plant. By 1988, Japanese firms were involved in 188 such renovation and retooling projects in China, many of which produced consumer goods for Chinese markets.[18]

Japanese firms have been among the most frequent participants in the expansion of joint ventures with the Chinese Government. Japanese overseas investment in general has been increasing since the Plaza Accord of 1985 devalued the dollar and eventually raised the value of the yen by almost 50 per cent. One way to deal with this 'yen shock' has been to shift production to lower cost sites in Asia. JETRO reported that in ·1989 alone Japanese investment in Asia grew by almost 110 per cent; in China it increased five-fold over the total for the previous year.[19] Japanese investment in China in 1988 totalled $380 million, and more than 80 per cent of all private and government loans to China originated in Tokyo.[20] As of September 1988, Japanese firms were involved in some 588 joint ventures in China, with a total investment of $2.77 billion. This commitment made Japan the third largest investor in China, trailing only the USA and Hong Kong.[21] The 1988 loan package from the Japanese Government was designed specifically to create a more favourable environment for private investment and joint ventures involving Japanese firms.

At the same time, it would be a mistake to portray Sino–Japanese relations as exclusively positive. The same decade that saw the rapid expansion of economic and political cooperation between the two nations also witnessed periodic conflicts and setbacks in bilateral relations that, in the eyes of some analysts, belie a profound underlying tension in Sino–Japanese relations that is deeply rooted historically and culturally. Indeed, Alan Whiting has gone so far as to argue that 'improvements in Sino–Japanese economic relations have often coincided with a deterioration in political relations'.[22] We turn now to a discussion of these tensions. If the strategic and economic incentives that motivated Japan's economic commitment to China during the 1980s have been altered with the end of the Cold War and the emergence of trade blocs in Europe and North America, then we must ask ourselves whether this commitment has, in the process, been rendered more susceptible to disruption by the kinds of issues that created periodic conflicts in Sino–Japanese relations during the 1980s.

RESIDUAL TENSIONS IN SINO–JAPANESE RELATIONS

The friction underlying Sino–Japanese political relations can be traced to China's historical perception of itself as the 'Central Kingdom' and, hence, the 'teacher' of Japan and the other 'student' nations of Asia. The modernization of Japan under the nineteenth-century Meiji Restoration coincided with the gradual disintegration of the Qing dynasty in China and left the once proud Central Kingdom under the domination of foreign powers, including Japan, its former tributary state. The culturally-based resentment in China over this reversal of roles in the asymmetric contemporary economic relationship between the two nations is exacerbated by Chinese enmity over their suffering at the hands of Japanese militarism during the Second World War. Most of China's current leadership experienced the hardships of Japanese occupation, and it remains a sensitive aspect of their dealings with Japan.

We can point to a number of specific incidents in which diplomatic tensions were sparked by the words or actions of key officials in the governments of China or Japan. Whiting describes a 1987 incident in which Deng Xiaoping gave a rather sternly pedantic lecture to a visiting Japanese official. This provoked the Japanese Vice-Minister of Foreign Affairs, Yanagiya Kensuke, to suggest publicly that Deng was becoming senile. The resulting diplomatic furore concluded with Mr Yanagiya taking 'early retirement' from the Ministry.[23]

The incident that provoked Deng's remarks and sparked this diplomatic flare-up was a ruling by the Osaka High Court that the Republic of China (Taiwan) was the rightful owner of a student dormitory in Kyoto that was claimed by both Taipei and Beijing. To the People's Republic, this resolution to an otherwise minor property dispute took on grave symbolic meaning as being tantamount to Japan's practising a 'two China' policy.[24]

Earlier, in 1985 Nakasone's official visit to the Yasukuni Shrine provoked student demonstrations in China protesting not only against Japan's contemporary 'economic invasion' of China but the perceived revival of Japanese militarism, as symbolized by the Prime Minister's visit to a memorial honouring Japan's war dead, including General Hideki Tojo.[25] Incidents such as this have periodically brought to the surface of Chinese politics deep resentments over the suffering and humiliation China endured as a result of Japanese expansionism and militarism in the first half of this century. Even the 1982 publication of a high-school history text that sanitized the severity of Japanese militarism during the Second World War drew official protests from the Chinese Government (as well as from the governments of other Asian nations who likewise had suffered under the domination of imperial Japan).

In 1987, the Nakasone Government increased its defence budget by 5.2 per cent to about $22 billion, breaking for the first time the informal '1 per cent of GNP' ceiling on Japanese defence spending (the total amounted to 1.004 per cent of GNP). This too drew official notice from Beijing. Chinese officials remarked that 'there has to be a limit to the growth of Japanese defence forces, which should not exceed its defence needs and make its neighbors uneasy'.[26] Deng Xiaoping reiterated China's concerns in direct talks with the Prime Minister, Noboru Takeshita, in 1987. Takeshita assured him that Japan 'will never pose a threat to neighboring countries'.[27] Since then, Japan's defence budget has fallen back below the 1 per cent ceiling, although this was a result of GNP growth that exceeded the growth in defence spending and not a consequence of any reduction in defence spending.

In 1990 Shintara Ishihara, the former Minister of Transport, said in a magazine interview that the Nanjing massacre – an incident in 1937 in which as many as 300 000 Chinese soldiers and civilians died during a six-week rampage of controlled violence and plunder by the Japanese army – was 'a lie fabricated by the Chinese'.[28] This provoked an extensive official rebuttal in *Renmin ribao*, as well as academic debates over the accuracy of the casualty count and over the validity of the rather mild treatment of the 'incident' in Japanese high-school textbooks.

In this context, it is perhaps surprising that the official Japanese reaction to the Tiananmen Square massacre was so mild and short-lived. It was not until three days after the 4 June crackdown that the Japanese Government condemned the violent repression of the pro-democracy movement, characterizing it as 'unacceptable from a humanitarian point of view'.[29] When the US Government announced on 20 June that it was suspending all high-level contacts between US officials and their Chinese counterparts, Japan followed suit by freezing the $6 billion loan package that the Takeshita Government had announced earlier. Still, Japanese leaders continued to adhere to the belief that to isolate China through severe sanctions would be more damaging to peace and stability in East Asia than would a policy premised on preserving and even enhancing China's interdependence with the developed market economies. Moreover, isolating China would only serve to strengthen the hand of the conservative faction involved in the ongoing leadership struggle in Beijing.[30] When the equally mild reaction of the Bush Administration was further undermined by the revelation that Brent Scowcroft, the National Security Advisor, and Lawrence Eagleburger, the Assistant Secretary of State, had visited China secretly in July 1989, in violation of the official US policy banning high-level contacts, the Japanese Government was free to pursue its preferred policy of keeping the door open to China. After a series of visits by both Japanese and Chinese officials, the Japanese Government finally unfroze the $6 billion loan package on 10 April 1990.[31] By 1991, the status quo ante in official relations between China and Japan was all but restored. Trade and investment flows resumed a growth trend.

TRADE BLOCS AND CHANGING JAPANESE INTERESTS IN CHINA

One might reasonably question whether this pattern of growth in Sino–Japanese economic relations will continue, given the altered strategic environment in Asia and the opening of new opportunities for Japanese trade and investment in the EC, North America, Eastern Europe and the former Soviet Union. While the Japanese Government in 1989–91 might have felt compelled to avoid isolating China for strategic reasons, the historic transformation of the security environment in Asia that resulted from the collapse of the Soviet Union necessarily alters and probably diminishes the long-term strategic importance of China to Japan's vision of a stable and secure Asia. The major threat to that stability – the Soviet Union – no longer exists as sovereign entity. Likewise, even if the Japanese Government actively supports a restoration of Sino–Japanese economic intercourse, one must ask whether for the longer term China's economic value to Japan, might diminish as a consequence of the profound structural changes occurring in the global economy upon which Japan's own further development is so heavily dependent.

We must keep in mind that the Sino–Japanese economic relationship is decidedly asymmetric: China's trade with Japan is unlikely to surpass more than 4–5 per cent of Japan's total foreign trade by end of decade, whereas Japan has consistently commanded at least one-fifth of China's total trade volume. Moreover, China's exports to Japan remain concentrated in unprocessed commodities, which are subject to replacement by alternative suppliers. For instance, over half of China's exports to Japan consists of mineral products, with oil alone accounting for over 40 per cent and coal another 4.2 per cent. Textiles make up another 15 per cent of China's exports to Japan, and agricultural commodities comprise most of the remainder. Virtually all of these categories of goods are easily replaceable on world markets. China's exports comprise only 4.4 per cent of Japan's total imports of coal and only 5.2 per cent of its crude oil and refined petroleum products imports.[32] Thus, China's share of these commodities is easily replaceable. Moreover, Japan's strategy of reducing its dependence on fossil fuels and diversifying its sources (now including joint resource development projects with Russia) makes it clear that this component of China's exports will probably diminish in volume and in importance to Japan. The further modernization of China's own economy and the depletion of easily extracted energy resources will also reduce the availability of coal and oil for export.[33]

The Japanese business community might have been loath to impose harsh sanctions on China in 1989 for fear of the repercussions for the substantial amount of existing Japanese private investment in China and current or pending trade contracts with Chinese enterprises. After all, Japan had invested $380 million in China during 1988 alone, and total Japanese investment in China came to $2.6 billion by the end of 1989.[34] China's foreign debt is estimated to have reached $49 billion in 1989, with foreign exchange reserves amounting to only $17.5 billion.[35] Thus China was already faced with the likelihood of a serious repayment crisis at some point in the next decade, and a substantial proportion of that foreign debt is owed to the Japanese Government or Japanese banks. The events of June 1989 found Japan with its financial sector exposed. Japanese banks did not want their government to impose sanctions that might incite the Chinese Government to retaliate by delaying payments on loans, defaulting or taking other measures that might jeopardize Japan's public and private financial commitments in China.

The 'adjustment programme' that China implemented after the Tiananmen Square massacre affected Japanese firms negatively. It curtailed credit availability to Chinese enterprises, including those with Japanese partners. The result was the cancellation or postponement of several projects, including several in which Japanese firms were involved. Although Japan's exports to China grew in the first half of 1989 at almost the same rate as imports, they fell for every month after June. The shortage of funds following China's 'readjustment' programme in the autumn of 1988 weakened demand, and the state imposed further restraints on imports through the recentralization of importing authority. This resulted in a sharp decline in Japanese exports of consumer durables to China during in the second half of 1989.[36]

By 1991, the momentum for economic liberalization that had been curtailed in the immediate aftermath of Tiananmen Square seemed to be returning. Foreign banks were allowed to open branches in Guangzhou, Dalian and Tianjin. The government undertook policy reforms to bring China in closer compliance with GATT regulations in order to enhance its prospects for membership in GATT. The renewed efforts at reform began to pay off, as the total value of foreign investment contracts in 1991 rose 47 per cent over the previous year's total to $17.8 billion. In the first quarter of 1992, the value of new contracts was $6.54 billion, an increase of 140 per cent over the first quarter of 1991.[37]

However, having suffered through yet another Chinese 'readjustment', the Japanese private sector may not be as anxious to commit itself over the long term to the same or increasing levels of investment capital as before Tiananmen Square. Likewise, Japanese firms may view the opportunity costs and risks to investment differently in the aftermath of Tiananmen Square, especially in the context of the emergence of new opportunities in North America, the EC, Eastern Europe and the CIS. It is perhaps noteworthy that, despite the return to liberalization on the part of the Chinese Government, Japan's share of China's total trade dropped from 16.9 per cent in 1989 to 14.4 per cent in 1990, and experienced no recovery in 1991. In contrast, Hong Kong increased its share of China's total trade from 30.9 per cent in 1989 to 36.6 per cent in 1991, and the US share actually rose during 1989 (over the 1988 figure) and experienced little if any decline or increase in the aftermath of Tiananmen Square.[38]

In assessing the impact of changes in Japan's international environment on its willingness to continue its relationship with China at the level that evolved during the last decade, it would perhaps be wise to maintain the distinction between the Japanese Government's willingness to continue its support of China's development efforts and the Japanese private sector's interest in China as a business partner. As Alan Whiting notes, the geopolitical and strategic interests that led the Japanese Government to treat China as being too large and important to ignore or isolate do not apply to the Japanese private sector, which responds more strictly to considerations of risk and profit.[39] These two sets of actors in Japan are thus motivated by different interests in their dealings with China, and they will respond differently both to political turmoil and economic uncertainty in China and to the transformations of the global economic environment brought about by the emergence of trade blocs in Europe and North America and by the availability of Eastern Europe as an alternative partner in trade and investment.

Private Sector Interests in China

The Japanese private sector appears to be less sanguine than its government about the long-term stability of the Chinese modernization programme. Likewise, they find less credible any long-term commitments by the Chinese Government or private interests with whom they negotiate agreements. Their willingness to invest or commit themselves to long-term contracts with China is tempered by a number of business considerations. China lacks a stable currency, and it cannot guarantee firms access to the foreign exchange needed to purchase equipment and spare parts abroad. Japanese firms must cope with a huge, complex bureaucracy that is rife with corruption and prone to periodic policy swings in the extent and forms of the control that the state exerts over the economy. There has been a rise in corruption during the 1980s, as Chinese officials extort bribes or kickbacks in exchange for their approval of lucrative contracts with foreign firms. Japanese businesses executives complain about the 'invisible fees' that result from various forms of state intervention in commercial transactions. Managers of Japanese factories lack complete control over hiring and firing of workers. Ownership issues and managerial control of enterprises are both subject to the shifting tides of the policy struggles between conservative and reformist factions in the ageing Chinese leadership, as are questions of the repatriation of profits and state-imposed limits on access to (and use of) foreign exchange.

The Japanese business community's concern about the reliability of China as a business partner and about the risks inherent in the periodic policy retrenchments in Beijing are compounded by the inadequacy of China's infrastructure – especially communications and transportation – to support industrial investment and by the uncertainty that prevails with respect to the supply, cost and quality of locally-sourced raw materials and other production inputs. Foreign investors of all nationalities have also expressed disappointment with the amount of access to domestic markets they are permitted. Finally, Japanese businessmen complain about the exorbitant price of office space and living costs in China.[40] MITI reported in 1988 that so far only 10 per cent of the 360 Sino–Japanese joint ventures could be deemed profitable.[41] Whiting and Xin report that a survey of 159 Japanese firms operating in China found that 42 per cent reported being negatively affected by the changing business and political climate following the Tiananmen massacre.[42]

The Japanese private sector has consistently demonstrated less willingness to make long-term commitments in China, at least compared to the Japanese Government. Several times during the post-Mao era, the Japanese business community has been burned by unanticipated disruptions in the Chinese economy that redounded on the value of their investments in China. The wave of trade and investment expansion that followed the signing of the 1978 Long-Term Trade Agreement came to a sudden halt as a consequence of China's 'adjustment' policies of 1981. These adjustments included suspension of payment on a number of large Japanese contracts, cancellation of others, and scaling back a number of major joint venture projects, including the notorious Baoshan steel complex.[43] Between 1981 and 1985, China's 'economic adjustment' policy meant that plant and technology contracts dropped to less than $5 billion, or about half of the level of the previous five years. Moreover, American and Western European firms began to compete more actively for these contracts, with the result that Japan's share of plant and technology contracts declined to 24 per cent over the course of the 1980s.

Beginning in 1985, the Chinese Government began relaxing restrictions on foreign investment. Prior to Tiananmen Square, the Chinese Government had embarked upon an extensive effort to improve the business environment in China and thereby to make it more attractive to foreign investors. Over 200 pieces of legislation had been issued by Chinese officials to regularize investment and tax procedures. Some 22 bilateral investment agreements had been made with 23 different countries. China extended especially favourable treatment to Japan when in August 1987 its Premier, Li Peng, signed an agreement with Takeshita that offered to Japanese firms the same protections and legal treatment for their investments as those available to Chinese investments. No other nation's investments enjoy this status.[44]

By end of 1988, 15 000 ventures with foreign capital had been approved by the Chinese Government with a contract value of FDI in China reaching $28.2 billion, of which $11.59 billion was in paid-in capital.[45] In 1988 alone, the Chinese Government approved a record 5903 foreign-invested enterprises, worth $2.6 billion. This represented a 260 per cent increase over 1987 and a 59 per cent increase over the total for the previous eight years. It made China the site of the largest volume of foreign investment in Asia for that year.[46]

Despite the resurgence of plant and technology contracts between 1985 and 1988, Japan's share continued to decline, to 16.6 per cent for the period 1985–88 and to 7.7 per cent in 1988.[47] Prior to Tiananmen Square, the Chinese Government had already begun expressing grave concerns about their persistent trade deficit with Japan. In the aftermath of Tiananmen Square, they took unilateral steps to remedy the situation by restricting imports and recentralizing the authority over imports. As a consequence, Japanese private interests have shown a tendency since then to channel their capital into short-term service industries such as hotels, restaurants and electronic assembly plants. Even these have fallen victim to renewed concerns about the security of investments in China. A number of Japanese-owned plants temporarily shut down operations during the turmoil of June 1989, including Sanyo Electronics in Beijing and Yokogawa Electric in Xian. NEC and Canon closed operations in Beijing, and Koito suspended operations at its Shanghai plant. Indeed, perhaps as much as half of the Japanese firms pulled out their expatriate staff until order could be restored. When the USA asked Japan to observe COCOM rules on technology transfer to China more stringently, Matsushita Electric's efforts to co-produce videocassette recorders with China had to be suspended.[48] Finally, public opinion in Japan appears to be taking a negative turn towards China. A 1989 survey indicated that 43 per cent responded negatively to whether they had friendly feelings towards China (up from 26 per cent in 1988), and 33 per cent had negative feelings on Sino–Japanese relations generally (up from 23 per cent the year before).[49]

Thus it appears that despite the resurgence of the Chinese economy in the aftermath of Tiananmen Square, there is a residue of disillusionment among the Japanese private sector that may dampen their willingness to participate in and contribute to the further development of the Chinese economy. The periodic policy swings that affect their ability to import production inputs and their autonomy over enterprise management (among other things), as well as the growing negative sentiments among the Japanese public towards China, combine to make it less attractive as an investment and trading partner.

These sentiments, determined by conventional business considerations of risk and opportunity, are further exacerbated by the emergence of new opportunities and challenges to Japanese market shares in North America and Europe, which are more important by far to the Japanese private sector. The appeal of China as a partner in business ventures must now also be assessed in comparison to the newly emerging opportunities in Eastern Europe and the former Soviet Union as well. For these reasons, we can expect the Japanese private sector's assessment of China to be altered by events not only within China, but also in Europe and North America. Increasingly, the limits of their willingness to invest in and trade with China will be defined by the extent to which the Japanese Government, through its overseas assistance programmes and other financial instruments, is willing to insure them against the risks inherent in doing business with China. We turn now to an assessment of changes in the Japanese Government's interests in China and how these interests have been altered by the same events both there and in the global economy.

Government Interests in China

The motivations underlying the Japanese Government's policy towards China have been grounded in geopolitical and strategic considerations, with support for China's economic modernization being the instrument by which to advance those strategic interests. As was discussed earlier, the primary motivation behind the Japanese Government's cultivation of ties with China has been the desire to strengthen the latter's interdependence with the developed democracies so as to pre-empt the re-emergence of a Sino–Soviet alliance. With the relentless Soviet military build-up in Asia under Brezhnev, a demilitarized Japan found it prudent to hedge against the tensions in its military alliance with the USA by cultivating China as a mainland counterweight against the mounting Soviet threat.

In addition, we have noted that the Japanese Government was actively engaged in diversifying its sources of energy as a hedge against future oil shocks. China became a prime target for Japanese development assistance aimed at expanding China's energy production for export. As we have seen, the Japanese private sector has been an active partner with the government in these energy development projects, with Japanese firms serving as the prime (if not sole) contractors hired with the credits provided by the Japanese Government. Japanese firms have been major participants in the development of coal mines in the Shanxi, Shandong and Hubei provinces as well as the many infrastructure projects (road, rail and port facilities) needed to support these extractive operations in interior provinces. Japanese oil companies have been the recipient of many of the Japanese Government-financed offshore oil and gas exploration projects.[50] However, the limits of Japanese private sector involvement in these projects has always been defined by the extent of Japanese Government financing of these projects.

Beyond this, the prospect of economic development in a market of over one billion potential customers was sufficient for the Japanese Government to enlist the support of its private sector in service of its China policy. The series of generous loans and credits extended to China by the Japanese Government, beginning in 1978, was intended to create an environment in which the Japanese private sector would find it profitable to do business with China. In other words, government support of expanded economic ties with China was intended to overcome, at least in part, many of the infrastructure, regulatory and market weaknesses that otherwise would have deterred Japanese firms from doing business with China on purely economic grounds.

As a consequence of these differing motivations, the Japanese Government demonstrated an obvious reluctance to join in the international criticism of China following Tiananmen Square. In contrast to the flood of official condemnations and economic sanctions from other world capitals, the government of Japan was far more cautious in its expression of criticism and far more reluctant to initiate sanctions. Its Prime Minister, Sosuke Uno, explained this reaction by arguing, 'Japan invaded China forty years ago. Japan cannot do anything against a people who experienced such a war. Sino–Japanese relations differ from Sino–United States relations.'[51] One might also note that, in the aftermath of revelations of secret meetings between Chinese leaders and officials of the Bush Administration, and the later unwillingness of the Bush Administration to initiate additional sanctions or accept those enacted or recommended by Congress, perhaps Mr Uno may have overstated the difference, at least as far as the Bush Administration was concerned.

The question today is whether the Sino–Japanese relationship will continue on the same expansive course that has characterized bilateral relations for the past fifteen years, or will the changed international environment – the emergence of major trade blocs in North American and the EC, the collapse of Communism in Eastern Europe and the disintegration of the

Soviet Union – combined with the instability and uncertainty in the Chinese domestic environment – the cyclical crises in the Chinese economy, the intra-elite struggles over development strategy and economic policy, and the additional economic and strategic uncertainties that will assuredly emerge with the imminent leadership transition – so alter the strategic interests of the Japanese Government that it will be tempted to shift attention and resources elsewhere?

First, the collapse of the Soviet Union has meant the evaporation of Japan's major strategic motivation underlying its policy of cultivating ties with China. The Soviet Union no longer exists as a military threat to Japan. The Russian Federation, inheritor of most if not all of the Soviet military forces arrayed in East Asia, will not be able to maintain force levels or capabilities at nearly the level of the former Soviet Union. Furthermore it is apparent that the government of the Russian Federation is more interested in cultivating economic ties with Japan than it is in trying in vain to maintain the preponderant military force in the region. Indeed, the prospects for some sort of breakthrough on the Northern Territories issue, the traditional stumbling block to Soviet–Japanese relations, appear to be constrained more by Boris Yeltsin's fear of undermining the increasingly fragile coalition for his domestic reforms that by any continued Russian concern with the strategic value of the four disputed islands.

With the demise of the Soviet Union as a security threat in Asia, Japan has less interest in building a strong China to serve as the mainland counterweight to Soviet expansionism. Indeed, China's recent use of force in seizing the disputed Spratly Islands in the South China Sea may raise a new set of concerns in Tokyo: a strengthened China unconstrained by the Soviet Union may come to replace the Soviet Union as the greatest threat to a stable security environment in East Asia. In March of 1988 China used its naval forces to seize the Spratly Islands in the South China Sea. The seabed surrounding the Spratly and Paracel island groups is rich in resources, including petroleum, but is subject to competing claims by seven Asia–Pacific states: Brunei, China, Indonesia, Malaysia, the Philippines, Taiwan and Vietnam. The fact that China used military force unilaterally to settle this dispute should be cause for some concern in Tokyo about the value of a militarily revived China, unchecked by the Soviet Union. At the very least, the Japanese Government may find it prudent to re-evaluate its support of Chinese modernization in the light of the diminished Russian threat and the new opportunities and risks for Japan's position in the global economy that are emerging with the creation of the North American and European trade blocs, as well as the transition to market economies in much of Eastern Europe and the former Soviet Union.

Second, as we have seen, the importance of China as a source of energy has diminished over the course of the last decade. Japan has diversified its energy sources during the 1980s and reduced its dependence on oil by substituting coal, gas and nuclear power as fuels for electric power generation.[52] The fact that China resorted to arms to enforce its claims to the disputed Spratly Islands will probably diminish the willingness of Japan to undertake joint energy development projects with them, if for no other reason than the fear of offending other nations which have claims to the disputed territory and are also suppliers of petroleum to Japan. With new opportunities for joint energy development opening up with Russia, it seems less likely that the Japanese Government will seek expansion of their partnership in China's energy development when China has shown itself willing to risk a military confrontation with other nations in order to extend its claims to additional oil reserves. In time, the risks that accompany Japanese investment in Chinese energy production should direct Japanese attention to safer opportunities emerging elsewhere in the Pacific Basin.

TRADE BLOCS AND THE FUTURE OF JAPAN'S RELATIONS WITH CHINA

With the erosion of Japan's strategic interests in contributing to China's development, we would expect the government's decisions on all forms of development assistance to China to be based increasingly on questions of profitability for the Japanese private sector. Certainly other opportunities for such assistance are emerging in Eastern Europe and the former Soviet Union. Whether they are deemed to be potentially more lucrative than China remains to be seen, but in 1989 they did not even exist as alternatives to compete with China for Japanese development assistance. Furthermore, the Japanese Government must consider how trade blocs in North America and Europe will affect the interests of the Japanese private sector in these markets. The resources required to assist Japanese businesses in maintaining their competitive position in these markets will probably take priority over claims for assistance to the Chinese economy, since the North American and European markets are far more lucrative and far more critical to Japan's continued economic prosperity and position in the global economy than is the China market. Eastern Europe may become especially attractive as a site for investment in production facilities for goods destined for the single market of the newly integrated EC. Proximity to the EC, the quality of the Eastern European labour force (compared to China's), and the more developed (compared the China) infrastructure of Poland, Hungary and the

CSFR should make them strong competitors with China for Japanese private investment.

This same logic applies to Japan's willingness to expand further its FDI in China. The risks to such investment are non-trivial and the pay-offs, while lucrative during the 1980s, may become relatively less attractive compared to new opportunities emerging in Eastern Europe and the former Soviet Union. Japanese investment in China must also now be evaluated against the added pressure to increase investment in North American and the EC as a hedge against possible protectionist barriers to these two markets and increased competition for market share from within each of the blocs. The Japanese business community may have been burned one time too many by the periodic 'readjustment' programmes of the Chinese Government. Consequently, their interest in China may extend no further than the limits of the Japanese Government's financial guarantees: that is, loans and credits from the Japanese Government may do no more than define the upper limits of the Japanese private sector's commitment to China; they will not serve as the catalyst for a burgeoning private sector commitment that develops a self-sustaining momentum of its own.

The other leg of Japan's 'grand design' with respect to China involved trade. Increasingly, however, Japan has been under pressure from the People's Republic to reduce its trade surplus with China. In compliance, the Japanese Government has taken steps to shift the balance of trade in favour of China and to alter the structure of trade by increasing the share of manufactured goods in its imports from China. When Japan's actions have proven insufficient to satisfy the Chinese leadership, Beijing has demonstrated a willingness to take steps of its own to alter the trade balance by restricting imports from Japan and cancelling, delaying, or scaling down contracts with Japanese firms to supply equipment for major Chinese industrial projects.

With the emergence of trade blocs in North America and Europe, and the emergence of new markets in Eastern Europe and the former Soviet Union, one must question how long Japan will be willing to run an artificially induced trade deficit with China or continue to finance Chinese infrastructure projects in order to create a more favourable investment climate for Japanese private firms. Prior to 1991 the primary motivations for Japan to accommodate China's demands were geopolitical. With the demise of the Soviet Union, those motives have largely dissolved. Thus the willingness of the Japanese Government to accommodate China on such matters is now more strictly economic. Japan's interests in China have lost the 'special' character that Cold War strategic concerns imparted to Japan's China policy. Now China must compete with Japan's other trading partners for the attention of the Japanese Government, and it must do so on strictly economic grounds.

The uncertainty surrounding the benefits of expanded Japanese economic intercourse with China seems to be increasing rather than diminishing with the resumption of rapid growth in the Chinese economy. These uncertainties were magnified by the power struggle surrounding the Tiananmen Square incident and the imminence of a major leadership transition in China. The fact that China represents such a small share of Japan's total trade may work to China's advantage in the sense that the threats to Japan's overall international trade position posed by a trade deficit with China pale in comparison to the risks Japan faces to its market shares and export volumes in North America and the EC. By the same token, however, trade with China is not sufficient to offset any potential losses of market share in North American and Western Europe either. As alluded to earlier, the one billion consumers in China have yet to develop into a lucrative market for Japanese exports, and the Chinese Government is clearly willing to restrict the flow of Japanese products available to them in the interest of its own trade balance. So far, Japanese consumers have not demonstrated an appetite for Chinese manufactured goods, and with Japan increasing its imports of manufactured goods from the Asian NIEs, Chinese goods face stiff competition for a share of the Japanese market when the access it is granted is based more exclusively on economic considerations. Finally, the Spratly Islands incident indicates that China could replace the Soviet Union as the primary security threat to stability in the Pacific Basin.

CONCLUSION

For much of the past decade, cultivating closer and more diverse economic ties with China has been a major priority of the Japanese government. Strategic interests – specifically, the containment of the Soviet Union – were the major motivation underlying these interests, and government support for rapidly expanded trade and investment with China on the part of the Japanese private sector was the major policy instrument by which these interests were served. With the collapse of the Soviet Union and the shift to market economies and democratic governments in the republics of the former Soviet Union and Eastern Europe, the major strategic threat that motivated Japan's China policy dissolved. While China remains an attractive overseas site for Japanese-owned production facilities (owing to the low production costs), the economic advantages to investment in and trade with China have always been tempered by the risks of periodic policy swings by the Chinese Government. It has been argued that, in addition to these risks associated with doing business with China, the emergence of trade blocs in North America and Western Europe as well as the opening of new opportunities in Eastern Europe and several of the republics of the former Soviet Union have altered the opportunity structure for Japanese businesses in such a way that the relative attractiveness of China as a site for overseas investment and as a partner in trade relations has diminished. The uncertainty surrounding the imminent leadership transition in China, and the disturbing evidence from the 1989 Tiananmen Square incident and the Spratly Islands incident of China's willingness to use force against its neighbours and its own citizens, should further diminish the willingness of the Japanese Government and private sector to accept the risks that have accompanied business transactions with China for the past fifteen years. The extent to which these factors will actually reduce the volume of economic intercourse between Japan and China remains to be seen, and the remarkably high rates of growth in the Chinese economy certainly represent a powerful force to offset, at least partially, these risks as well as the competition from alternative opportunities emerging in North America, the EC, Eastern Europe and the former Soviet Union. However, the conventional wisdom that China's consistently high growth rates promise to make it the economic miracle of the 1990s may be a bit too sanguine when considered in the context of the profound changes in the structure of the global economy represented by the emergence of trade blocs in North America and Western Europe and the emergence of market economies in Eastern Europe and the former Soviet Union.

Notes

1.   Tomozo Morino, 'China–Japan Trade and Investment Relations', in F.J. Macchiarola and R.B. Oxnam (eds), *The China Challenge: American Policies in East Asia* (New York: The Academy of Political Science, 1991) p. 88.
2.   Harry Harding, *China's Second Revolution: Reform After Mao* (Washington, DC: Brookings, 1987) pp. 147–8.
3.   See T. David Mason, 'US–Japan Security Cooperation amid the Shifting Security Environment in Asia', pp. 158–92 in T.D. Mason and A.M. Turay (eds), *US–Japan Trade Friction: Its Impact on Security Cooperation in the Pacific Basin* (London: Macmillan, 1991) for an elaboration of this thesis; see also Christopher Howe, 'China, Japan, and Economic Interdependence in the Asia Pacific Region', *China Quarterly*, 124 (December 1990) pp. 676–80.
4.   Ibid, p. 676; for a more extensive case study of the restoration of Sino–Japanese relations, see Haruhiro Fukui, 'Tanaka Goes to Peking: A Case

Study in Foreign Policy-Making', in T.J. Pempel (ed.), *Policymaking in Contemporary Japan* (Ithaca, NY: Cornell University Press, 1977).

5. See Yasuo Imai, 'Energy Cooperation between the US and Japan', in Mason and Turay, *US–Japan Trade Friction*, pp. 78–87; Ronald Morse, 'Energy Cooperation and the Future of US–Japan Security Relations', in Mason and Turay, *US–Japan Trade Friction*, pp. 67–77.

6. Shigeru Ishikawa, 'Sino–Japanese Economic Co-operation', *China Quarterly*, 109 (March 1987) p. 7; Howe, 'China, Japan', p. 676.

7. Morino, 'China–Japan Trade', p. 90.

8. Allen S. Whiting, 'China and Japan: Politics Versus Economics', *Annals of the American Academy of Political and Social Science*, 519 (January 1992) p. 42.

9. Hong-nack Kim, 'Perspectives on Sino–Japanese Relations', *The Journal of East Asian Affairs*, 4 (Summer/Autumn 1990) p. 405.

10. Uldis Kruze, 'Sino-Japanese Relations', *Current History*, 90 (April 1991) p. 157.

11. Kim, 'Perspectives', p. 405; Morino, 'China–Japan Trade', p. 90.

12. Harding, *China's Second Revolution*, pp. 147–8; Morino, 'China–Japan Trade', p. 90.

13. Whiting, 'China and Japan', p. 41.

14. Howe, 'China, Japan', p. 683; see also Chapter 8 in this book.

15. Kim, 'Perspectives', p. 405.

16. Yoichi Yokoi, 'Plant and Technology Contracts and the Changing Pattern of Economic Interdependence Between China and Japan', *China Quarterly*, 124 (December 1990) pp. 698; see also Ishikawa, 'Sino–Japanese Economic Co-operation', pp. 8–11.

17. Kim, 'Perspectives', pp. 405–6.

18. Ibid, p. 406; see also Ishikawa, 'Sino–Japanese Economic Co-operation', pp. 14–16.

19. Kruze, 'Sino–Japanese Relations', p. 156.

20. Ibid, p. 156.

21. Kim, 'Perspectives', p. 407.

22. Allen S. Whiting and Xin Jianfei, 'Sino–Japanese Relations: Pragmatism and Passion', *World Policy Journal*, 8 (Winter 1990) p. 107; see also Allen S. Whiting, *China Eyes Japan* (Berkeley, CA: University of California Press, 1989) for a more thorough elaboration of the roots of this tension.

23. Ibid, p. 157.

24. Kim, 'Perspectives', pp. 411–12; see also Hidenori Ijiri, 'Sino–Japanese Controversy since the 1972 Diplomatic Normalization', *China Quarterly*, 124 (December 1990) pp. 652–6.

25. Ibid, pp. 648–652; Kim, 'Perspectives', p. 410.

26. Quoted from Kim, 'Perspectives', p. 411; see Hua Xin, 'Defence Budget Stirs Controversy', *Beijing Review* (19 January 1987) p. 12.

27. Kim, 'Perspectives', p. 411.

28. Quoted in Whiting, 'China and Japan', p. 45.

29. Quoted in Kim, 'Perspectives', 418.

30. Ibid, pp. 420–2.

31. Ibid, p. 432.

32. Dick K. Nanto and Hong Nack Kim, 'Sino–Japanese Economic Relations', pp. 453–71 in Joint Economic Committee of the Congress of the United

States, *China's Economy Looks Toward the Year 200, Vol. 2: Economic Openness in Modernizing China* (Washington, DC: US Government Printing Office, 1986) pp. 460–2.
33. Whiting, 'China and Japan', p. 41.
34. Kruze, 'Sino-Japanese Relations', p. 156; Morino, 'China–Japan Trade', p. 93.
35. Ijiri, 'Sino–Japanese Controversy', p. 659.
36. Denis Fred Simon, 'After Tiananmen: What is the Future for Foreign Business in China?' *California Management Review*, 32 (1990) pp. 111–13.
37. Thomas R. Gottschang, 'The Economy's Continued Growth', *Current History*, 91 (September 1992) pp. 268–9.
38. Ibid, p. 269.
39. Whiting, 'China and Japan', p. 43.
40. Simon, 'After Tiananmen', p. 112.
41. Kruze, 'Sino–Japanese Relations', p. 157.
42. Whiting and Xin, 'Sino–Japanese Relations', pp. 109–11.
43. See Howe, 'China, Japan', pp. 676–7.
44. Kruze, 'Sino–Japanese Relations', p. 157.
45. Simon, 'After Tiananmen', pp. 106–7.
46. Ibid, p. 111.
47. Yokoi, 'Plant and Technology Contracts', p. 698.
48. Kruze, 'Sino–Japanese Relations', p. 158.
49. Whiting and Xin, 'Sino–Japanese Relations', p. 111.
50. Kim, 'Perspectives', pp. 406–7.
51. *Asahi shimbun*, 7 June 1989; quoted in Ijiri, 'Sino–Japanese Controversy', p. 656.
52. Morse, 'Energy Cooperation', p. 74; see also Imai, 'Energy Cooperation'.

11 Can Japan Lead in the International System?[1]

Kenneth B. Pyle

In the late twentieth century, it has become fashionable to write of long cycles in history, the rise and fall of the great powers, the passing of hegemonies, and the dynamics of change in the international political economy. This is doubtless a reflection of major structural changes that are thought to be imminent in international politics. As much as any factor, the emergence of Japanese economic power is responsible for this phenomenon.

The role that Japan will play in the future of the international system is a subject of mounting interest. It is widely asserted that through its export of goods and capital and through its scientific and technological creativity, Japan has the potential to play the role of a world leader. Moreover, the obligation of Japan to 'share the burden' of leadership of the liberal international economic system is also widely asserted. But questions immediately arise. What evidence is there that this potential will be realized in the near future? Are Japanese leaders formulating a new foreign policy to reflect its growing potential influence? Are there forces in Japanese society of sufficient strength to bring about a reorientation of its mercantilist policies of the past? Is a free trade coalition taking shape that can provide a new direction? Or will it continue to require outside pressures to overcome the legacy of these past policies? What, in short, are the prospects that Japan can fashion a new foreign policy consensus that would support a role of international leadership?

This chapter examines the effort of the Japanese elites during the past decade to prepare Japan to play the role of an international leader by defining a Japanese national purpose that is broader and more inclusive than the narrow mercantilist view of the Japanese role that has prevailed since the end of the Occupation. Their view is that, having caught up with the West and having a confident vision of Japan's future economic and technological prowess, Japan's own interests will no longer be served by pursuit of mercantilist policies, or even by passive acceptance of and adjustment to prevailing international conditions. This new world view, as expounded by some of Japan's most prominent leaders, rests on the belief that so great is

219

Japan's stake in the international political-economic order, owing to its export of goods and capital, that now more than ever before to be a Japanese nationalist is to be an internationalist.

THE 'NEW INTERNATIONALISM' IN JAPAN

There are three fundamental tenets of this new internationalism: (1) it is in Japan's national interest to give support and leadership to the institutions of a liberal international economic order; (2) Japan must of its own initiative and to its own advantage reform its institutions to bring them into harmony with international norms and expectations; and (3) the Japanese must develop a global consciousness and a liberal nationalism which, while taking pride in their own heritage, is open to and tolerant of other nationalities and cultures.

On the face of it, the notion of a genuine Japanese internationalism must evoke scepticism. Nothing stirs greater exasperation from foreign observers of Japan, even those who have devoted their careers to understanding Japanese culture, than Japanese parochialism. Edward Seidensticker wrote in his last column for the *Yomiuri* in 1962, '[The Japanese] are not like other people. They are infinitely more clannish, insular, parochial, and one owes it to one's self-respect to preserve a feeling of outrage at the insularity.'[2] Ambassador Reischauer was of the same mind. He wrote in 1978, '[The Japanese] must overcome their sense of separateness and, to put it bluntly, show a greater readiness to join the human race.'[3] Dan F. Henderson, galled by the persisting legal restrictions of this 'quasi-state-trading-regime', characterized Japan in 1986 as 'a homogenous insular enclave' whose liberal rhetoric was little more than an 'insular internationalism'.[4]

A recent series of highly publicized incidents would seem to confirm the persistent ethnocentrism of Japanese political leaders and belie an expressed commitment to a new internationalism. For example, in May 1988 the Director-General of the National Land Agency had to be dismissed from the Cabinet by Takeshita for public remarks glossing over Japanese responsibility for the invasion of China during the 1930s. Less than a year later, Takeshita himself, on the eve of Emperor Showa's funeral, expressed uncertainty about Japanese responsibility for aggression in the Second World War and was also vague as to whether Hitler's policies were aggression. Similarly, in 1986 the then Prime Minister, Nakasone, dismissed the Education Minister for arguing that the colonization of Korea had been legitimate and that the Rape of Nanking did not violate international law.[5] Nakasone himself, however, was not infrequently guilty of remarks extolling the homogeneity of the Japanese people, as in his slighting reference in 1986 to the multiracial character of American society. With little difficulty, one could multiply the examples of such insular statements by Japanese politicians. The weight of Japanese history and culture is undoubtedly on the side of a deeply ingrained and persistent ethnocentrism. Nevertheless, we need to examine the effort of the Japanese elite leadership to shape a different kind of national consensus because it represents their first attempt to adjust to changes in the international environment and to the new era that Japan confronts. During the 1980s leading members of the Japanese political, business and bureaucratic elites have sought, albeit in an often confused and contradictory fashion, to articulate a historic shift of Japan's national purpose. This shift would entail replacing Japan's traditional narrow definition of its national interests with a broader definition that recognizes Japan's own advantage in actively supporting a liberal international economic order.

To accomplish this shift of national purpose will be truly revolutionary, entailing a kind of Japanese *perestroika*, for such a shift would go contrary to the policies of the past century and the historical disposition of the Japanese people. It is by no means clear that a people can make such changes in their institutions, values and patterns of behaviour in the short run. It is not simply Japan's unique cultural identity that is an obstacle: the burden of Japan's own historical struggles to catch up with Western nations also constrains it from readily accomplishing this shift of national purpose and fulfilling the role of an international leader. For purposes of stark comparison, it may be said that America's history gave it certain natural advantages that paved the way for it to be an international leader: the universal values that came out of the American revolution, the continental abundance of resources, the geographical position that gave it free security in which to develop, and the historical struggle to assimilate different races and creeds. Ernest May wrote in the conclusion to his book on America's unplanned rise to world power at the beginning of this century, 'Some nations achieve greatness; the United States had greatness thrust upon it.'[6]

Japan's national experience has been quite the contrary. Stature among nations was a goal to be achieved; it was not bestowed. From the beginning of its modern history in 1868 Japan struggled for national power. Powerful bureaucratic structures were erected to mobilize the people and their resources for a single-minded pursuit of industry and empire. Greatness had to be achieved; it would not be thrust on Japan. Mercantilist policies to enhance state power were devised at the great expense of the Japanese people.

Japan's emergence in the 1980s as a world economic power was the outcome of this century-long all-consuming struggle. Paradoxically, however, the Japanese leaders are considering which of the policies and practices of nationalist struggle that were responsible for the successes of the past are the ones to bring success to Japan in its new circumstances. The issue for them is not whether Japan will still be nationalist and still pursue its own national interests: that, after all, is the purpose of the nation state. The issue, rather, is what form should nationalism take in the new circumstances of the late twentieth century?

As the structure of Japan's economy changed over the past several decades, and particularly since the oil shocks of the 1970s, as Japan emerged as the second biggest free market economy in the world and as its share in world trade, especially trade in manufactures, became conspicuously large, it became apparent to some Japanese leaders that Japanese prosperity was increasingly dependent upon the existence of a healthy, open free trade order. And as American commitment to a liberal international political economy showed signs of wavering, these leaders' appreciation of its benefits grew.

Fundamentally, this realization was a matter of the dramatic improvements in Japan's industrial capability and its comparative advantage. In the early post-war decades Japan's comparative advantage was in labour-intensive products that were dependent upon cheap but high-quality labour. Over time the economy was able to move ahead under the aegis of the high growth system, and by the late 1970s 'the pattern of Japan's comparative advantage shifted toward processing and assembling-type manufacturing industries that depend on mass-production methods and medium to high technologies'.[7] As the industries in which Japan had a comparative advantage moved up the product cycle and as these products gained competitiveness, Japan had less reason to oppose liberalization and correspondingly greater reason to support a liberal international order. Komiya and Itoh succinctly sum up the reasons for Japan's growing confidence:

> Japan's comparative advantage today is based on such factors as organizational and managerial skills, intelligent and cooperative labour, efficient use of information, and flexibility in shifting resources from one sector to another. Such technologies in a wider sense are of a versatile character and can be applied over a fairly wide range of manufacturing industries. It appears that Japan will lead other countries in this kind of technology and hence in a fairly wide range of sophisticated manufacturing industries for some time to come.
>
> Some such technologies can be applied to many new industries in which technological innovation is taking place or for which the world

demand is increasing rapidly, and since Japan has a severe comparative disadvantage in industries dependent on natural resources and land, free multilateral world trade will be most advantageous for Japan.[8]

In sum, to perceptive leaders of the business community and to bureaucrats in some (but by no means all) of the ministries, Japan's stake in the continuation of the international order prescribed a fundamental change in its foreign policy.

During the early 1980s such views gained ground in MITI, excluding some sections of the Ministry with jurisdiction over industries still being protected. The evolution of MITI views could be well charted by tracing the changing views of Amaya Naohiro, former vice minister for international affairs. Known for his advocacy of the *chonin kokkaron*, he signalled his change in a 1987 essay entitled 'Farewell to the Merchant Nation'.[9]

In addition to the evolution of comparative advantage, another change in the structure of the Japanese economy which favoured the new internationalism was the rapid rise in FDI after 1985, when Japan became the world's leading net creditor. The benefits of FDI for Japan included new markets, lowered production costs, the easing protectionist pressures, and the acquisition of benefits from the preferential policies of host governments. FDI required a greatly enhanced sensitivity, tact, and knowledge of foreign conditions and sensibilities. As a MITI advisory report put it:

For direct investment to remain fruitful over the long run, close relations must be maintained with local [i.e., foreign] employees, firms, and local society, and the investing firm must strive to contribute to the development of the host country. Care should be taken lest the locals feel that foreign ways are being imposed on them. If Japanese enterprises can blend into the local socioeconomic system and become an indispensable part of local society, then the host government will be much less likely to take measures prejudicial to the Japanese firms because such measures would hurt the local economy as well. Negligence in such efforts will not only increase the risk of jeopardizing the investment but will draw a dark cloud over all of the firm's activities, including exports from Japan.[10]

In short, if the vastly expanding FDI were not implemented with the utmost care and finesse it could jeopardize not only FDI but Japan's domestic economy itself.

The new internationalism gained impetus not only from the growing strength of the economy as manifested in dramatic improvements of its comparative advantage and in overseas investment, but also from a new conception of Japan's future. Japan's new internationalism is based on a confident belief that Japan is destined by its unique economic, scientific and cultural skills to be the pioneer of a new stage of technology, and this will project Japan into the role of global leadership. A tone of national pride clearly suffuses the new internationalism, as does an air of inevitability and technological determination. The 1986 MITI advisory report stated the premise: history teaches that leadership in a technological revolution also entails leadership of the international system. In the nineteenth century, England's pioneering role in the creation of steam and iron technology and its application to rail transport and oceangoing vessels laid the basis for the *Pax Britannica*. In the twentieth century, America's leadership in electric and chemical technology and its application to the motor, aeroplane and consumer durables industries laid the basis for the *Pax Americana*. In sum:

In the past, major changes in technological structure invariably wrought changes in the international system as a whole: the country which held the overwhelming advantage in a specific industry or a specific technology that was the key in the technological paradigm for the world's economic development in a given era became the leader of international society and took the initiative in the formation of the international order of that era.[11]

For Japan, in short, its century-long pursuit of stature among nations required one final, revolutionary step. In its own interest, it must set aside the narrow conception of national interest that had motivated it and replace it with a global perspective that would see Japan as a leader of the international system. As the most efficient and competitive economy, Japan had a powerful incentive to encourage and maintain the rules of a liberal open world economy. True nationalism for Japan was now the new internationalism. As MITI's report stated succinctly, 'Japan cannot expect to grow or prosper unless the rest of the world grows and prospers.'[12]

Accordingly, the first principle of the new internationalism is that Japan must give support and leadership to the institutions of a liberal international system. This is urgent because the Japanese perceive the US leadership as declining. Throughout the last decade the decline of the USA has been a common theme of public discourse. A major thesis of the Ohira Research Group on Comprehensive National Security, which issued its report on 2 July 1980, was that:

the days are gone when Japan could count on [an international] system maintained single-handedly by the United States, be it in terms of military security, politics and diplomacy, or the economy. Japan must now contribute to the maintenance and management of the system as an influential member of the free world. There has been a shift from a world of '*Pax Americana*' to the world of 'peace maintained by shared responsibilities'.[13]

The new internationalism believed, in the light of the Reagan military build-up, that the USA would continue in the near term to provide military–security leadership but that the international economy would be supervised by a 'collective management system'. Japan must join other nations in providing the 'public goods' required by the international system such as an open trading system, development assistance, expenditures on R&D, and as lending agencies of last resort for nations facing massive debts. Although some internationalists, like Nakasone, believe that economics and politics can no longer be separated, the mainstream concludes that 'Japan must not aim to be a hegemonic power preponderant in all fields – economic, military, and international political – but should define its role in the world primarily in terms of economic strength', following the examples of Venice, Holland and other leading trading states in history. This role will entail active Japanese leadership in expanding free trade and in promoting coordination of international fiscal and monetary policy.[14]

A second fundamental tenet of the new internationalism is more controversial because of the immediate threat it represents to institutions and social practices as well as to a vast array of private interests in Japan. This tenet is what the internationalists call

a commitment to harmonize national actions with global interests. This will necessitate reform and/or reorganization of political, economic, social, and educational and other domestic institutions ... These efforts ... will no doubt be accompanied by considerable friction and turmoil, imposing severe strains on the nation. The responsibility of Japanese, in view of their country's position in the world, is to surmount these difficulties ... and to cultivate a global perspective ... Needless to say, strong political leadership and popular support will be needed if Japan is to successfully shoulder these responsibilities.[15]

Harmonizing Japanese institutions with international practice recalls a US Commerce Secretary's assertion to the Japanese: 'You will have to change your culture.' To take this revolutionary step, Nakasone proclaimed the goal of transforming Japan into an 'international state' (*kokusai kokka*). The century-long pursuit of equality with the West had left its mark on all Japan's institutions. They were designed to promote a uniform and disciplined national effort to achieve this goal. They were also designed to insulate Japan from direct influence by foreign companies and individuals. To play the new role of international leader, Japan's economic, social and educational institutions have to be made more open, flexible, tolerant of diversity and responsive to the expectations of Japan's new status.

The new internationalism is thus addressing the difficult and controversial issue of international norms versus domestic autonomy. Formerly, adherence to the norms of a liberal open economic system meant maintaining non-discriminatory tariffs and refraining from overt quotas on imports. The growth of interdependence of national economies, however, has increased the relevance of domestic social structures and economic policies to the smooth operation of a liberal international economy. As Gary Saxonhouse writes,

> The thrust of international economic diplomacy has moved from tariff to quotas and from quotas to standards, subsidies and government procurement. The agenda for international economic harmony seems now to include the demand that much of the domestic affairs of participants in the international economic system should be governed by fully competitive, open, and contractual relationships.[16]

Probably more than any other single factor, it is the Japanese system that has created this clash between domestic autonomy and international norms in international economic negotiations. 'Western liberal societies,' Gilpin observes, 'find Japanese economic success particularly threatening because it is the first non-western and nonliberal society to out compete them. Whereas Western economies are based on belief in the superior efficiency of the free market and individualism, the market and the individual in Japan are not relatively autonomous but are deeply embedded in a powerful nonliberal culture and social system.'[17] Saxonhouse has compiled a formidable list of distinctive Japanese economic institutions and policies which, from an American if not from a West European perspective, constitute an 'illiberal' way of conducting economic affairs.[18]

To reform these institutions and practices would constitute a challenge to central features of Japanese culture, social relations and political structure. The new internationalism seeks a liberalization of institutions partly because they are remnants of the catching-up process, partly because they may inflame protectionist sentiment in other countries and partly because liberalization will better qualify Japan for leadership.

A major attempt to address this clash of international norms and domestic autonomy was made in the Advisory Group on Economic Structural Adjustment for International Harmony, chaired by the former governor of the

Bank of Japan, Maekawa Haruo, who was appointed by Nakasone in the autumn of 1985. The so-called Maekawa Report unveiled the next spring announced that 'the time has come for Japan to make a historical transformation in its traditional lifestyle'. It acknowledged that trade surpluses had to change in order 'for Japan to become a truly international state', and it promised expansion of domestic demand through promotion of housing construction and urban redevelopment, changes in preferential tax treatment for savings, increased imports and a five-day working week. A second Maekawa Report issued a year later, in April 1987, extended the commitment to restructure the economy, lessen economic friction with other countries and play a leadership role in the world economy. It recommended further changes to shift to domestic-led growth; reform of the distribution system; removal of barriers to trade in a number of industries; measures to relieve Third World debt; and a greater role in providing development assistance.

The third fundamental tenet of the new internationalism is, as the MITI advisory report stressed, cultivation of a 'consciousness of the global community' or 'internal internationalism'. True internationalism meant not only institutional change; it required 'a transformation of the national consciousness' to leave behind the old catching-up mentality and prepare the Japanese for international leadership. Becoming an international state in the twenty-first century entailed revolutionizing the educational system and the patterns of thinking it imparted to new generations of Japanese. Nakasone persuaded the Diet to establish the Ad Hoc Council on Education Reform in 1984 to propose ways that the existing school structure, which was characterized by standardization, centralization and uniform thinking, could be liberalized and deregulated to permit greater diversity, tolerance and individual expression. A convert to internationalism and a former Vice-Minister of MITI who served on the Council, Amaya Naohiro, observed:

> During the stage when Japan was catching up companies welcomed a mass-produced supply of workers equipped with a uniform, homogeneous education. The resounding success of total quality control is closely tied to the uniform educational background and ability of Japanese workers. The big question now is whether what has succeeded in the twentieth century will also lead to success in the twenty-first century.[19]

The Japanese had been successful because they had been quintessential organization men, attentive to detail, loyal to the group, highly skilled in group management and human relations. The problem so far as Japan's future was concerned was that this accentuated a narrow, inward-looking perspective. 'Our schools,' wrote one of the leading neo-conservatives,

Kôyama Kenichi, 'do not train people for international communication by nurturing their ability to express themselves, to debate, and to interact with people of other countries.'[20] What is necessary, the Education Commission recommended, is a shift from a single-track system to a diversity of schools; a loosening of the requirements for licensing and accreditation of schools in both secondary and higher education; greater latitude for competing teaching methods, curriculum and teacher qualifications; consideration of a wider range of achievement than simple test scores in school admissions; and removal of obstacles to the hiring of foreign teachers and acceptance of vast numbers of foreign students. The product of a new educational system would be a student with a 'broad mind, sound body, and rich creativity' and possessing 'the spirit of freedom, autonomy, and civic-mindedness'.

The indispensable innovation that would establish Japan as an international state was a new liberal nationalism, which would have more open and universal characteristics than the traditional nationalism. Professor Otake has termed it an 'international nationalism' (*kokusaiteki nashonarisumu*).[21] The education report stressed formation of 'Japanese identity in a global context'. This meant a sure sense of Japanese traditions and strengths, but not in the exclusive sense of pre-war nationalism:

> It is essential for Japanese not only to be assertive about the distinctive character of Japanese society and culture [but also to] deeply understand the excellence of other cultures in the world. Although one is expected to love Japan as a Japanese, he must avoid judging things on the basis of narrow nationalistic interests only, and try to build his character with a broad international and global perspective that covers all humanity.

The new internationalized Japanese would be self-confident, at home in the world, not clinging to other Japanese when abroad, but rather communicating easily with foreigners and understanding their mores.

The internationalists believe that the global strategy of Japan to become a leader of the international system in the next century depends on the success of their agenda. As the 1986 MITI advisory report stressed, 'Future Japanese influence can only be achieved by participation in the international community. It is for its own benefit that Japan must make efforts at international exchange and to develop a global perspective.'[22] In short, Japan's new internationalism was not to be an empty idealism; it was instead based on a new vision of Japan's future self-interest. Not without some justification progressive critics described the reforms as a plan so that 'Japan can both consolidate the economic gains it has won over recent years and increase its already powerful advantages in the global economy.'[23]

THE BURDENS OF HISTORY

By the end of the 1980s, the new internationalism envisaged by the Ohira Research Groups at the beginning of the decade had met with only limited successes. Nakasone left office in 1987 with a wry remark that the outcome of his 'grand design' to transform Japan's international role was 'yet to be seen'.[24] The most egregious features of a closed economy, the formal barriers, had been largely laid aside. Whether through foreign pressure or out of self-interest, or because the economy was so demonstrably strong, the Japanese dismantled some of the mercantilist policies of the past. 'By the mid-1980s the Japanese had become, at least in their formal trade barriers with respect to manufactures, the least protectionist of the advanced capitalist countries.'[25]

There had been some liberalization of domestic institutions. Administrative reform, for example, did succeed in creating a blueprint for a leaner, more streamlined and better rationalized administration. Progress was made in the privatization of public corporations, inducing greater competition, and generally loosening some aspects of bureaucratic control of the economy. The Education Council stimulated a vigorous debate about the shortcomings of the educational system, but reform petered out. Innovations were limited to such items as the introduction of information technology in the curriculum and the development of continuing education. Progress was made in some of the Maekawa Commission recommendations, such as the abolition of the *maruyu* system of incentives for savings and steps to liberalize the financial markets. However, the distribution system remained an impediment, and changes in the exchange rate were not passed through to the consumer in the form of lower prices. Domestic demand picked up in spite of rather than because of government policy. Japan increased its overseas development assistance to become the world's largest aid donor and increased its support of international organizations such as the World Bank, the IMF and the Asian Development Bank. Japan became 'one of the world's largest producers of internationalist rhetoric', a faithful participant in the GATT negotiations and in the annual economic summit meetings among the economic powers. But still, Japan rarely showed the qualities of leadership and initiative that the new internationalism demanded. The nation still resisted support for the framework of military security that had protected the open economic order. The vision of changing the structure of the economy to achieve international harmony had barely begun to be implemented. What were the obstacles?

A new foreign policy consensus is constrained by what we may call, in general, the burdens of history. The legacy of the century-long forced march to catch up with the West has become, in the new circumstances, a barrier to the achievement of the internationalist consensus. Part of the burden of history is unquestionably therefore institutional, structural and systemic. To overtake the West, Japan built institutions and political structures that it felt could most efficiently mobilize and allocate resources. For the first three decades of the post-war period, the bureaucracy dominated the political system and worked effectively with business. A strong consensus supported the strategy laid out in the post-war years by Prime Minister Yoshida of concentrating on economic recovery while avoiding involvement in international political–strategic affairs. This consensus held firm until the 1970s when issues of distribution of the national wealth began to emerge, and foreign criticism of and pressures on Japan's industrial policies mounted. Partly for these reasons and partly because of the evolution of political processes, the bureaucratic leadership weakened and the political system became more complex. New issues arose that divided the bureaucracy and stimulated in-fighting among the ministries. Senior LDP politicians who had acquired expertise in areas of policy specialization that served special interests made common cause with bureaucrats having jurisdiction over these special areas of interest.

The political scientist, Inoguchi Takashi, a leading student of this phenomenon, writes that increasingly powerful triangular relationships 'binding specific vested interests, ministries, and cliques [*zoku*] of Diet members' offer almost insurmountable obstacles to policy initiatives.

As a result of this three-way alliance, Japan became a society in which vested interests were virtually inviolable. In such a society government policy initiatives must pass through tortuous channels before their effects can be felt, and the more ambitious the plan is, the more it will be diluted before it can be adopted ... Reform efforts evaporate like drops of water on a hot griddle.[26]

Nakatani Iwao, an economist from Osaka University, finds the lack of a strong executive tradition partly responsible for the ponderous decision-making process and the absence of a new sense of national purpose. 'The present administration system,' he writes, 'resembles a massive corporation whose separate divisions are engaged in totally discrete operations and are oblivious to overall corporate goals.' The fundamental problem in his view, however, is the alliance of bureaucrats, interest groups and politicians:

The most problematic Japanese system of all is doubtless the rigid bureaucracy. And one of the biggest problems associated with this system is the activities of politicians aligned with private-sector interest groups who take advantage of it. It is the alliance of bureaucrats, industrial and agricultural interests, and politicians that has closed Japan tight to the rest of the world. Although linkages between specific government agencies and specific industries were effective in many ways during the period of rapid economic growth in the 1960s, they have since acted counter to national interests by intensifying bureaucratic sectionalism. The pace of change has been slowed and international friction intensified by clannish bureaucrats who, with the support of industry-aligned members of the National Diet, have opposed specific reform measures even while endorsing the idea of reform.[27]

Nakasone's 'grand design' of remaking Japan into an international state ran head on into interest alliances. Initially he excoriated them for obstructing reform. While he was still Director of the Administrative Management Agency he took the unprecedented step of threatening obstinate bureaucrats with penalties and disciplinary measures. Subsequently as Prime Minister he resorted to the appointment of private or *ad hoc* advisory councils to highlight his ideas, build popularity and evade the intransigence of the bureaucracy. In some cases these strategies were successful, but in other cases they were not. When he left the prime ministership he remained dissatisfied with the slow pace of innovation. Leaders of business with dependence on international trade and investment shared his feelings. In the summer of 1988, Gotô Noboru, a retired president of the Japanese Chamber of Commerce, wrote that if Japan was to reform itself as an international state the bureaucracy must be radically restructured.[28]

Nakasone's successor, whose low profile contrasted with his ebullient predecessor, did succeed in making some progress at market opening measures in construction and agriculture through painstaking negotiations. But, as a veteran high-ranking official of the Ministry of Finance, Sakakibara Eisuke, concluded, the political system is now heavily weighted in favour of the status quo. Bold and aggressive policy departures with more than a one-year time horizon are 'quite difficult if not impossible'. Sakakibara believes that, in the light of 'the increasing pluralization and decentralization' of the decision-making process, achieving structural change in the socio-economic system will be 'by no means an easy proposition'. He concludes his examination of the decision-making process by observing that 'reforming the process will be extremely hard, if not impossible, given that the present decision-making process is the result of a long historical evolution'.[29]

In view of the growing strength of the Japanese economy and the consequent self-interest in the maintenance of an open international economy, it might seem that there should be strong enough support in Japanese society to overcome bureaucratic in-fighting, parochial interests and the immobilism of the political system. Is a free trade coalition possible? Clearly there are groups that are committed to free trade that would favour most of the larger aims of the new internationalism. Komiya and Itoh identify these as consisting of leaders of government; MITI, except some bureaus in charge of specific industries; the Ministry of Foreign Affairs; part of the Ministry of Finance; leaders of big business; the EPA; and the Fair Trade Commission. It is significant that Japanese labour has not generally taken a stand against free trade as labour has elsewhere.[30]

Is it then possible that a free trade coalition can take shape to press the larger agenda of restructuring the economy and in the process transforming the Japanese world view? It appears not. Japanese policy making is so highly segmented and policy arenas so self-contained, as Okimoto argues, that horizontal public interest coalitions emerge only rarely, either in or out of government.[31] A consumer movement, for example, has not been strong enough to overcome the price distortions created by the distribution system. The shallowness of liberalism keeps it from overcoming the many interest groups that resist liberalization and the politicians and bureaucrats who support them. Komiya and Itoh identify the Ministries of Agriculture, Public Welfare, Transportation, Post and Telecommunications and some sections of MITI as resisters.[32] Murakami finds the 'new middle mass' of Japanese voters still wedded to the status quo and unenthusiastic about assuming international responsibilities.[33]

In addition to this systemic handicap that combines a weak executive tradition, a ponderous decision-making process and vast encroachment of parochial interests, the bold policy initiatives of the new internationalism are handicapped by Japan's traditional reactive stance in the international system. Japan has progressed in the modern period by assessing international conditions and turning them to its own advantage. Prior to the middle of the nineteenth century, Japanese history was almost entirely an indigenous affair; and since then for the most part Japan has been a reactive state in international affairs. As a late developer, Japan learned to be responsive to conditions established by other powers and to react to opportunities that presented themselves. The industrial civilization of the advanced countries provided an image of Japan's future not only in the form of technology but also models of institutional innovation. Japan's peculiar dependence on trade left it, in addition, with a vulnerability that further engendered a cautious and deliberate foreign policy.

Since the end of the Second World War, the reactive nature of Japan has been even more pronounced. Partly this was the result of defeat, occupation and being reduced to the status of pariah in the international community; but it was also a result of the constraints of the Constitution and the character of the post-war state. Still another reason for Japan's reactive nature after 1945 was that it was a matter of conscious national policy, the so-called Yoshida Doctrine, to concentrate on economic growth while depending on the USA to maintain Japanese security. The path to economic recovery lay in shrewdly taking advantage of the international order and its rapidly expanding free trade regime. As a Vice-Minister of International Trade and Industry said in 1986, 'Japan has usually considered the international economic order as a given condition and looked for ways in which to use it.'[34] Another leading official of MITI, Otsuka Kazuhiko, Director of the Industrial Structure Division in MITI's Industrial Policy Bureau, agrees with this assessment of Japan's reactive nature to the international system: 'This passive posture has now become so entrenched that the Japanese have a hard time taking action even on economic problems that are largely of their own making – until, that is, they are forced to move by outside pressure.'[35]

Outside pressure (*gaiatsu*) is, in fact, another dimension of Japan's reactive stance in international affairs. One of the greatest handicaps to the new internationalism is that Japan has usually not been able to respond institutionally, even in its own best interest, without the intervention of forces from outside its system. *Gaiatsu* has become a dynamic of the change, reform and liberalization that is essential to the agenda of the new internationalism.

A recent authoritative study of Japanese industrial policy concludes that American pressure was decisive in liberalizing bureaucratic controls over the Japanese economy. The various policy tools that the Japanese Government used in the catching-up period – control of the interest rate structure and the capital market, the use of cartels to limit competition, and a variety of other policies regarding trade protection, subsidies and promotion of technological innovation – could only have been limited or discontinued through outside pressure:

> To discontinue the policies or to change their character sufficiently to meet the needs of the post-catch-up decades, Japan needed some force sufficiently strong to overcome the opposition of politically powerful interest groups. Such a force would have been extremely difficult to forge within the Japanese body politic ... The force should ideally come from outside. And, it did.[36]

Indeed, former MITI Vice-Minister Amaya observed recently that:

> looking back it becomes obvious that almost all liberalization policies effected by Japan in the postwar period were implemented due to foreign pressure. Trade liberalization in the early 1960s and capital liberalization

in the 1970s, for example, were undertaken reluctantly by industry or the government because of pressure from outside. Financial and communications liberalization in the 1980s, meanwhile, was commenced because of pressure from the US.[37]

In the absence of a strong national consensus in support of the new internationalism, the institutional rigidities of the Japanese system allow the reactive nature of the Japanese state to persist. 'Japan must not view the "global community",' says the 1986 MITI advisory report, 'as a society of nations which it can enter at a minimal cost while reaping maximum profit.'[38] Nonetheless this remains the prevailing attitude. Tokuyama Jiro, a representative spokesman of the leading Japanese business circles, sums it up:

This is what Japan has come to. One by one, outside shocks have become necessary to make any changes – a shameful state of affairs. So these destructive forces that pave the way for market liberalization and other policy changes are welcome, as it seems that this is the only way Japan can proceed with the necessary structural realignments to build a stronger and more efficient economy.[39]

The dilemma for the internationalists of having to rely on *gaiatsu* is that it runs the risk of creating a siege mentality in Japan and thereby inflaming a narrow nationalism, which is another burden of Japanese history. The external pressures for liberalization and for harmonization of Japanese institutions with international norms have created a serious dilemma for Japanese leaders, challenging central features of Japanese culture, social relations and political structure, and arousing nationalist resentment of foreign interference with domestic institutions. Such apparent infringements on Japanese autonomy have rallied xenophobia and ethnocentrism since the beginning of modern Japanese history, and the present is no exception. The young writer Hasegawa Michiko finds *kokusaika* (internationalization) too deferential to Western ways: '*Kokusaika* is a word redolent of the ruthless coercive power to which all non-Western nationals are perforce subject.'[40] Similarly, Nishio Kanji, a relentless critic of neo-conservatism, writes that Nakasone's advocacy of making Japan an 'international state' amounts to a continuation of post-war deference to US demands.[41] Shimomura Osamu, an architect of the policies and institutions of high growth in the 1960s, wrote a best selling book entitled *Japan is Not at Fault, America Is*, in which he castigated the Maekawa Report for its submission to American views and agreeing to reforms that would deprive the Japanese economy of its strength and vitality: the propensity to save, work longer hours, and maintain patterns of work that are culturally sanctioned by Japanese values.[42]

The Japanese are perplexed by the issues that are raised by the expectations that its new economic status requires it to adopt a proactive approach to support of the international order. *Kokusaika* implies changing Japanese culture in a wide variety of threatening ways: putting foreigners in executive positions of Japanese organizations, admitting foreign labour, accepting women on a more equal basis into social groups, shortening the working week, changing savings habits, reforming the distribution and sales systems, putting foreign teachers on university faculties and opening research laboratories.

Surveys indicate a deep ambivalence in Japanese attitudes toward *kokusaika*. A 1986 survey by the EPA showed strong support for what we might call 'superficial internationalization'. Over 70 per cent of respondents were favourable to increases in 'news from abroad', 'technology from overseas', 'overseas telephone calls and mail', and other categories of information exchange. Similar support existed for short-term human exchanges, such as foreign tourists and students. On the other hand, for what we might call 'profound internationalization' (such as increases in foreign employees and marriage to foreigners) less than 30 per cent approved.[43]

In pre-war days the elites used nationalist resentments to mobilize the population for the sacrifices required to catch up with the advanced nations. Now they are wary of an emotional reaction, instead seeing Japan's future interest in accommodation. For Yamazaki Masakazu, Japan has no choice:

> As long as the Japanese economy continues to make its presence felt globally, Japan will find it increasingly difficult to ignore the global community's demands for the internationalization of Japanese culture. Unless Japan is prepared either to conquer the world by force or to stage an economic retreat on all fronts, it has little choice but to accede to these demands.[44]

For Satô Seizaburo, an ardent internationalist, the further advancement of Japan's international position requires such accommodation:

> If we want to attract the world's first class minds to Japan we must resolve to use English ... To really strengthen Japan we must open the country to the world. If we stick stubbornly to the Japanese language and Japanese culture the world's superior human talent will simply not come. If we really want to create a *Pax Japonica* in the twenty-first century we

must do things like giving our lectures in English ... If we don't Japan cannot in the true sense take intellectual leadership in the world.[45]

Similarly a former MITI Vice-Minister, Amaya, in a 1987 address to a business group, stressed Japan's self-interest in opening its universities and institutes to foreign researchers: 'Repressing nationalism and promoting internationalism will eventually lead to long-term national benefits, particularly in the field of high technology.'[46] Yano Tôru, author of a book on Japanese internationalization, writes that, 'I see little likelihood of the tightly held nature of the Japanese sense of national identity giving way to an enthusiasm for racial mixing or multinational and ethnic community living.' He argues that a cosmopolitan or liberal internationalization is not in the cards. Instead it will proceed only as it serves Japan's national interests. This is of course appropriate, but the issue becomes how to define those interests.[47]

CONCLUSION: FROM FOLLOWERSHIP TO LEADERSHIP

The existence of a liberal international economic order in which norms are established for the free flow of goods and capital based on impersonal market principles is a relatively recent development. It depends on the leadership and self-restraint of the most powerful states in the system. Further, as Charles Kindleberger argued, a great power (hegemon) is needed to give stability to such an order and to maintain its norms.[48] Great Britain performed this role in the nineteenth century and the USA has done so since 1945. They acted not out of idealism or *noblesse oblige* but rather out of their own long-run self-interest as they perceived it. As Gilpin writes, 'Free trade is the policy of the strong. The conversion of the British from colonialism and formal imperialism to free trade and the Open Door did not reflect a shift in British ultimate objectives; it represented only a change in methods. The objectives of British policy remained the expansion of British wealth and power.'[49]

The most advanced and efficient economy has no need for tariffs to protect it; instead it requires open markets to sell its superior products and to buy raw materials. 'Free trade,' Kindleberger remarks, 'is the hypocrisy of the export interest, the clever device of the climber who kicks the ladder away when he has attained the summit of greatness.'

In the modern world of industrial civilization, in two cases the leading nation has taken responsibility for maintaining an open liberal trading order, sometimes at some short-term cost to itself but ultimately in its own long-term interest. This was a role that the leader did not at first accept. Instead it was accepted only after protracted struggle between social forces representing the previous economic stage and forces representing the interests of the new wave of industrial innovation. Decades passed before the inertia of the past – the burdens of history – and the resistance to the best interests of the new industrial phase were overcome. In so doing, old institutional arrangements had to be put aside, special economic interests representing the previous order were subdued and interests representative of the leadership of the new wave of industrialism constructed a new liberal institutional framework of global economic order.

In the 1970s Japan reached the stage where the strength and competitiveness of the Japanese economy would allow it to remove many formal tariff barriers and also to have a substantial and growing self-interest in the maintenance of the free trade order. Of course, there were important advanced industries where Japan had not established an advantage and would continue the strategy of 'industrial pre-emption', denying foreign producers market access until Japan attained dominance in cost and quality. Nevertheless, the logic of their economic strength in many fields and their confident vision of the future were leading the elites to rethink the nation's international role. The transition from followership to leadership will undoubtedly be a trying process. Other examples in history of shifting from economic nationalism to liberalism have been so. In England at the close of the Napoleonic Wars the Tory landholding class used their control of Parliament to pass a new Corn Law and other protective legislation to stem the tide of imported agricultural imports and the collapse of farm prices and rentals. The gentry and their farmers benefited, but wage-earners had to contend with the high price of foodstuffs. It took a generation of struggle by the Whigs and liberals, representing the new business interests created by industrialization, to overcome the mercantilism policies of the Tories. Reform of Parliament in 1832 gave greater representation to the new industrial interests, but still it was not until 1846 that the Corn Laws were repealed and Britain entered on its leadership of a liberal international order.

Similarly, the USA struggled for a generation after the First World War, when its economic and technological pre-eminence was established, before shouldering the burden of leadership in restructuring the international economic order. Internationalists like Cordell Hull, arguing that the Great Depression was brought on by mercantilist policies and economic nationalism, revived the Wilsonian vision of an 'open and integrated liberal-capitalist world system in which America, with her maturing power and exceptional virtue, would naturally take the leading role'.[50] The passage by Congress of the Reciprocal Trade Agreements Act in 1934, which empowered the President to negotiate the reciprocal lowering of tariffs, was a first victory for Hull, but it was another decade before the pressures of export-oriented industries, the need for unimpeded access to raw materials and the outcome of the Second World War made America's self-interest clear. The establishment of the IMF–GATT regime marked the victory of internationalism and the commitment to a liberal international order.

The obstacles that Japan faces in making the transition to being a world leader are much more formidable than the two examples cited. An accommodation between her domestic institutions and values and the norms of the liberal international order must be achieved. The internationalists know this will take time; perhaps more time than Japan's trading partners are willing to permit. Moreover, as Amaya has written, Japan lacks two essential qualifications for leadership: an ideology of universal appeal and military power. For the time being, Japan must be content as 'Number Two'.[51] Kosaka Masataka, similarly, has stressed Japan's lack of experience in foreign affairs as an additional reason for maintaining a 'special relationship' with the USA.[52] Murakami Yasusuke likewise agrees that continued American leadership, albeit in modified form, is required. He advocates a '*Pax Americana* Mark Two' in which America remains pre-eminent but shares leadership in economic affairs.[53] A June 1988 MITI report, *Nihon no sentaku (Japan's Options)*, advocates a transition from *Pax Americana* to the US-centred *Pax Consortis* in which existing macroeconomic policy coordination among industrialized nations is extended to cooperation in dealing with Third World debt, environmental problems[54] and development assistance.

For the near future, an international division of labour will be needed. But for the longer term Amaya, a quintessential internationalist and neo-conservative, expresses a growing sentiment:

> At the moment, Japan is somewhere between being a mercantile nation and a true world leader. Our choice is whether to continue the way we are – a strong silver medalist – or go for the gold. Do we have the strength and guts to make it?
>
> As long as Japan remains a merchant-cum-industrialist, we must always defer to the United States. We have to swallow our pride, accept insults and not argue back. Otherwise, we may lose the American market.
>
> If that is too high a price to pay, we have to raise our sights and become a leader. We would need our own ideology, independent defense and economic policies, and leaders who can perform on the world stage.
>
> Shortages of land and resources preclude Japan from ever becoming a classic imperialistic state. But by keeping our government apparatus small and efficient, we can compete with the best.

No matter what Japan decides, the future is fraught with peril. But for me, the choice is clear. Failure in the quest for glory is more noble than failure in the pursuit of profit.[55]

Notes

1. This chapter first appeared in Kenneth B. Pyle, *The Japanese Question: Power and Purpose in a New Era* (Washington, DC: American Enterprise Institute, 1992). It is reprinted here with the permission of the author.
2. See Edward Seidensticker, *This Country, Japan* (Tokyo: Kodansha, 1984) pp. 331–2.
3. Edwin O. Reischauer, *The Japanese* (Cambridge, MA: Harvard University Press, 1978) p. 420.
4. Dan F. Henderson, 'Access to the Japanese Market: Some Aspects of Foreign Exchange Controls and Banking Law', in Gary R. Saxonhouse and Kozo Yamamura (eds), *Law and Trade Issues of the Japanese Economy: American and Japanese Perspectives* (Seattle: University of Washington Press, 1986) p. 133.
5. Fujio Masayuki, '"Hogen daijin" oi ni hoeru' (The Big-Talking Minister with the Big Bank), *Bungei Shunju*, October 1986.
6. Ernest R. May, *Imperial Democracy: The Emergence of America as a Great Power* (New York: Harcourt Brace, 1961) p. 270.
7. Ryutaro Komiya and Motoshige Itoh, 'Japan's International Trade and Trade Policy, 1955–1984', in T. Inoguchi and D.I. Okimoto (eds), *The Political Economy of Japan: The Changing International Context*, Volume 2 (Stanford, CA: Stanford University Press, 1988) p. 213.
8. Ibid, p. 214.
9. Amaya Naohiro, 'Saraba, Chonin kokka' (Farewell to the Merchant Nation), *Voice*, October 1987.
10. The report has been translated: Yasusuke Muramaki and Yutaka Kosai (eds), *Japan in the Global Community: Its Role and Contribution on the Eve of the Twenty-first Century* (Tokyo: University of Tokyo Press, 1986) p. 69.
11. Ibid, p. 9.
12. Ibid, p. 35.
13. Ohira Research Group, *Sogo anzen hosho senryaku* (Comprehensive Security Assistance Strategy) (Tokyo: Okurasho, 1980); see also Nagatomi Yuichiro (ed.), *Masayoshi Ohira's Proposal to Evolve the Global Society*, (Tokyo: Foundation For Advanced Information and Research, 1988) pp. 224, 237.
14. Muramaki and Kosai, *Japan in the Global Community*, pp. 36–7.
15. Ibid, p. 34.
16. Gary R. Saxonhouse, 'Comparative Advantage, Structural Adaptation, and Japanese Performance', in Inoguchi and Okimoto, *The Political Economy of Japan*, p. 246.
17. Robert Gilpin, *The Political Economy of International Relations* (Princeton, NJ: Princeton University Press, 1987) pp. 391–2.

18. Saxonhouse, 'Comparative Advantage', pp. 246–7.
19. 'Mirai shiko ka, genjitsushugi ka' (Futuristic or Realistic?), *Chuo koron*, April 1985. Translation in *Japan Echo*, XII (1985) p. 52.
20. 'Kakuitsu seini shi o' (Uniformity kills the spirit), *Next*, March 1985. Translation in *Japan Echo*, XII (1985) p. 45.
21. Otake, 'Nakasone seiji no ideorogi' (Nakasone: Political Ideology), *Leviathan* (Autumn 1987) p. 83.
22. Maramaki and Kosai, *Japan in the Global Community*, p. 118.
23. Horio, *Educational Thought*, p. 61.
24. Text of the former Prime Minister's address to the Asia Foundation, San Francisco, 11 March 1988. See also Kenneth Pyle, 'In Pursuit of a Grand Design: Nakasone Betwixt the Past and the Future', *Journal of Japanese Studies*, 13 (Summer 1987) pp. 243–70.
25. Gilpin, *Political Economy*, pp. 389–90.
26. 'Zokueki, shoeki ga naiju kakudai o sagai suru' (Political Changing Preventing the Extension of Domestic Demand), *Ekonomisuto*, 8 September 1987. Translation in *Japan Echo*, XIV (1987) pp. 56–8. See also T. Inoguchi and Iwai Tomoaki, *'Zokugiin' no kenkyu* (Tokyo: Nihon keizaishimbunsha, 1987).
27. Nakatani Iwao, 'Sekinin kokka, Nihon e no sentaku' (The Choice for Japan in the Last Term), *Asuteion*, Autumn 1987. Translation in *Japan Echo*, XIV (1987) pp. 7–18.
28. Gôto Noboru, 'Watakushi no Nihon keizai kaizo an' (My Plan for Improving the Japanese Economy), *Bungei shunju*, July 1988.
29. Eisuke Sakakibara, 'Is Japan Governable?', *International Economy*, May/June 1988, pp. 92–9.
30. Komiya and Itoh, 'Japan's International Trade', p. 210.
31. Daniel I. Okimoto, 'Political Inclusivity: The Domestic Structure of Trade', in Inoguchi and Okimoto, *Volume 2 The Political Economy of Japan*, pp. 334–7.
32. Komiya and Itoh, 'Japan's International Trade', p. 210.
33. Murakami Yasusuke, 'The Japanese Model of Political Economy', in Kozo Yamamura and Yasukichi Yasuba (eds), *The Political Economy of Japan: The Domestic Transformation*, Volume 1 (Stanford, CA: Stanford University Press, 1987) pp. 89–90.
34. *Look Japan*, 10 September 1986, p. 4.
35. Otsuka, 'Charting a New Policy Course', *Economic Eve*, June 1986.
36. George C. Eads and Kozo Yamamura, 'The Future of Industrial Policy', in K. Yamamura and Y. Yasuba (eds), *The Political Economy of Japan*, Volume 1, p. 466.
37. *Japan Economic Journal*, 31 January 1987.
38. Murakami and Kosai, *Japan in the Global Community*, pp. 113–14.
39. Tokuyama Jiro, *Far Eastern Economic Review*, 4 August 1988, p. 51.
40. Hasegawa Michiko, '"Kokusaika" to iu kotoba o saiko suru' (Rethink the Word 'Internationalization'), *Shokun*, December 1985. Translation in *Japan Echo*, XIII (1986) pp. 49–55.
41. Nishio Kanji, 'Senryaku toshite no "sakoku" e no ishi' (The Will towards Isolation on a Strategy), *Seiron*, January 1988.
42. Shimomura Osamu, *Nipon wa waruku nai: warui no wa Amerika da* (Japan Is Not at Fault, America Is) (Tokyo: Bungei shunju, 1987).

43. Takeuchi Hirotaka, 'Jinteki sakoku taisei kara dappi seyo' (Outgrow the System of Cultural Isolation), *Chuo koron*, October 1987.
44. Yamazaki Masakazu, 'Nihon bunka no rekishiteki jikken' (Historical Events in Japanese Culture), *Chuo koron*, June 1986. Translation in *Japan Echo*, XIII (1986) pp. 56–63.
45. Satô Seizaburo, 'Kokusaika e no Nihon no kakugo' (Japan's Commitment to Internationalization), *Seiron*, November 1987.
46. Amaya Naohiro 'The Dawning of a New Era', *Speaking of Japan*, 9 (May 1988) pp. 21–2.
47. Yano Tôru, *Kokusaika no imi* (The Meaning of Internationalization) (Tokyo: NHK Bukkusu, 1986); see also the essays by Yano in *Japan Times*, 28 and 29 September 1986.
48. Charles Kindleberger, *The World in Depression, 1929–1939* (Berkeley and Los Angeles, CA: University of California Press, 1973) Chapters 1 and 14.
49. Robert Gilpin, *U.S. Power and the Multinational Corporation: The Political Economy of Direct Foreign Investment* (New York: Basic Books, 1975) p. 84.
50. David P. Calleo and Benjamin M. Rowland, *America and the World Political Economy* (Bloomington, IN: Indiana University Press, 1973) p. 58.
51. Amaya Naohiro, *Nippon wa doko e iku no ka* (Where is Japan Headed?) (Tokyo: PHP, 1989, pp. 201–5.
52. Kosaka Masataka, 'Nichibei "tokubetsu kankei" no honshitsu' (The Foundation of the American–Japan Special Relationship), *Voice*, January 1988.
53. Murakami, 'Japanese Model of Political Economy'.
54. *Tsūshosangyosho Daijin kanbo* (ed.), *Nihon no sentaku* (Japan's Options), (Tokyo: MITI, 1988), pp. 30–5.
55. *Tokyo shimbun*, 24 June 1987, Asia Foundation Translation Service.

Index

Abe, Shintaro 143
'adversarial trade' 58
Agnelli, Giovanni 64
Airbus Industrie, and Canada–US FTA
11
Andean Pact (1969) 28
Andriessen, Frans 80, 84, 99
Anti-dumping measures 41
and NAFTA 22
complaints by EC 80
Argentina, and MERCOSUR 28
ASEAN (Association of South East
Asian Nations) 164, 168
and Japanese FDI 166
concerns about Japan 178
FDI in 169
relations with Australia 191
ASEAN–Japan Development Fund
179
Asia Development Bank, and Russia
161
Asia-Pacific Economic Cooperation
(APEC) Conference 58, 165,
178, 191
and Russia 161
Asia-Pacific region, regional
integration 191, 192
Asian NIES 164, 168
investment in ASEAN 169
trade with US 167
Asian trade bloc 170
Australia 189
and APEC 192
and Pacific Basin 176
relations with China 193
relations with Japan 175, 189, 190
relations with US 192
Austria, European Free Trade
Association 3
Automobile industry, and NAFTA 8,
17, 22, 25
Automotive Products Trade Agreement
of 1965 (US–Canada) 11

Bangemann, Martin 80
Bank of Tokyo, in Russia 158
Baoshan Iron and Steel complex 201
Belgium, Treaty of Rome 1
Brazil, and MERCOSUR 28
Brezhnev, Leonid, military build-up in
Asia 210
Bulgaria
relations with EC 117
relations with Japan 123
state of the economy 123
Bush, George
and NAFTA 23, 28
and Tiananmen Square incident
204

Cambodia 193
Canada
and NAFTA 20
and Pacific Basin 176
relations with Japan 175
trade with US 10–11
Canada–United States Free Trade
Agreement 10–12, 38, 53
dispute resolution 12–13, 46
Canada's motives 11, 40
effects on Canadian economy 13
effects on trade 13
effects on US economy 13
impact on multilateral trade
negotiations 50
objectives and scope 43
rules of origin 44
services 45
US motives 12, 42
Central American Common Market
(Caricom) (1963) 28
Cecchini Report 6, 65
Charlottetown Accord 27
Chile
and NAFTA 28
and Pacific Basin 176

China, People's Republic of
  'adjustment' programmes 206
  'readjustment' programmes 206
  and Asia-Pacific integration 193
  corruption 208
  joint ventures 201
  military 212
  oil industry 198
  prospects for GATT membership
    206
  restrictions on FDI 208
  trade agreement with Japan (1978)
    199
  trade with Japan 195, 200, 201,
    215
  Yunnan and Hainan Island
    development 199
Chrétien, Jean, and NAFTA 16
Clinton, Bill 9
  and NAFTA 15, 16, 25
Cockfield White Paper 64
COCOM
  and China 209
  Toshiba incident 159
Colombia
  and NAFTA 28
  trade agreement with Mexico 20
Common Agricultural Policy (CAP)
  9, 77
Computer equipment
  and NAFTA 24
  software 8
Consumer safety legislation, European
  Community 5
Council of Mutual Economic
  Assistance (CMEA) 115, 121
  collapse 122
Countervailing duties 41
Cresson, Edith 61
Currency devaluation, Canada 13
Cyprus, application for EC
  membership 4
Czech and Slovak Federal Republic
  (CSFR) 5, 8
  and EC 92 116, 196
  relations with Japan 127
  state of the economy 125
Czechoslovakia
  partition 5
  relations with EC 4

Data privacy directive 8
Daqing Petrochemical Complex 201
De la Madrid, Miguel 18
Delors, Jacques 2, 4, 6–7, 64
Deng Xiaoping 203
Denman, Sir Roy 68, 69
Denmark, Maastricht Treaty 5
Dispute resolution, and NAFTA 23
DRAM chips 102

Eagleburger, Lawrence, and
  Tiananmen Square incident 204
Eastern Europe
  and EC 92 114
  MFN status 132
  and NAFTA 114, 120
  as gateway to EC 197
  impact on Sino–Japanese relations
    196
  relations with Japan 115, 120, 129,
    134
Echeverría, Luis 18
Enterprise for the Americas Initiative
  (EAI) 28
Entertainment industry, and NAFTA
  22
Environmental protection
  European Community 5
  and NAFTA 28
ESPRIT (European Strategic Programme
  for Research and Information 99
'Europe 1992' (EC 92) 7, 94
  economic benefits 7
  internal market 94, 96
  impact on Sino–Japanese relations
    196–7
  Japan's perspective 105
European Bank for Reconstruction and
  Development 9
European Commission 2, 5
  and anti-dumping 103
European Community 1–2
  Common External Tariff 78
  Council of Ministers 95
  domestic market 7
  investment policy 97
  investment in Japan 76
  rules of origin 98
  trade 72
  relations with Japan 58, 63–6, 70–2

European Council
    and the SEA   95
    Japan policy   70
European Court of Justice   5
European Economic Area (EEA)   4
European Free Trade Association
    (EFTA)   4, 9, 98
European Monetary System   2
European Parliament   2, 95
'Eurosclerosis'   2, 101
Exchange rates   63

Financial services industry
    and NAFTA   22, 24
    Canada–US FTA   46
Finland, European Free Trade
    Association   4
Foreign direct investment (FDI)
    and NAFTA   23
    in China   209, 214
    Japanese   22
    by Japan in Asia   166
'Fortress Europe'   9, 104
France, Treaty of Rome   1
Fraser, Malcolm   176
Fukuda Doctrine   176

GATT (General Agreement on Tariffs
    and Trade)   1, 10
    'safeguard clause'   78
    1993 agreement   9
    and anti-dumping   81
    and regional trade agreements   29
    Kennedy Round   52
    prospects for China's membership
        206
    Tokyo Round   52
    Uruguay Round   53, 83
General Motors   80
Generalized System of Preferences
    (GSP), and Eastern Europe   132
Germany
    economic strength   5
    unification   4
Gilpin, Robert, theory of hegemonic
    stability   173
Glass–Steagall Act   46
Gorbachev, Mikhail   141
    China policy   160

Japan policy   144
    Vladivostok speech   143
    government procurement contracts
        and NAFTA   23, 25
        and SEA   7
Gramsci, Antonio, theory of
    hegemonic stability   173
Great Britain, trade balance   5
Greece, admitted to European
    Community   2
Green Party (Germany)   5

Hawke, Robert   165, 178
Hegemonic stability   63, 169–72, 174,
    181
    and Japan   171
    Japan   226
    role of military power   172
High-definition television, in EC   9
Hong Kong   167, 168
Human rights, and NAFTA   26
Hungary   196
    privatization   117
    relations with EC   4, 116
    state of the economy   127

Import surges   44
Intellectual property rights
    Canada–US FTA   48
    and NAFTA   22
Intermediate Nuclear Forces (INF)
    agreement   148
Ishihara, Shintaro   81
Italy, Treaty of Rome   1

Japan
    and Asian economic integration
        165
    and NAFTA   33
    and Pacific Basin   176
    and regional hegemony   175, 182–3
    Cambodia peacekeeping   158
    corporate strategy   108
    defence spending   203
    education reform   228
    effect of Canada–US FTA   14
    exchange rate policies   136
    keiretsu system   85–6
    new internationalism   221, 227, 229
    non-tariff barriers   67

OECD membership 66
oil dependence 199
overseas development assistance
(ODA) 168, 198–9, 230
private sector interests in China
207
relations with Australia 189–90
relations with China 195, 198–9,
200–1, 210, 215
relations with Eastern Europe 131,
134
relations with EC 8, 58, 73, 100,
161
relations with Russia/Soviet Union
145, 148, 156, 158
savings rate 110–11
self-defence forces 158
trade policy 136
trade surplus 74, 110
voluntary export restraint 70
'Japan bashing' 60, 111
'Japan, Inc.' 169
Japan–Soviet Scientific and
Technological Cooperation
Committee 143
Japan–Soviet trade 148, 150–1,
153–5, 157, 159, 162
Japanese automobile industry
and NAFTA 26
exports to Europe 69
Japanese foreign direct investment
(FDI) 22, 76, 224
in ASEAN 167
in Asia 162, 167, 202
in China 202, 205
in Great Britain 109
in the EC 67, 71, 75, 100–1
JESSI (Joint European Submicron
Silicon Initiative) 99

Keiretsu system 85–6
Keohane, Robert, theory of hegemonic
stability 174
Konigsberg Vaapenfabrikk, COCOM
violations 159

Labour regulations, and NAFTA 28
Li Peng 209
Local content regulations 82
Luxembourg, Treaty of Rome 1

Maastricht Treaty 3–6
Maekawa Commission 230
Maekawa Report 228
Major, John 6
Malaysia 167, 176
Malta 4
Maquiladora 25
Maquiladora factories 24
Matsushita Electric, and China 209
MERCOSUR 28
Mexico
debt crisis 18
impact of NAFTA 18, 25
micro-electronics industry 9
Miki, Takeo 175
MITI (Ministry of International Trade
and Industry) 224
New Asian Industries Development
Plan 179
and Asia-Pacific integration 179
Morita, Akio 81
Most Favoured Nation (MFN) 65
Motor Iberia, S.A. 70
Mulroney, Brian 10, 12, 42
1993 elections 14

NAFTA (North American Free Trade
Agreement) 1, 15–16, 53, 108
accession clause 26, 28
agricultural marketing boards 22
and automobiles 17, 25
and Eastern Europe 120
and GATT negotiations 30
and government procurement 25
and human rights in Mexico 26
and Japan 58
and service sector 22
anti-dumping 22
Canada's motives 20
dispute resolution 23
government procurement 23
impact on Mexico 18, 25
impact on US 23
implications for Sino–Japanese
relations 196–7
Mexico's motives 18
provisions 21–2
US motives 17, 18
Nakasone, Yasuhiro 221, 226, 228
and Sino–Japanese relations 203

Nanjing massacre, and Sino–Japanese
  relations 204, 221
Netherlands, Treaty of Rome 1
New Zealand, relations with Japan
  175
Newly Industrializing Economies
  (NIES) 164, 167–9
Nippon Telegraph and Telephone
  Corporation (NTT) 104
Nissan Motor Co., and EC 70, 82
'Nixon shocks' 198
Non-tariff barrier (NTB) 67
Northern Territories dispute 141,
  143, 145–7, 159
  Soviet armed forces 147
Nuclear proliferation, in Northeast
  Asia 193

OECD (Organization for Economic
  Cooperation and Development)
  66
  positive adjustment policies 99
Ohira, Masayoshi 176
oil shocks 198
Okita, Saburo 168
Omnibus Trade and Competitiveness
  Act 1988 43
orderly marketing agreements (OMAs)
  61, 78
original equipment manufacturing
  (OEM) 166
Organization of Pacific Trade and
  Development (OPTAD) 176
Organization of Petroleum Exporting
  Countries (OPEC) 7

Pacific Basin Cooperation Concept
  (PBCC) 177
Pacific Basin Economic Council
  (PBEC) 176
Pacific Cooperation Committee (PCC)
  177
Pacific Economic Cooperation
  Conference (PECC) 176
  and Russia 161
Pacific Free Trade Area (PAFTA)
  175
Pacific Trade and Development
  (PAFTAD) conference 176
Paraguay, and MERCOSUR 28

PHARE (Poland–Hungary Aid for
  Restructuring of Economies)
  116, 120
Philippines, and Pacific Basin 176
Plaza Accords (1985) 22, 42, 165,
  202
Poland 116, 196
  EC membership 6
  privatization 117
  relations with EC 4
Portugal, admitted to European
  Community 2
Preferential Trade Area 122

Qilu Petrochemical Complex 201
Québec separatism 4, 26

RACE (Research in Advanced
  Communications Technologies in
  Europe) 99
Reagan, Ronald
  and Canada–US FTA 10, 12
  military build-up 226
  trade policy statement 42
Recruit scandal 144
Romania
  relations with EC 117
  state of the economy 127
Rules of origin 82
  Canada–US FTA 44
  for EC 98
  in NAFTA 22–3
Russian Federation
  and Sino–Japanese relations 212
  trade with Japan 153
Ryzhkov, Nikolai 142

Salinas de Gortari, Carlos 15
  National Development Plan 19
Sanyo Electronics 209
Scowcroft, Brent, and Tiananmen
  Square incident 204
Service sector 8
  Canada–US FTA 45
  and NAFTA 22
Shevardnadze, Eduard 141
Singapore 167, 168
Single European Act 1, 6, 64
  impact on Eastern Europe 116

348

248 *Index*

Sino–Japan relations 198, 202, 205
diplomatic conflicts 202
economic relations 198, 205
joint ventures 208
trade 160
Treaty of Peace and Friendship
(1978) 195
Sino–UK Investment Agreement 133
Solovyev, Nikolai 143
South Korea 167–9
South Yakutian coal fields 151, 154
Soviet Union
and Sino–Japanese relations 160,
196, 205, 212
civil strife 5
end of Cold War 4
relations with Japan 141
Spain
admitted to European Community
2
Japanese investment 70
Spratly Islands 212, 213
Structural Impediments Initiative 77,
85–6, 111
Super 301 111
Sweden, European Free Trade
Association 4
Switzerland, European Free Trade
Association 3

Taiwan 167–9
Takeshita, Noboru 144, 180, 203,
209, 221
and Tiananmen Square incident 204
Tariffs, and NAFTA 23
Technology transfer, to China 209
Telecommunications industry 8
and NAFTA 24
European Community 7
Thailand 167–9
Japanese FDI 167
Tiananmen Square incident (1989)
and Sino–Japanese relations 195,
204
impact on Sino–Japanese trade 200
Toshiba Machine Company, COCOM
violations 159
Trade remedy legislation 41

Transportation industry, and NAFTA
24
Treaty of Rome 1
European Free Trade Association 4
Turkey, application for EC
membership 4

United Kingdom, Maastricht Treaty
5
United States
and Asia-Pacific region 192
and EC 92 7
and Pacific Basin 176
as hegemonic power 59
investment in Europe 8
savings rate 110
trade 7, 17
trade deficit 7, 29, 68
trade with Canada 10, 11
trade with China 207
Uno, Sosuke 145, 190, 211
Uruguay, and MERCOSUR 28
Uruguay Round of GATT 10, 53
and Canada–US FTA 12
and agricultural subsidies 29
US–Japan alliance 192
US–Japan trade imbalance, impact on
Russia 160

Venezuela
and NAFTA 28
trade agreement with Mexico 20
Vietnam 193
Visegrad Countries (Poland, Hungary,
and CFSR), relations with EC
116
voluntary export restraints (VERs)
41, 61, 70, 78
by EC 79
in EC 79

Warsaw Pact 4, 5

Yangzi Petrochemical Complex 201
Yeltsin, Boris, Japan policy 141
Yen bloc 169
Yoshida doctrine 60
Yugoslavia, civil war 5